WORK, FAMILIES AND ORGANISATIONS IN TRANSITION

European perspectives

Edited by Suzan Lewis, Julia Brannen and Ann Nilsen

This edition published in Great Britain in 2009 by

The Policy Press
University of Bristol
Fourth Floor
Beacon House
Queen's Road
Bristol BS8 1QU
UK

Tel +44 (0)117 331 4054
Fax +44 (0)117 331 4093
e-mail tpp-info@bristol.ac.uk
www.policypress.org.uk

North American office:
The Policy Press
c/o International Specialized Books Services (ISBS)
920 NE 58th Avenue, Suite 300
Portland, OR 97213-3786, USA
Tel +1 503 287 3093
Fax +1 503 280 8832
e-mail info@isbs.com

British Library Cataloguing in Publication Data
A catalogue record for this book is available from the British Library.

Library of Congress Cataloging-in-Publication Data
A catalog record for this book has been requested.

ISBN 978 1 84742 220 0 hardcover

Cover design by The Policy Press
Front cover: image kindly supplied by Flavio Takemote
Printed and bound in Great Britain by TJ International, Padstow

To Jake, Tim and Sam, Rosa and Joe, and Idar and Sanna

Contents

Acknowledgements

The editors and contributors to the book would like to acknowledge the work of the rest of the Transitions team: Michaela Brockman, Jeanne Fagnani, John Howarth, Polona Kersnik, Atanas Matev, Jana Nadoh, Rob Pattman, Christina Purcell and Marijke Veldhoen-van Blitterswijk. They would also like to acknowledge the support of the European Commission for funding the Framework Five project 'Gender, Parenthood and the Changing European Workplace'. Gratitude is also due to all the organisations that took part in the study and to the parents and managers who gave up their valuable time.

Notes on contributors

Pedro Abrantes is a PhD researcher at the Centre for Research and Studies in Sociology (CIES-ISCTE), in Lisbon, Portugal. During the last few years, he has been involved in various projects on youth, education and work–family balance. He is currently developing research on educational programmes and teaching sociology in Universidade Aberta and in Instituto Politécnico de Leiria. In addition, he collaborates with the Portuguese Ministry of Education in the Schools' Evaluation Programme.

Margareta Bäck-Wiklund is Professor of Social Work and Family Policy at Göteborg University, Sweden. She is heading the research programme 'Parenting and Childhood in Modern Family Cultures'. Among her publications are *Det moderna Föräldraskapet: En studie av familj och kön i förändring* [*The modern parenthood: A study of family and gender in transition*] (Natur och Kultur, 1997, 2002, 2005), *Nätverksfamiljen* [*The network family*] (Natur och Kultur, 2004), 'New trends in the time bind: the Swedish case', in M. Jacobssen and J. Tonboe (eds) *Arbeidssamfundet* [*The work society*] (Hans Reitzel Forlag, 2004) and, with Lars Plantin, 'The workplace as an arena for negotiating the work–family boundary: a case study of two social service agencies', in R. Crompton et al (eds) *Women, men, work and family in Europe* (Palgrave, 2007). She is currently directing the Swedish part of QUALITY – a European project about working and family life.

Julia Brannen is Professor of Sociology of the Family in the Institute of Education, University of London, UK, and Adjunct Professor at the University of Bergen, Norway. Based in the Institute's Thomas Coram Research Unit, she has carried out national and international research studies of the lives of working parents, young people and children for over 20 years. She has a particular interest in methodology and has written extensively on mixed methods. Recent books include *Working and caring over the twentieth century: Change and continuity in four-generation families* (with Peter Moss and Ann Mooney) (Palgrave Macmillan, 2004), *Coming to care: The work and family lives of workers caring for vulnerable children* (with June Statham, Ann Mooney and Michaela Brockmann) (The Policy Press, 2007) and *The handbook of social research* (with Pertti Alasuutari and Leonard Bickman) (Sage Publications, 2008). She is a co-founder and co-editor of the *International Journal of Social Research Methodology*.

Nevenka Černigoj Sadar is a senior researcher in the Organisations and HR Research Centre and Professor of Social Psychology in the Faculty of Social Sciences at the University of Ljubljana, Slovenia. Her main areas of research are changing life patterns, gender divisions in paid and unpaid work in relation to social policy measures, quality of life in various life spheres, and women and the labour market. She lectures on organisational behaviour and career management.

She has participated in several Slovene and international comparative projects. She has been a visiting scholar at the Centre National de la Recherche Scientifique, Paris, and at the Manchester Metropolitan University and the University of Bath, UK. Her most recent publications are 'Work–family arrangement in organisations', in I. Svetlik and B. Ilič (eds) *HRM's contribution to hard work* (P. Lang, 2007), *Delo in družina: s partnerstvom do družini prijaznega delovnega okolja* [*Work and family: With partnership towards family-friendly work conditions*] (with Kanjuo A. Mrčela; eds) (Fakulteta za družbene vede, 2007), 'Viskanju izmikajočega se cilja' [In search of the elusive goal] (with D. Podmenik), in M. Sedmak and Z. Medarič (eds) *Med javnim in zasebnim: Ženske na trgu dela* [*Between public and private: Women in the labour market*] (Založba Annales, 2007).

Maria das Dores Guerreiro is Professor in the Department of Sociology, ISCTE (Instituto Superior de Ciências do Trabalho e da Empresa), Lisbon, Portugal, and Member of the Scientific Council of ISCTE. She is research coordinator at CIES, where she is the editor of the scientific Portuguese journal *Sociologia, Problemas e Práticas*. Her research covers young generations, work–life balance, women and work, equal opportunities, family, organisations and professions, social policies, and new forms of work and employment. She has published many books, and articles in scientific journals and social policy publications. Her most recent book publication is *Transições Incertas* (Comissão Para a Igualdade no Trabalho e no Emprego, 2007).

Laura den Dulk is an assistant professor at the Department of Sociology, Utrecht University, the Netherlands. Her main area of expertise is cross-national research regarding work–life policies in organisations in different welfare state regimes. In 2001 she completed her PhD in Social Sciences on the presence of work–family arrangements in organisations in different European countries. In 1999 she co-edited a book on work–family arrangements in Europe. Her latest co-edited book is *Flexible working and organisational change: The integration of work and personal life* (Edward Elgar, 2005). Current research interests include the attitudes, opinions and behaviour of top managers towards work–life policies and the social quality in European workplaces. She participates in various EC research projects: 'Quality of life in a changing Europe' (QUALITY) and 'Gender, Parenthood and the Changing European Workplace: young adults negotiating the work–family boundary' (Transitions).

Lise Granlund achieved her Master's degree in Sociology at the University of Bergen, Norway, in 2003 with her thesis entitled 'The school's plural values: definition and legitimation of problem behaviour in a Waldorf school and a public school'. Following the Transitions study she has since been employed in the Department of Sociology, Bergen. She also has had responsibility for executing several evaluation projects.

Siyka Kovacheva is Assistant Professor in Sociology and Social Policy at the University of Plovdiv and Head of the New Europe Centre for Regional Studies in Bulgaria. Her research has focused on the social transformation of Bulgarian society, changes in family life, including gender and intergenerational relations, and work–life balance. Recent publications include 'Work–life balance of employees in Bulgarian service sector companies' (with Stanimir Kabaivanov), *Quality of Life Journal*, 1-2 (2008), 'Social change, family support, and young adults in Europe' (with Andy Biggart), in M. du Bois-Reymond and L. Chisholm (eds) *The modernisation of youth transitions in Europe* (Wiley, 2006) and 'Changing cultures in changing workplaces: UK and Bulgaria compared' (with S. Lewis and N. Demireva), *Sociological Problems*, Sofia, Special Issue (2005). She is the editor of a special issue of the journal *Sociological Problems* 'Work-life dilemmas: Changes in work and family life in the enlarged Europe' (2008) vol IL.

Suzan Lewis was coordinator of the Transitions project. She is Professor of Organisational Psychology in the Department of Human Resource Management, Middlesex University Business School, UK. Her research focuses on work–personal life issues and workplace practice, culture and change in different workplace and social policy contexts. She is a founding editor of the international journal *Community, Work and Family* (Taylor and Francis). Her recent authored and edited books include *Work–life integration: Case studies of organisational change* (with Cary L. Cooper) (Wiley, 2005), *The myth of work–life balance* (with Richenda Gambles and Rhona Rapoport) (Wiley, 2006) and *Women, men, work and family in Europe* (with Rosemary Crompton and Claire Lyonette) (Palgrave, 2007). She is currently a member of the European Commission Expert Group on Women in Science and Technology (WIST2).

Ann Nilsen is Professor of Sociology in the Department of Sociology, University of Bergen, Norway, where she is also Vice Dean in the Faculty of Social Sciences. She publishes on biographical and lifecourse research, methods, gender studies and environmental sociology. She has been a partner in various EU projects. Her many publications include *Young Europeans, work and family: Futures in transition* (with Julia Brannen, Suzan Lewis and Janet Smithson) (Routledge, 2002), based on a previous EU study.

Bram Peper is an assistant professor at the Erasmus University Rotterdam, the Netherlands. His main area of expertise is cross-national research regarding work–family arrangements in organisations in different welfare state regimes. Presently he is working on several research projects. one regarding the well-being of employees, and one regarding boundary management in relation to work–life issues. His latest co-edited book (with Laura den Dulk and Anneke van Doorne-Huiskes) is on flexible work, organisational change and the integration of work and personal life.

Inês Pereira graduated in sociology and has a Masters degree in Culture, Communication and Information Technologies (both at ISCTE, Lisbon). She is a researcher at the Centre for Research and Studies in Sociology (CIES-ISCTE). She has been involved in several research projects focusing on work–family balance, organisational policies, youth, information/network society and social movements. She is currently developing a PhD in Urban Anthropology at ISCTE/URV-Tarragona.

Lars Plantin is Associate Professor of Health and Society in the Department for Social Work, University of Malmö, Sweden. His main area of expertise is family sociology with a special focus on fatherhood. His PhD thesis 'Mäns föräldraskap: om mäns upplevelser och erfarenheter av faderskape' [Men's parenting: on men's perceptions and experiences of fatherhood] (2001) drew on a collaborative project between the University of Sunderland in England and the University of Göteborg in Sweden 'Fatherhood and masculinities: a comparative study of the ideals and realities of fatherhood and masculinities in Britain and Sweden' (2000). He has published related articles including 'Talking and doing fatherhood: on fatherhood and masculinity in Sweden and Britain', *Fathering*, 1(1) (2003). Recently he has also worked for the World Health Organization (WHO) in Geneva and is the author of the WHO report *Fatherhood and health outcomes: The case of Europe* (WHO, 2007). Currently he is working on a research project on parenthood and the internet.

Janet Smithson is a research fellow at the University of Exeter, UK. Her main research interests are in cross-national comparative research on work–family, youth, transitions to adulthood and parenthood, gender, discourse and qualitative methodology. One of her many publications is *Young Europeans, work and family: Futures in transition* (with Julia Brannen, Suzan Lewis and Ann Nilsen) (Routledge, 2002), which is based on a previous EU study. She was Project Manager of the Transitions project.

Sevil Sümer is Associate Professor of Sociology at the University of Bergen, Norway. Her research interests include gender, family, work and welfare regimes with an emphasis on the Scandinavian model. Currently she is working on a book entitled *European gender regimes and policies: Comparative perspectives*.

Anneke van Doorne-Huiskes is Emeritus Professor of Sociology in the Department of Sociology and ICS Research School at Utrecht University, the Netherlands. Her research interests lie in the areas of welfare states, labour market and gender, gender and organisation, organisational culture and work–life balance. She is currently participating in an international comparative project on the quality of life and work of European citizens, funded by the European Union (EU). She represented the Netherlands in an EU-Network on Family and Work (1995–2001) and participated in the research project 'Defining Family Obligations in Europe: A Cross-National Research'. Since 1987 she has been a senior partner of VanDoorneHuiskes and Partners, a research and consultancy firm in Utrecht.

ONE

Work, family and organisations in transition: setting the context

Suzan Lewis, Julia Brannen and Ann Nilsen

Most young Europeans expect to combine paid work and parenting at some time in their lifecourse, although they do not always have a clear idea about how easy or difficult it will be to manage, nor what support might be necessary (Brannen et al, 2002). Indeed, it is difficult for them to do so, as people's circumstances vary and in some national contexts there are no clear normative models that apply to both mothers and fathers. Most of the research on working parents' needs and experiences focuses either on national public policy and regulation or on workplace policies, but important as these are, they are only a part of the overall picture. National context matters as does economic, social and ideological context. Labour market and workplace policies can make a difference to parents' lives (Lewis, 1997; Brandth and Kvande, 2001, 2002; Haas et al, 2002; Allard et al, 2007). However, changing economic climates and global trends also have a part to play in shaping practices and cultures in specific workplaces in specific contexts and societies.

Policies and practices to support the reconciliation of work and family or 'work–life balance'[1] in Europe, whether stemming from government regulation or voluntary organisational initiatives, are being implemented at a time when employing organisations are undergoing massive and rapid changes in the context of global competition and efficiency drives. In emerging economies in post-communist societies, huge social and economic transformations are taking place. Moreover, whatever the context, the experiences of parenthood are different for men and women while education and occupational level also influence parents' opportunities to negotiate work and family boundaries. Gender ideologies, the domestic division of labour and kinship networks all play a part too in this complex web of structural and cultural supports and constraints for employed parents.

In this volume we recognise the importance of several interacting and dynamic layers of context on employees who are attempting to reconcile the ever-growing demands of paid work with the equally demanding tasks of parenting young children. We also explore the ways in which managers manage employees' need for work–life balance while also fulfilling the organisation's goals of profitability and/or efficiency. We focus primarily on the workplace and the changes taking place therein, but we also touch on the other layers of context that influence and are influenced by employing organisations.

The volume consists of a series of case studies of changing European workplaces carried out as part of an eight-country study entitled 'Transitions: Gender, Parenthood and the Changing European Workplace' (hereafter referred to as the Transitions study), which was funded by the European Union (EU).[2] The project examined experiences of employed parents and their managers, and the ways in which parents are able to negotiate work–family boundaries in diverse national contexts and rapidly changing organisational contexts. A specific objective was to develop an understanding of the impact of the welfare state, workplace context and organisational change on young adults who become parents, in the following partner countries: Bulgaria, the Netherlands, Norway, Portugal, Slovenia, Sweden and the UK. The organisational case studies generate understandings of the processes whereby contexts (global, national and local) create limiting and enabling conditions for working parents to manage their everyday lives. In the remainder of this chapter we briefly consider aspects of various layers of context that are relevant for understanding and comparing parents' experiences of combining paid work and parenting, before overviewing the chapters in the book.

Global context

The global context is important because the spread of global capitalism impinges on local practices and ultimately on parents' experiences of paid work and family. Changes at the workplace level in response to global competition and efficiency drives can undermine both regulatory and voluntary initiatives to support working parents.

Employer strategies to compete in increasingly internationalised product and service markets have resulted in many changes in employment and the organisation of work in European private sector workplaces. The perceived need to enhance competitiveness in the world market has led employers to flexibilise their employment contracts and increase job precariousness. For employees, the fear of job insecurity (objective or perceived) is exacerbated by the increase in mergers, acquisitions and alliances experienced in many of the private sector organisations discussed in this volume. Feelings of job insecurity can constrain parents from taking up opportunities to work flexibly, for example, although fears of job loss vary across different European countries. The drive for functional and temporal flexibility, through multiskilling and various forms of flexible working arrangements, also have implications for employed parents and may, in some circumstances, enhance opportunities to manage work and family boundaries although often at a cost, resulting in an intensification of work.

Globalisation also impacts on the provision of public services, as regulatory regimes are liberalised to allow entry into national markets of foreign-owned service providers. The EU (Bolkestein) Services Directive will reinforce this trend by opening up a public service market within the EU (Grahl, 2007), while the World Trade Organization General Agreement on Trade in Services (GATS) will have the same effect.

Consequently, many employers in both public and private sectors have reassessed their labour costs. This has resulted in trends towards subcontracting or outsourcing peripheral or lower-skill functions. For core workforces strategies such as high commitment management techniques (Appelbaum and Berg, 2001), including widespread target setting and team working replacing hierarchical-based divisions of labour, also stem from the need to compete in global markets or cost-cutting and efficiency drives and can increase workplace pressures.

Thus, in Europe, as elsewhere, employers adapt to the challenges of globalisation and demand more and more of their workers. This can be particularly problematic for employed mothers and fathers. Greedy organisations (Coser, 1974) develop family-unfriendly practices, which create the need for, but also undermine, flexible working arrangements purporting to support parents. Nevertheless, some recognition of the potential and actual social impacts of these processes has led to demands for some regulation to tame unfettered market forces in some contexts, including at the EU level.

The European context

Public policy discussions at the EU level address the challenges raised by the globalisation process as well as rapid technological developments. While the drive for competitiveness of national and organisational economies is an important objective, there is a recognition that this should not be at the expense of quality of working life and quality of life more generally (Eurofound, 2002, 2008; EU, 2007). It is argued that economic performance has to be balanced with socially sustainable forms of work organisation, with quality jobs, and with the maintenance and improvement of the quality of life in its broadest sense, including gender and other forms of justice (Webster, 2004).

European Union social policy objectives include further increasing women's employment rates, which, it is recognised, will involve enhancing opportunities to reconcile employment and family life, for both women and men. The EU focus is mainly on Directives negotiated by social partners to influence state policies, such as parental leave, rights for part-time workers and working-time regulation, which have been introduced at different times and implemented very differently across European welfare states (den Dulk, 2001; den Dulk and van Doorne-Huiskes, 2007). The promotion of better jobs is seen as a key element of the EU approach. Better jobs include more supportive ways of combining working and personal life. For example, although part-time work is not widely available in all EU states, where it is available it is now legally protected. Following EU initiatives, part-time workers (still predominantly women) increasingly enjoy equal rights to their full-time counterparts, although in the contexts of organisational cultures based on the model of the ideal workers who always prioritise work over family, they are not always equally valued in practice.

There is also some recognition in the EU that change is necessary at the level of workplace structures, cultures and practices to support or extend the impact of state policies (Webster, 2004). However, this is more difficult to address in the context of the massive changes taking place in organisations across Europe as they adapt to the challenges of globalisation and demand more and more of their workers. These changes are particularly acute in some of the new member states that are making the transition from a planned to a market economy.

National contexts

Various aspects of national contexts impact on the formal strategies available to working parents, including working hours, taking up family-related leave, childcare provision and flexible working arrangements.

Working hours

There are country variations in patterns of labour market regulation that impact on opportunities for working and parenting. These include the regulation of working hours and working-time flexibility. In Norway, the 1977 Work Environment Act (updated in 2005) regulates daily and weekly working hours, while the EU countries are subject to the European Working Time Directive, which restricts working hours to 48 per week, although Britain has a partial 'opt-out'. Neoliberal policies place few restrictions on working hours, making Britain the country with the longest average working hours in Europe for full-time employees. In the UK, fathers spend, on average, almost 47 hours each week at their jobs. Portugal also has long working hours. In terms of the number of hours spent at work, gender differences are apparent whichever country is considered (Fagnani et al, 2003).

The availability and affordability of part-time work also varies considerably across European states. Part-time work is more prevalent in the Netherlands, Norway, Sweden and the UK and less commonly available in Bulgaria, Portugal and Slovenia. In Norway and Sweden, women typically work 'long part-time hours' (20 hours or more per week) compared to the 'short part-time hours' (less than 20 hours per week) of women in the Netherlands or the UK. These factors also interact with economic factors. For example, part-time work would not be an option, even if it was available, in low-wage contexts such as Bulgaria and Portugal. Moreover, where part-time work is available, since it is usually carried out by women, it can also disadvantage them in career terms and economically. Full-time work, however, is not inevitably associated with pay equity. The gender pay gap is relatively large in post-communist regimes where full-time work has long been the norm but the domestic division of labour is very traditional (Domsch and Ladwig, 2000; Metcalfe and Afanassieva, 2005). Women in all the partner countries are more likely to work in the public sector, notably in the care workforce, which, like other female-dominated work, tends to be characterised by lower pay.

Most of the countries also have some form of entitlements to temporal flexibility for parents of young children or at least the rather weak entitlement to request flexible hours, for example a reduction or a change in hours. Although in the Netherlands and the UK, parents have the right to request such flexible forms of work, employers can still reject employee requests if they can show that proposed flexible working arrangements would seriously damage their business interests.

Family-related leave

Table 1.1 summarises the national policies on leave arrangements for working parents, when the study was carried out in 2004.[3] In terms of maternity, paternity and parental leave and leave to care for sick children, considerable inter-country differences existed at the time. The duration of parental leave varied between three and 36 months across the seven countries under study. The Netherlands, Portugal and the UK were characterised by less generous parental leave arrangements. In Bulgaria, not only parents but also one grandparent were entitled to take parental

Table 1.1: Parental leave schemes in the seven countries in 2004

	Maternity leave	Paternity leave	Parental leave	Sick child leave
Bulgaria	19 weeks on 90% pay	No specific	21 months for mother or father, or grandparent, basic rate	60 days per year for mother or father on full pay
Netherlands	16 weeks on full pay	2 days	13 weeks each parent, basic rate	10 days on 70% pay
Norway	42 weeks on full pay or 52 weeks on 80% pay	4 weeks on full pay, not transferable	29 weeks on full pay, 39 weeks on 80% pay, shared; one year unpaid. Father's quota 4 weeks.	10 days per year on full pay
Portugal	16 weeks on full pay	5+15 days on full pay, 10 weeks of mother's leave can be shared	3 months unpaid	30 days per year unpaid
Slovenia	15 weeks on full pay	15 days on full pay, 75 days on minimum wage	260 days on full pay	14 days on 80% pay
Sweden	8 weeks on 80% pay	8 weeks on 80% pay + 10 days basic rate	38 weeks on 80% pay, shared; 12 weeks on basic rate. Father's quota 18 weeks.	60 days per year per child on 80% pay
UK	6 weeks on full pay, 20 weeks on statutory fixed rate pay	2 weeks flat rate	13 weeks unpaid per parent	None specified

Source: Fagnani et al (2004)

leave. In addition, with the exception of the UK, most countries also offered leave in the case of a sick child, varying between 10 and 60 days per year.

Only the Scandinavian countries had a generous period of paid leave for fathers. In the Nordic countries, a father's quota of paid non-transferable leave represents efforts to redefine the fatherhood role, in terms of active parenting rather than just economic provision (Ellingsæter, 2003). Although none of the countries in the study, other than Norway and Sweden, had special daddy quotas in their parental leave systems, there were some developments regarding paternity leave. The Netherlands, Portugal and Slovenia all introduced paid paternity leave for fathers to be taken shortly after the birth of the child. The length of paternity leave varied between two days in the Netherlands and 90 days in Slovenia (Fagnani et al, 2003).

Legal entitlement, however, is not always reflected in a subjective sense of entitlement to take up family-related leave or flexible working options (Lewis and Smithson, 2001). The take-up of parental leave in our study was gendered everywhere, albeit less so in the Nordic countries. Men still, on average, took less parental leave than women. Moreover, specific workplace and occupational contexts, availability of childcare, economic and other factors all contributed to parents' experiences of and capacity to take up formal entitlements. Experiences of some of the parents participating in the Transitions study illustrate this (see Box 1.1).[4]

Box 1.1

In Bulgaria, parents – specifically mothers – can take up to three years of maternity leave, and Rosa, with a job in the lower ranks of social services, took full advantage of this. On the other hand, Nelly, a Bulgarian social worker, who saw her job as a career with promotional opportunities, went back to work after only four months. Meanwhile, Anna, working for a private Bulgarian bank, took minimal maternity leave because of fear of getting behind, given the fast pace of change in the industry and its young profile and the fear of losing her job. In Norway, Gro, an engineer in a private sector company, also took less leave than she was entitled to, but still took eight fully paid months of the 12 months to which she was entitled. Her partner took extended parental leave of four months rather than just the one month to which he was entitled in his own right. This contrasts with the Bulgarian fathers who were minimally involved in childcare.

Childcare

Affordable childcare is crucial for working parents. Where there is limited state childcare support it is generally women who have to be resourceful and put together complex and often fragile arrangements (Fagnani et al, 2003). Three of our seven countries studied are characterised by a strong tradition of childcare support for working parents – Bulgaria, Slovenia and Sweden. In Norway, unlike the other Scandinavian countries, investment in public childcare started only in the 1990s. However, nowadays the level of childcare support is relatively high (although supply does not fill the demand, see Table 1.2), and more substantial than in the Netherlands, Portugal and the UK. In 2002, 66% of Norwegian children between one and five years of age were enrolled in public daycare centres. Another option for Norwegian parents is the 'cash-for-home-care scheme'. Within this scheme, parents can choose a cash benefit instead of using publicly funded childcare. In Sweden, parents with children between one and 12 years of age are entitled to public childcare, with affordable fees linked to parental income.

After the transition from communism in Bulgaria in 1989, the number of childcare places decreased and fees for parents increased. Since the 1990s, grandparents have become more important in caring arrangements. All the Bulgarian families in the study relied heavily on the support of their own parents to supplement publicly available childcare for their children. Similar developments as far as fees for childcare are concerned are visible in Slovenia. Especially since the cost of childcare has increased, grandparents are nowadays important caretakers of children. In 2001/02, 55% of children under school age were enrolled in childcare centres in Slovenia. Both the Dutch and Portuguese government promoted the development of public childcare in their countries in the 1990s. However, provisions are less advanced compared to the Nordic and post-communist countries. The UK offers childcare provision largely provided by the market (commercially run nurseries and childminders).

However, childcare issues are increasingly complicated by current workplace trends such as the growth of atypical and casualised work and it is difficult for state-sponsored childcare services to cover all care needs and contingencies in a 24/7 society. Meanwhile, public debates on the quality of childcare and the desirability of long childcare days are growing across many European countries.

Finally, another important and interrelated layer of context is the household and wider family. The dual-earner family model is the norm (among two-parent families) across most of Europe. Nevertheless, the unravelling of the 'male breadwinner model' towards more egalitarian models of work and family integration across Europe is in practice multidimensional, uneven and a very slow process (Crompton et al, 2007). In Norway and Sweden and among some families in the other countries there is an ideal of gender equality in the family. This raises expectations of spouse support and independence from families of origin, although workplace pressures can undermine those expectations (Brandth and Kvande, 2002; Gambles et al, 2006). In other contexts, notably in Bulgaria and Slovenia, there is little expectation that fathers will be involved in childcare. In the Northern European countries, small but increasing numbers of fathers are taking time off from paid work or they are working flexibly for childcare reasons, so that workplaces and policy makers are increasingly reconsidering the role of fathers in the family (Brandth and Kvande, 2001; Haas et al, 2002; Brannen and Nilsen, 2006; Allard et al, 2007). Nevertheless gender continues to shape experiences

Table 1.2: Support for parents according to evidence from national reports

State	Workplace	Partner	Wider family	Community/friends	Access to childcare
Sweden	High level of support. Childcare is a *public issue*.	Colleagues' support. Many mothers work part time.	Ideals of gender equality. Mothers do more domestic work. Fathers do some childcare.	Some practical support for parents' *leisure time*.	Some babysitting.	Publicly funded and subsidised. Widespread access.
Norway	High level support. Childcare is a *public and private issue*.	Colleagues' and some manager support. Many mothers work part time	Ideals of gender equality. Mothers do more domestic work. Fathers do some childcare.	Some practical support for parents' *leisure time*.	Not mentioned.	Publicly funded. Expensive. Demand exceeds supply.
Portugal	Low level support. Childcare is a *private issue*.	Public sector 'continuous working day' – ie, a shorter day but without a break (mothers or fathers of children under 12). Full-time norm for all.	Traditional gender ideology. Mothers responsible for domestic arena.	Practical *everyday support in addition to* formal and informal childcare.	Some exchange of childcare.	Some publicly funded. Severe shortage.
UK	Some support. Childcare is a *private issue*.	Depends on job level and manager. Some mothers work part time.	Mothers mainly responsible for domestic arena. Fathers give some practical support.	Some *practical support in addition to* formal childcare.	Not mentioned.	Severe shortage. Private and expensive. Some tax credits for lower-income families.
Netherlands	Some support. Childcare is predominately a *private issue*.	Flexible employment. Mothers have a high part-time rate (short and long hours).	Mothers mainly responsible for the domestic arena. Fathers give some practical support.	Some practical support for parents' *leisure time*.	Not mentioned.	Privately funded and recent public–private partnerships in poor areas. Shortage. Expensive unless on a low income.
Slovenia	Rather high level of support. Childcare is a *public and private issue*.	Inflexible hours. Full-time norm for all.	Traditional gender ideology. Mothers responsible for domestic arena.	Practical *everyday support in addition* to public childcare. Financial support.	Children play in the neighbourhood	Publicly funded. Subsidised. Good access. Short opening hours.
Bulgaria	High level of support. Childcare is a *public and private issue*.	Inflexible hours. Full-time norm for all.	Traditional gender ideology. Mothers responsible for domestic arena.	Practical *everyday support in addition* to public childcare. Financial support.	Not mentioned.	Publicly funded. Subsidised. Good access.

of work and family everywhere, and social class and the regional economic and cultural context are also important. Wider community can also be important for providing informal care. Table 1.2 shows differences in informal and formal support for working parents in the seven countries studied based on the national reports from the study. Some of the variations in support for working parents – in this case mothers – are illustrated by the cases discussed in Box 1.2 (Brannen and Nilsen, 2005; Brannen, 2006).

Box 1.2

Dália, a care worker in social services in Portugal, has two children. Following the birth of her second child, she took four months' parental leave, and says that her manager is supportive, allowing her to take the occasional day off for her children's illnesses. Key to Dália's experience of managing work and family boundaries is the support she receives from her parents, her mother in particular. Dália's husband has been unemployed for more than a year. He does no housework or childcare except to *"stay with the baby for an hour or two, now that she is a bit grown up"*. Dália does not appear to be critical of this: *"domestic work is for the women of the house"*.[5]

Susanne, from Sweden, is a care worker in a centre for people with learning disabilities. She and her husband shared parental leave. They took 16 months' leave between them in order to be at home as long as possible: *"We were very poor during that time but it was worth it. That's why I could stay home for nine months and my husband seven months"*. They were able to see themselves as *"good parents"* by postponing their children's start in daycare. They have high-quality, affordable public childcare that is locally available. But, unlike Dália, they have no parents living close by to fall back on in case of emergencies. Having recently moved to their new house, they have no extended family and few friends in the neighbourhood to help with babysitting. Under Swedish law, Susanne was able to reduce her hours on her return to work; she works four days a week. There is no official flexitime in her centre and as her work involves contact with clients she cannot work from home. However, she is able to take time off if she makes it up later. She has negotiated with her manager to leave work 15 minutes earlier each day and to arrive 30 minutes later than her colleagues *without* a reduction in her wages. This enables her to catch trains without having to wait for long periods. Unlike Dália's husband, Susanne's husband shares responsibility for their son, for example taking him to and collecting him from daycare. They share the household work between them equitably, with Susanne conscious of how rare this is even among Swedish couples.

Carol works in a social services centre for adults with learning disabilities in London. After her child was born she took the available paid maternity leave of six months and then returned to her full-time job. Her partner was not supportive and within months their relationship broke down. Carol found working full time very difficult and managed to negotiate slightly shorter hours so that she could collect her child earlier from the childminder. However, her manager soon pressed her to return to full-time hours by which time Carol was separated

---

from her partner and having to manage on only her own income. Without a partner, part-time work was not a possibility. She now has a new partner. She does not seek childcare support from him as he is not the child's father but seems resentful of the fact that he does not pull his weight in other ways, for example he does not pay half the bills. In practice, Carol feels she is a lone mother. Unlike Dália but like Susanne, Carol lacked close kin living in London except for her father who provides some support with childcare. Carol's access to childcare is also more problematic than it is for the other mothers as the UK has no history of public childcare for young children. Unlike Susanne but like Dália, Carol could not rely on locally provided public childcare that she could readily afford. Carol had some initial difficulties with the childminder and moved the child to a private nursery near her workplace when the childminder put up her fees.

Thus, both formal and informal support is important although many factors impact on these mothers' experiences of managing work–family boundaries.

Workplace context

Flexible working arrangements

It is in the workplace that national public policies are implemented and are supported or undermined by workplace practices and trends. Employing organisations can affect employees' opportunities and strategies for integrating work and parenting, by the supports they provide and also the demands they make on parents – both of which are changing in contemporary contexts. On the one hand, there appears to be some growth in what are often called 'family-friendly', 'work–family' or 'work–life balance' policies or what we generally refer to here as 'flexible working arrangements' (den Dulk, 2001; Evans, 2001). These are introduced into organisations in response to national social policy or voluntarily. At the same time, however, employees face growing demands, manifested in the intensification and insecurity of work, as employers introduce organisational change strategies to deal with the challenges of global competition in the private sector and of economic cutbacks in the public sector. The growth of workplace supports for working parents in some contexts is not uniform or unequivocal in its effects. First, the nature and extent of such support differ across national contexts. In Scandinavian and some Eastern European contexts, the development of work–family policies stems from social concerns, especially concerning the promotion of gender equality. In neoliberal contexts, notably the UK, where state provision for employed parents is not particularly generous, government strategy is to support and encourage employers to develop such policies for business reasons. Such 'voluntary' employer provision often lags behind that of the more generous and egalitarian welfare states (Evans, 2001). On the other hand, high levels of state provision in the Scandinavian countries and Eastern European countries can absolve employers from providing additional policies. Supports for employed parents in this study differed not only across national contexts, but also across sector (public and private), type of workplace and occupation, influenced by national policy and its implementation, the nature of the work and normative working practices.

Second, even when flexible working arrangements are introduced, their effectiveness depends on implementation so that there is very often a gap between policy and practice (Lewis, 1997, 2001; Bond et al, 2002; Gambles et al, 2006), as we demonstrate in the case studies discussed in this book. There are a number of reasons for this. Policies tend to be introduced by organisations as human resource management initiatives rather than as strategic imperatives. They are therefore often marginalised and so do not achieve systemic change in organisational structures, cultures and working practices (Lewis and Cooper, 2005).

In turn, take-up of both state and workplace policies is often low, particularly among fathers, because of organisational cultures, which influence everyday working practices (Lewis, 1997, 2001; Brandth and Kvande, 2002; Haas and Hwang, 2007). Such failure by men to take up these policies sustains a 'male model' of full-time, long-hours work, predicated on outdated assumptions of separate and gendered work and family spheres (Bailyn, 1993, 2006; Lewis, 2001; Rapoport et al, 2002) and is intensified in contemporary high-pressured settings. In this context, if part-time or flexible forms of work are available, those who take up these arrangements are regarded as less valuable or committed than those who work in more normative ways (including, in many organisations, long working hours that are not compatible with parenting). The policies and those who use them are undervalued, and employees pay a career and/or earnings penalty. It is mainly women who take up flexible working, which can reproduce gendered norms and inequalities (Smithson et al, 2004). Managers also play a central role in determining which employees can take advantage of official entitlements to reduce or change working hours (Lewis, 1997, 2001; Yeandle et al, 2003). The important role of management discretion, and the crucial but often inconsistent response of line managers in permitting flexibility, emerged in all the case studies discussed in this volume. We also find that in the context of managerial trends such as the development of autonomous work teams, colleague support becomes increasingly important and often problematic. Dilemmas face both managers and parents in these pressurised contexts as illustrated in the case studies in this volume.

The presence of state and workplace policies relating to flexible working does not necessarily create a subjective sense of entitlement among employees. Sense of entitlement is not only shaped by available policies but is also influenced by the interaction of national context, workplace culture, management discretion and support (Lewis and Smithson, 2001). Gender is also important. Women tend to feel more entitled than men to take up family-oriented policies, but face major constraints on occupational advancement if they do so.

Nevertheless, workplace policies can be positive, especially where national policy provides a positive infrastructure of provision. For example, the father's quota of parental leave in Norway and Sweden has been associated with some increase in take-up by fathers, especially but not exclusively in public sector workplaces (Haas et al, 2002; Brandth and Kvande, 2006; O'Brien et al, 2007).

In other organisations, however, positive national policies are undermined by workplace trends in response to global competition and pressures (Brandth and Kvande, 2001, 2002; Allard et al, 2007). Reorganisations and efficiency drives result in more work being accomplished by fewer people, and/or employers' drive for functional flexibility results in jobs being enlarged to include more functions. New management approaches such as high commitment management provide employees or teams with more autonomy and flexibility to work towards ever-increasing targets, resulting in an internalisation of organisational goals (Lewis, 2003a). These trends can make it difficult for parents to take advantage of formal flexible working arrangements, as will be shown in this volume. In these contexts, the impacts of changes purporting to be family friendly are far from clear as many current working practices, including flexible working arrangements, are often double edged. When policies are implemented as a way for employers to manage 24/7 demands, they can result in atypical hours of work. In intensified work contexts, flexibility can also result in the flexibility to work longer hours, blurring work–home boundaries, which is then often regarded as a 'choice'. Thus, the pressures of competitive capitalism and modern managerial techniques can have a negative impact on employed parents of young children, whatever the national context or formal workplace policies purporting to support work and care. It is significant that an intensification of work was reported in all the case studies discussed in this volume.

Overview of the book

This book explores the impacts of public and workplace policies on employees managing contemporary forms of work and parenting, within the various layers of context discussed above. It does this via case studies of public and private sector organisations selected from seven countries. Although each case study raises some specific issues, there are many common themes arising from the study of these organisations whatever their national context. Interrelated themes include:

- the experience of flexible working arrangements alongside high-pressure working practices, including the widespread intensification of work;
- the crucial role of line managers;
- impacts of team working;
- persisting gendered organisational cultures that idealise those who prioritise work over family; and
- a widespread implementation gap between policy and practice.

The chapters in this book apply a range of lenses to the case studies, reflecting the multidisciplinary as well as cross-national nature of the research team, and provide diverse and complementary insights. The authors approach the case studies from different standpoints, focusing on:

- the nature of human service organisations;
- the role of social capital;
- historical legacy;
- organisational learning;
- sense of entitlement to support; and
- methodological issues.

Part One comprises case studies of social services in the UK, Sweden and Bulgaria. Case studies from the finance sector in Slovenia, the UK and the Netherlands are then presented in Part Two. Moving to a comparative approach in Part Three, within-country comparisons are made between private and public sector organisations in Norway and Portugal, and this is followed by two broader comparative and integrative chapters.

In Chapter Two, Julia Brannen, Ann Nilsen and Suzan Lewis discuss the research design and methods, providing insights that contextualise the discussions in subsequent chapters. In this chapter the logic of the different phases of the Transitions study is outlined, with a particular focus on the organisational case studies. Although data from these case studies are the main empirical material for the book, this phase must be seen within the methodological design and framework of the whole Transitions study. What sets the Transitions study apart from similar studies of how parents negotiate work and family boundaries is the interplay of the different layers of context in which mothers' and fathers' lives are embedded and that shape the ways in which individuals and families arrive at choices and decisions. This particular design thereby allows for a grounded and contextualised analysis of the different data collected in this study.

In Chapter Three, Julia Brannen, drawing on a case study of social services in a large metropolis in the UK, takes a methodological slant. She first explores issues of context, both national and organisational, reminding us that the results of a study cannot be divorced from the research methods and the settings in which research participants' experiences and views are elicited. The chapter also focuses on and explores some interactive dynamics of the focus groups in this case study in which parents complain about the constraints on their ability to take up work–life policies or work flexibly.

In Chapter Four, Lars Plantin and Margareta Bäck-Wiklund discuss a social services organisation in Sweden. Social services is conceptualised as a loosely coupled system with uncertain lines of decision making in which frontline workers, specifically social workers, have a great deal of discretion in their working practices. Tightening budget restrictions contribute to continuous change within a national context characterised by generous family policies. A considerable gap is evident between national policy and the local level in terms of both how support for parents is perceived and how practice is reported. A focus on the professional group of social workers illustrates the contingencies of this type of work and its implications for work–family strategies.

In Chapter Five, Siyka Kovacheva discusses the support available to parents of small children working in a state agency for social assistance in a city in Bulgaria, drawing on a social capital perspective. The main focus of the chapter is on the formal and informal practices of social workers and other social service workers in balancing professional and family responsibilities, and the reasons why working parents are concerned about improving legal provision since they have no access to formal employer support. In practice, most rely on informal help from line managers, colleagues in the team, wider family and public nurseries for their children.

Part Two focuses on private sector case studies. In Chapter Six, Nevenka Černigoj Sadar discusses the rights of employed parents in a recently partly privatised finance company in Slovenia. She explores the ways in which these rights bequeathed under a former Socialist regime are played out in the changing context of Slovenia's transformation to a market economy. The case study illustrates how the legacy of paternalism from the former Socialist regime contributes to the continued construction of work–family issues as both individual and state responsibilities rather than employer concerns or business issues. In this context, parents, especially mothers, bear the brunt of political and organisational changes associated with the transition to a market economy and increased global competition.

The UK private sector finance organisation discussed in Chapter Seven, by Suzan Lewis and Janet Smithson, claims to have moved beyond work–life policy implementation to address organisational culture change. A drive for culture change stems from the need to develop a single new organisational culture and identity following mergers and acquisitions. The workplace policies and practices the authors document are interpreted through a conceptual framework based on organisational learning theory and the concept of a dual agenda for change in which workplace policies aim to meet the complementary rather than conflicting needs of the organisation and its employees. This chapter questions how far a cultural change in this workplace represents a form of transformational learning. The authors conclude that change is a complex and dynamic process, with pockets of transformational change taking place alongside some management resistance.

In Chapter Eight, Bram Peper, Laura den Dulk and Anneke van Doorne-Huiskes describe the context in the Netherlands where current public policy defines work–family 'balance' as a shared responsibility between government, employers and employees. However, assumptions about gendered responsibilities remain rather traditional. Drawing on a case study of a Dutch finance company, the authors describe an organisation that adopts many formal supportive policies and experiences many tensions. They show how work–family policies play out in contradictory and ambivalent ways in the organisation at different levels, and the consequences for working parents and their managers. They argue that, although employers recognise that work–family policies and supports make sense in the context of changing economic environments and are intended to enhance employee satisfaction, in practice these policies do not feature in senior management's strategic business planning and thus are not embedded in the organisational culture. Consequently, workers do not feel entitled to take advantage of them.

Public and private sector organisations are compared within countries in Part Three. In Chapter Nine, Ann Nilsen, Sevil Sümer and Lise Granlund compare a private sector company and a social services organisation in Norway. The chapter demonstrates the importance of developing a grounded approach in understanding the experience of change within specific organisations as a basis for exploring parents' gendered experiences of reconciling work and family life. The chapter shows that the discourses of change tend to be individualistic in the private sector organisation in contrast to a more relational focus in social services. In the analysis of the private company the authors draw out a number of subsidiary themes concerning the way the organisation impacted on working parents.

In Chapter Ten, Maria das Dores Guerreiro, Pedro Abrantes and Inês Pereira compare organisational change as it affects working parents in social services and a finance consultancy. They show how the consultancy company abided by general labour laws and had no specific workplace policies for working parents, but followed an informal policy of flexible hours. In practice these were taken up to keep up with the large volume of work and because of its seasonal nature. Policy interpretation in the public sector was much stricter. Another theme pursued in the chapter concerns asymmetries in terms of age, education, qualifications and access to refresher training, with the resulting repercussions on pay and more or less job insecurity. While such asymmetries were found in both organisations, the private company had a more highly qualified workforce while this was not the case in the social services.

Chapter Eleven is in two parts with a common focus on parents' need for flexible working arrangements in order to manage their everyday lives. The first part focuses on organisational change in public sector social services, and the second part on private sector for-profit companies. The discussion in the first part takes as its point of departure some of the aspects of change in the social services case studies in the book. These receive comparative attention and a 'secondary' analysis of these highlights some of the pitfalls of assuming cross-national similarity within a single sector. In the second part of the chapter, private sector organisations are explored with reference to how issues raised by this sector's more exposed position in the global market affects working parents' experiences of both national and workplace policies.

The final chapter (Chapter Twelve) seeks to create a comparative synthesis of the findings from all the cases studies with respect to one of the key questions addressed in the book: how do public policy and workplace policies play out in practice in parents' lives in the different layers of context in which they live? It also explores some broader implications of the findings discussed in this volume for the current and future reconciliation of employment and family life.

Notes

[1] The term 'work–life balance' has attracted much criticism (see, for example, Caproni, 2004; Smithson and Stokoe, 2005; Lewis et al, 2007) but is nevertheless much used in policy debates.

[2] For more details of this EU Framework 5 project, see www.workliferesearch.org/transitions

[3] There have been changes in parental leave and a number of other family policies since the research was completed. The changes, however, do not impact on the interpretation of data from our case studies since these are embedded in the historical context of the time of the data collection.

[4] See Nilsen and Brannen (2005).

[5] See Nilsen and Brannen (2005).

TWO

Research design and methods: doing comparative cross-national research

Julia Brannen, Ann Nilsen and Suzan Lewis

Doing cross-national research is complex and challenging. In this chapter we discuss the project design and methods but also the challenges we met and the strategies we adopted to meet them.

The study on which this book is based adopted a comparative cross-national framework. The study design involved the use of several methods in order to address several layers of the social context. The three contextual layers in this study are:

- the macro layer of societal trends, national institutions, public policies and public discourses;
- the organisational layer of the workplace;
- mothers and fathers located in their households, wider families, workplaces and communities.

For a cross-national study to be context sensitive, it is necessary to take account of several contextual levels or layers, while comparisons can be made at each level. While this book relates largely to the organisational layer, account is taken of the macro layer involving analysis of national surveys and public policy and literature reviews; and also the level of the individual parents.

Two types of organisation – namely public and private sector – were studied using a variety of methods. Human resources directors and between six and 11 managers were interviewed in each public and private sector organisation and a variety of documentary material was collected from each organisation. Working parents with a young child were selected from the cohort born between 1965 and 1975 and invited to take part in focus groups (4-11 groups) which were conducted in the workplace (see the Appendix for details of the numbers and composition of the focus groups and details of the manager interviews) (in total 283 parents took part in the groups). The upper age limit of 12 years for the children was originally set lower because of the study's focus on the transition to parenthood; plans were revised when we found that the number of parents with very young children in the organisations was insufficient. Parents from these workplaces were then selected to reflect those in high- and low-status jobs to take part in individual biographical interviews.[1] Interviewees across the organisations were matched on occupational status and other factors.[2]

The project design is an example of an *embedded case study* where the cases – countries, workplaces and parents – were selected from larger (linked) wholes (Yin, 2003a). In a case study, it is crucial to develop a research design that has clear theoretical rationales for the choice of cases at all the levels; cases must be 'cases of something'. Case selection took place at several phases of the Transitions study: at the research design phase, at the fieldwork stage and in the data analysis (Nilsen and Brannen, 2005; Brannen and Nilsen, forthcoming).

The Transitions study involved a spatial distribution of countries from Northern, Southern and Eastern Europe, a decision governed by the funding prerequisites of the European Union (EU) at the time. Countries were, however, chosen on both practical and theoretical principles. One criterion related to the countries' welfare provision at the time of the study: two Nordic countries with egalitarian welfare states (Norway and Sweden); two countries that had liberal welfare states (the Netherlands and the UK); and three countries from Southern and Eastern Europe that had no or weak welfare states (Bulgaria, Portugal and Slovenia). However, the latter classification by welfare regime was not considered adequate for the study's purposes since the study also needed to take account of the *historical* context, for example in recognising the provision of support to workers (paid leave and daycare) that still exists in Eastern European countries that was inherited from the communist era (Nilsen and Brannen, 2005). Likewise in Portugal, the institutions of the Roman Catholic Church have historically provided assistance to the poor and remain a key part of the provision available to working parents for the care of children.

The organisations within the countries were also selected on the basis of principles of similarity and difference. We sought organisations from the private and the public sector in each country since type of sector affects employee experiences: social services in the 'human services' public sector and finance organisations in the 'for-profit' private sector. In most countries, wages are higher in the private than the public sector; jobs tend to be more secure in the public sector; more women are employed in public sector occupations and so on.

The organisational case studies

In the organisational case studies, our focus was on workplace structures, working practices and cultures that set the conditions for employed parents to manage their paid work and their family and care responsibilities. Our aim was also to identify and describe organisational changes and change initiatives that might act as barriers to working parents in combining their work and family responsibilities. A grounded approach to the analysis of the organisational cases was largely adopted. However, a strong steer was given in the kinds of questions and data that each national team was expected to collect and analyse (in the focus groups with parents and interviews with managers).

Choice of methods ought to be framed by the research problem. However, too often in recent years methodological strategy is seen to be determined by underlying philosophical positionings that shape what is known as the qualitative–quantitative divide while in practice more practical issues take priority (Bryman, 1988; Lincoln and Guba, 1985; Alasuutari et al, 2008; Brannen and Nilsen, forthcoming). Case study research typically combines qualitative and quantitative methods. However, in the analysis phase, the use of different data drawn from different methods is, or should be, governed by the ways in which the research questions are framed, with consequences for the ways in which these data are integrated (Bryman, 2001; Brannen, 2004).

Single or multiple cases can be used to address specific research questions in different social fields, and they are particularly appropriate for studying organisations (Crozier, 2000) and their contexts (Sainsaulieu, 1997), either individually or severally. Cases may be studied either iteratively or in parallel. In some countries (Bulgaria, Norway, Portugal and the UK), two cases were conducted – one from the public and one from the private sector – while in the Netherlands, Slovenia and Sweden, only one case study was carried out (largely because of the preferences and resources of the latter teams).

Case studies of organisations have a number of advantages. They provide in-depth, contextualised data on complex organisational structures and processes. Case studies can be more rigorous than other research strategies because of their focus on real-life contexts and their use of a range of methods, generating different forms of data gathered from multiple sources and stakeholders in organisations. Together these provide a holistic and in-depth understanding of social or organisational phenomena and processes. Multiple (and sometimes conflicting) perspectives are generated by collecting and comparing reports from diverse participants at various levels in the organisations and often from stakeholders beyond the organisation, such as family members (Hochschild, 1997).

In the Transitions study we could have employed a different research design such as a survey and studied many workplaces. However, surveys cannot tap into the specificities of either the organisational context or the particular situations of the workers in the specific organisations. On the other hand, case studies may employ surveys and other methods as part of their methodological repertoire. As Yin (2003a: 20) puts it, case studies allow 'investigators to retain the holistic and meaningful characteristics of real-life events' (see also Stake, 2002). The use of multiple methods in case studies – for example a combination of documentary analysis, surveys, interviews, focus groups, participant observation and action research – is particularly apposite for understanding context and reflecting multiple perspectives. Moreover, case studies are helpful for making analytical distinctions between the different layers of context, thus making the process of analysis suitable for cross-national comparisons where it is necessary to take account of social context, including historical context (Nilsen and Brannen, 2005).

A case study approach is particularly appropriate to investigate a contemporary phenomenon in a real-life context, where boundaries between the phenomenon and context are not clearly evident (Yin, 2003a). In such contexts, where there is limited historical or past evidence, or where there is rapid social and organisational change, the investigator sets out to focus on contextual conditions believed to be highly pertinent to the topic or process in question. In several of the organisations studied there was considerable pressure for change both from within and from outside the organisation. In the public sector the influence of New Public Management ideas – providing client services at cost-efficient terms (Christensen and Lægreid, 2002) – was evident in several countries while the effects of global competition were significant especially in the finance sector organisations in the study. In some Eastern European countries, other changes were evident relating to the break with the communist era.

Like other research strategies, case studies can be used for exploratory, descriptive or explanatory purposes. They are particularly appropriate for addressing 'how' and 'why' questions – for example, how does flexible working impact on workers and the organisation and why is it effective or of limited effectiveness? They help to explain processes and examine links over time in relation to specific interventions and contexts. Case studies can provide explanations suggesting causal processes analogous to statistical analysis (see Hammersley et al, 2002, for a discussion), identifying and providing explanations for the conditions under which phenomena occur.

Case studies have a further benefit – they can inform and be informed by theoretical propositions (Yin, 2003a). Theory is important for selecting the case or cases to be studied, in creating full and appropriate descriptions, in stipulating rival explanatory theories where this is their purpose and in generalising results to other cases and contexts (Yin, 2003b). However, case studies may also be used in a 'grounded' way where the 'thick descriptions' (Geertz, 2000 [1973]) they provide form the basis for theorising from the ground up. In the Transitions study we made use of both approaches.

Case studies are often subject to criticism. One major criticism is that they lack generalisability. However, this criticism is typically based on the assumption that statistical generalisation is the only basis for generalisability (Hammersley et al, 2002). Comparative case-based research (like all case studies) has its strength in the richness of thick descriptions of a *few cases*, which can make it possible to extrapolate from single cases features that are *transferable* across time and space. Moreover, as Mitchell (2002: 183) suggests, 'the validity of extrapolation depends not on the representativeness of the case but upon cogency of the theoretical reasoning'. This notion of generalisation in terms of transferability (Lincoln and Guba, 1985) is different from that adopted in variable-based research: generalisations based on *many cases* and few variables. Indeed, a weakness of many other approaches in work–life research, for example surveys of work–life policies and practices, is the failure to take account of the specificity and diversity of organisational contexts.

Selecting organisations and gaining access

The organisations were selected on the basis of principles of similarity and difference. On the one hand, we sought organisations from the private and the public sector in each country since type of sector affects employees' experiences: social services in the 'human services' public sector and finance organisations in the 'for-profit' private sector. In most countries, wages are higher in the private than the public sector; jobs tend to more secure in the public sector; more women are employed in public sector occupations and so on. On the other hand, we expected organisations to have some similarities, in particular that they would be undergoing constant change or be subject to discourses of change. In the current economic climate sweeping Europe and increases in global competition in the private sector this was manifest in a concern with 'flexibility' meaning flexibility for the employer. In the public sector, emphasis was on 'modernisation' based on the principles of New Public Management.

Getting access to organisations is always a key issue in case study research. Organisations may be resistant to investigation by outsiders. We encountered a number of constraints especially since we wanted as much *comparability* as possible: between organisations and across the occupational status ladder of the workers studied – social services departments within the public sector and finance within the private sector. A major issue in the Transitions study was that in almost every organisation and country, low-skilled workers such as cleaners and catering staff were outsourced to agencies and were not therefore formally part of the organisation. We were therefore unable to access most of them. This raises the issue of what is an organisation and what is the case? Which workers are included? If both core and peripheral workers are to be included in an organisational case study, access may have to be negotiated by other means.

Although social services were found in all the countries in the study they were organised differently. In some countries elder care was part of social services along with child protection and disability, whereas in others, elder care was covered by a separate organisation. We found that it was more difficult, however, to find comparable organisations in finance. Teams were forced to adopt different solutions with some countries gaining access to banks, others insurance and in one case a multinational company in another branch of business. As noted already, it was not possible to study both sectors in each of the seven countries. However, both cross-sector and same-sector comparisons were possible, if not for all countries.

Another constraint in gaining access related to variation in the hierarchies of management across sectors and countries. Complexity was particularly difficult in public sector bureaucracies where lengthy and complex negotiations were necessary with 'gatekeepers' before access could be agreed. Moreover, in social services, employees were often dispersed across local centres and the community, in contrast to the large office locations that prevailed in the private sector companies.

A further factor that constrained organisation comparability was the under-representation of minority ethnic groups in some workplaces. (All countries had minority ethnic groups.) In some instances this reflected the types of occupation and workplace, in others the particular cities where the study was carried out, including for example the costs of living and travel to the locality where the workplace was situated. Hence, this was a feature that could not be a criterion for similar case comparison: like could not be compared with like in this respect. Similarly, the absence of lone working parents in some countries (one criterion for selecting cases of working parents in the interviews) was a reflection of national demographic and historical trends in a society. The presence of trades union representatives as informants in some countries and organisations was another point of difference, reflecting the routes of research access (via management) or the absence of trades unions in some organisations.

We also experienced variation in organisations' responses to the invitation to take part in the study. Some companies fear 'intrusion': from their perspective, confidential information can be obtained and transferred to their competitors or used against their credibility in the market. The degree of threat that the study presented to management was therefore an issue in some contexts. In one Eastern European country, workers felt that their jobs were very precarious, an issue that was problematic in the private (finance) sector company that had only recently been privatised. It was less of a problem in organisations where the research fitted the goals of the organisation. In the UK, the study's focus on family-friendly issues facilitated access since this was a common discourse in organisations and in public policy. In other contexts, access was negotiated through recourse to different arguments. For example, being associated with a project funded by the EU was an important factor in Portugal while in the Swedish social services organisation, being connected to a project conducted at the local university's prestigious department of social work was important. Moreover, data gathering for the case studies made demands on participants' time. Time is rationed or monitored in most organisations and if managers do not see a clear benefit from their cooperation in a piece of research, they are reluctant to allow workers to take part.

In our study we made initial contact through senior management, human resources or other managers (the more senior the better). In some cases, agreement was granted on the basis of knowledge and contacts already made by the team from previous research. The means of gaining access involved informal and formal contacts by telephone calls, emails and letters. Managers were identified and sent letters from the Transitions coordinator or from national partners, together with a leaflet presenting briefly the main goals of the study; the countries and research teams and universities involved; information about the funder (the EU); and some ideas about the likely outputs of the study.

The process of identifying interviewees took different forms. With the exception of Portugal, no organisations' databases identified parental status while few had records of those who had recently taken maternity or parental leave. Because of this, strategies had to be developed, one method being to send a screening questionnaire to those in the relevant age group attached to monthly pay slips (not particularly successful). Access involved negotiation at other management levels, depending on the sector (social services organisations had many more levels) and the country. Once access to the local social services units was gained, however, recruitment was much easier since the unit managers knew their workers. Human resource managers were key informants providing not only contacts for and sometimes direct access to managers but also written documentation or internet information on workforce profiles (levels of pay, shift rotas and absenteeism rates, training programmes), workplace support, organisational charts and policies relating to change management. Whatever the levers used to engage organisational interest, persistence was necessary. However, in spite of obstacles, all teams were successful in gaining access and obtaining broadly comparable data.

Developing and piloting the research instruments

In field research, instruments have to be developed and piloted. In single case studies these can be designed with a very specific organisational focus, informed by the background information gained at the key informant stage. Where multiple case studies are used, a balance needs to be struck between both methods that are specific to the organisation and those aimed to achieve comparable data. In the Transitions study it was important that the research instruments reflected the different contexts. Account also needed to be taken of the fact that the national teams came from different research traditions.

A key issue in all cross-national research concerns the equivalence of concepts (Hantrais, 1999, 2009). Lack of equivalence arises from different traditions of theory, research methodology and policy. This is particularly important in a study employing qualitative methods that is concerned to examine subjectivity and meaning. However, differences in the ways that concepts are used are also of empirical interest. Understanding nuances in meaning and their application requires reflection and analysis within a cross-national team. To deal with differences in conceptual understandings, our strategy was to spell out as far as possible the conceptual issues that underpinned the questions posed in the research instruments and to operationalise these in semi-structured questions posed in the research. In developing the research instruments, we tried to ensure sufficient time for discussion at various project meetings. However, much of this took place via email, coordinated by the scientific coordinator of the project, since only two meetings per year could be scheduled for the whole team to meet.[3]

But while we sought a flexible and grounded approach to the interpretation of concepts, the constraints of EU Framework protocols prevented us from recasting our research strategy. (The specification of the timing and content of each work package means that researchers in practice have to stick closely to the proposal and the timetable.) For example, one particular concept that figured in the EU Work Programme that we believe contributed to our success in gaining funding was 'well-being', including organisational well-being. This concept did not translate well cross-nationally. Parents who took part in the focus groups were asked to fill in questionnaires about well-being (see Černigoj Sadar et al, 2005). The questionnaire included a number of constituent concepts – satisfaction, enjoyment and happiness. However, there was not a lot of agreement about their meaning in the different languages and cultures. Nevertheless, despite the realisation of the limitations of using these concepts we had to continue to apply them. But we did so in a 'sensitising' way (Blumer, 1956) through examining, for example, how working parents described their subjective states in particular situations and contexts. It was therefore vital that all members of the transnational team were involved in piloting and discussing the research instruments.

While these issues are particularly relevant to cross-national research, they have wider applicability. Methodological and theoretical terminology varies across social science disciplines. But also the terms used in the research instruments vary according to social context. As all research textbooks suggest, careful piloting is necessary. In cross-national research this is doubly difficult because of the need to translate into different national languages.

Analysing the data

As discussed, a feature of case-based analysis in cross-national research is its use of different types of data. In the Transitions study, attention shifted to different levels of context in different phases of analysis. According to Przeworski and Teune (1970: 50), the process of *analysis* typically proceeds at multiple levels: 'Even if the levels of observation are multiple but the levels of analysis are not, such studies will not be considered "comparative"'. Thus, understanding particular phenomena in a comparative study means taking into account the relevant layers of the social context in the analysis of data as well as in the research design.

In using methods such as interviews and focus groups that were employed in the organisational case studies with the aim of tapping into the meanings that actors place on their situations, the wider context is often missing and has to be filled in by the reader (Brannen and Nilsen, 2005). To avoid this problem, the national teams in the Transitions study were paired and exchanged drafts of national reports of the organisational case studies and summaries of individual working parent interviews that were translated into English. They were asked to report back on their understandings of these so that the corresponding team supplied the missing information, especially the structural context. The eyes of those who stand outside a society can be very helpful to the process of making manifest the wider social context that an insider researcher takes as given.

In the Transitions study, common analysis frameworks were developed for use by the cross-national team in order to facilitate comparability. However, the considerable volume of qualitative data could not for cost reasons be translated. (Translation was very expensive in some countries.) Therefore, an analysis framework organised around the main themes set out in the research instruments was employed to make the writing up of the material as detailed and grounded as possible. Each national team was required to write in English the following: full reports of the organisational case studies and interview studies; and lengthy case summaries of the interviews with working parents. The translated material thereby provided rich resources for analysis.

Language is a particular issue in cross-national comparative research (Mangen, 1999). The limitation is especially acute in the analysis phase of qualitative research in which interviews – the spoken word – are a primary source of data. Multilingual competence for the whole team is not feasible. So, ways of overcoming language differences have to be found. In the Transitions study, competence in spoken English was high and the only language spoken in common. Thus, although the fieldwork was conducted and written up in the language of the country, one method we adopted was for all the teams to write some material in English (see earlier).

The depth and length of the translated reports and case summaries in the Transitions study varied between countries. This may be related to competence in written English but may also raise questions about skill and experience in particular methods and types of research. Indeed, some of the fieldwork was carried out by relatively inexperienced researchers, which reflected the infrastructure of research expertise and methodological training available in a country.[4]

Partial translation and the exchange of material cannot fully replace the complete translation of the data but is more often than not the only viable way of making use of qualitative material for cross-national comparative purposes. All large research projects involve a *division of labour*. Time, costs and skill reasons often require that the translation and transcription of interviews are carried out by people other than those who collected the data. Inevitably, such division of labour creates further distance from informants' original meanings. This is a challenge in the analysis and writing phases. Steps taken to overcome such problems in the Transitions study included cross-readings of material by relevant partners where cross-national analysis formed the basis of a publication by a particular team or partner. In turn this raised another issue – that of co-authorship, which was adopted but will not be discussed here.

Maintaining anonymity and ethical issues

Ethics cannot be discussed fully in this chapter except to note that research ethics are as much an issue in cross-national research as they are in research generally, and are issues likely to rise up the international research agenda. One particular ethical issue faced in the Transitions study concerned the anonymity of the organisations and participants in the case studies. While anonymity may be easy to maintain in research that covers many organisations and individuals, in case study research this is more problematic. In reporting on the case studies in the Transitions study, each organisation was given a pseudonym and individual participants were either not named or given a pseudonym; in some cases, their details were changed to protect anonymity. As the project involved only two organisations in each country, each from a different sector, it would be fairly easy to guess which organisations were being studied. Particular attention was therefore given to guarding anonymity. The same caution was exercised regarding workers, especially those in smaller organisations where they could easily be identified by colleagues or managers.

Cross-national organisational case studies and the case of comparative research

In many instances of cross-national projects that involve several research teams, the outputs are often national reports and syntheses of the national findings rather than comparative analysis.[5]

Since organisations and their contexts are highly specific, we have chosen to structure this book around a series of organisational case studies (Chapters Three to Ten). However, we have also sought to make some cross-national comparisons (Chapters Eleven and Twelve). Drawing on the preceding chapters, Chapter Eleven draws out comparative elements from the cases presented in the book[6] to create an empirical foundation for 'secondary analyses' of the national material. The discussion in this chapter takes as its point of departure particular cross-cutting themes that invite comparison across the cases. The first is organisational change; three cases of social services are compared that highlight the processes of 'modernisation' that are occurring in the public sector and the different forms that this process takes across national contexts and how these affect parents' lives. This comparison turns our attention from the national to the cross-national level and the importance of taking account of different layers of context. The second theme of the chapter concerns the exposure of the private sector to global market competition. Here we highlight the ways in which globalising forces towards work intensification and work extension permeate many organisations across Europe and impact on the experiences of employees and their families. The concluding chapter (Chapter Twelve) compares all the case studies in all the countries and examines the relationships between public/national and workplace policies, parents' sense of entitlement to take up these policies, and the obstacles parents face in being able to work flexibly in practice, that is, in order to reconcile their responsibilities to their children as well as to their employers.

In this chapter we have described the methods adopted in the Transitions study and some of the methodological issues faced in carrying out a cross-national study that employed a case study approach to address the different layers of societal context in which the lives of working parents are conducted. We have highlighted particular features of case study design and comparative analysis, and identified some of the challenges faced in multinational team research and the methods used to deal with them. We have also shown how the type of cross-national design adopted in the Transitions study enabled several layers of context to be brought into the frame and how it provided an interpretive structure for understanding individuals within their societies.

Notes

[1] Data from the interview phase are not, for the most part, included in this book. Our aim here is to contextualise the individual cases of working parents in relation to the wider contexts of the organisation and the national welfare regimes and contexts in general. In the Transitions study, lifelines were also completed for each informant, thereby graphically depicting the phases and transition points in their lifecourse. A lifecourse perspective in the interviews was adopted to capture the sequence and timing of events and transitions in the person's life in relation to the cohort to which they belonged and the contexts (time and place) in which their lives unfolded. This approach is highly sensitive to the different layers of contexts within which people live their lives and therefore is well suited to cross-national research.

[2] In the interview study cases, 10 working mothers and fathers were matched across each organisation according to the mother's occupation, marital status, age of parent and age of child. We sought two lone mothers in each organisation (one high status and one low status), but this proved difficult in some cases.

[3] The scientific coordinator also made a visit to one of the national teams to develop capacity in qualitative research.

[4] In addition, expertise in the biographical methods used in the individual interviews was variable across the teams.

[5] A number of reports and papers have been written that apply a comparative analysis (Nilsen and Brannen, 2005; Sümer et al, 2008; Lewis and den Dulk, in press; Brannen and Nilsen, forthcoming).

[6] Also to some extent the national case study reports.

Part One
Public sector organisations

THREE

Working parenthood in a social services context: a UK case

Julia Brannen

This chapter is about the experiences of working parents with young children in the UK as they are located in and experience one particular kind of workplace – a social services department situated in a metropolitan area. The chapter's focus includes how the organisation was changing, its particular characteristics in relation to its local environment, its employment conditions and workplace policies, the practices and perspectives of its managers, and the ways in which these impact on the lives and experiences of working parents. It also has a methodological slant, describing and discussing how context is made manifest through the research methodology. In particular, it examines the use of the focus group method by which the accounts of working parents were elicited in the workplace studied and how the dynamics of the focus groups speak to people's experiences as both employees and parents. From a methodological perspective, it is important that the 'results' of a study are not divorced from the context of its research methods and the settings in which research participants' experiences and views are elicited (Brannen, 2004). In presenting this analysis, attention is paid to how 'talk' about work–family issues was generated through the dynamics of the group and the methodological encounter (see also Brannen and Pattman, 2005).

The first part of the chapter sketches the organisational context, including change and trends in the public sector more generally, and the workplace policies for parents, drawing on the literature and available data and documentation about the local authority and social services in question at that time (2003). Second, this is followed by an analysis of interviews carried out with managers at all the many levels of the social services department concerning their views about how the organisation accommodated employees' family responsibilities when they had young children while also responding to the need to manage public resources efficiently (Rapoport et al, 2002; Lewis and Smithson, this volume). Third, the chapter explores the main themes generated in the focus group discussions with working parents in social services who discussed issues related to managing their family responsibilities.

The organisational context

Social services in the UK are the responsibility of local government (referred to as a local authority or council). Directors of social services are responsible to chief executives of local authorities and elected councillors who form the local authority's social services committee. Councillors are elected by political parties from the different wards within the local authority. The services provided by social services are for those considered to be 'vulnerable' and cover a huge range of areas: fostering, adoption, child protection, children needing local authority care, mental health, dementia care, care for frail older people, disability, youth crime, and drug and alcohol abuse (Douglas and Philpot, 1998). Access in our study was negotiated with both adult and children's services and also with human resources, finance and training. Reflecting the diversity of its services and functions – central and local – the social services department was a typically fragmented organisation covering a number of different geographical locations.

The local authority area covered by this social services department had a population of almost 301,000 in the 2001 Census. As a major metropolitan area, it has had a long history of in-migration, with 41.3% from black and minority ethnic groups (compared with 9.1% nationally) at the time of the study. Three quarters of its population were born outside Britain. Although the area had pockets of poverty, it had a low unemployment rate. About one quarter of the population worked in health, education or public administration and the area was within reach of large employers outside the local authority. The area had a high concentration of middle classes and the cost of housing was very high. At the time of the study the local authority employed 7,332 staff with 1,100 in social services and an overall budget (general fund) of £613 million. Most employees worked full time: 88% of men and 72% of women. In some instances, staff requesting part-time work had to organise their own arrangements. Usually this meant that they had to work half time, thus precluding more flexible arrangements.

The local authority had a high percentage of minority ethnic groups in its employment and a workforce that was heavily gendered. Only 22% of the workforce were male. No data were available on age although it seems that public service employees tend to be older than average, peaking in the age group 45-54 (Simon et al, 2003). This contrasts with the banking and financial sector in the UK where employment peaks in the 25-34 age group and declines steeply thereafter.

The social services department employed a large proportion of its staff on temporary contracts as well as depending on agency workers (especially social workers), reflecting trends in social services nationally (Winchester, 2003). However, despite the fact that agency workers had access to fewer training and promotion opportunities, less entitlement to holiday and sick pay, and low job security, many preferred this option while permanent positions were hard to fill (Winchester, 2003). (At the time of the fieldwork, the local authority, like all employers, was required to move people off fixed-term contracts under the then new European Union law.) No centrally collected data were collected on parental status and it was not possible to find figures for the take-up of maternity, paternity or parental leave. Between 50 and 60% of employees were reported by the (acting) head of human resources to be trade union members, especially those in blue-collar jobs. (We were unable to interview trade union officials.)

In terms of qualifications, the vast majority of those working in social services nationally were in care work and at that time few had educational qualifications at upper-secondary level or above (only 12% of social services workers were social workers); care staff typically had only lower-level qualifications (Douglas and Philpot, 1998: 51). However, social services were being pressed by government to bring care workers up to upper-secondary educational level through a vocational training course (National Vocational Qualifications). Social workers varied in whether they had the equivalent of university degrees: many having left school without the necessary qualifications to go to university returned to further and higher education in adulthood. While pay levels for care staff in local authorities and for qualified staff were higher than many private sector jobs, the wherewithal to work and live in the area depended on having two decent incomes in order to be able to buy housing (there being little good-quality social housing since it was sold off in the 1980s). This meant that many employees had to travel from cheaper areas with corresponding increases in travel-to-work time. This was inconvenient particularly for staff with childcare responsibilities. Travel included expensive and often unreliable public transport or driving on very crowded roads. These obstacles in turn caused additional recruitment problems for the organisation.

At the time, social services was experiencing considerable change. At a macro level, social services, like most public sector organisations, had been subjected to pressures to make the sector more efficient in cost terms and to become more 'customer oriented'. Legislation and initiatives at the national level sought the 'modernisation' of public services and to make them more accountable financially. This led to the restructuring of service delivery (with larger groupings of staff at the local level) and to changes in the job roles of social care staff (for example, higher administrative content and increased public scrutiny). In the particular local authority, a major shake-up of senior management was taking place and new policies and practices were being implemented. The local authority was also experiencing problems at the time with its human resource function. The local authority was trying to extend equal opportunities policies beyond issues of 'race' to disability, and introduce a new information technology system.

Such changes were ongoing, reflecting wider changes in the delivery of public services, with budgetary controls in place and 'new-style managers' brought in at senior level to implement change. Yet the organisation remained curiously bureaucratic, with many layers of management and a rule-bound culture.

A particular feature of social services in the UK at the time was the poor press received as a result of a number of children killed by their parents/carers while under the 'care' of social services. These cases led to heavy public criticism of social workers and the resulting pressure created a flood of social workers leaving the profession and to a growth in independent, voluntary and private sector agencies whose services were being bought in by local authorities (Eborall and Garmeson, 2001).

Workplace policies for working parents in the national context

As described in Chapter One, working parents in the UK have access to rather little state support when they have children. Rather, the object of the UK government has been to make employers take on a family-friendly guise. Under UK law, parents are entitled to *ask* for flexibility or a reduction in working hours but they are not entitled to have such requests granted. There was no state childcare and limited public financial support for working parents at the time of the study. Decent affordable housing was a particular problem in the metropolitan area under study for public sector workers, in particular for lone parents a significant number of whom were to be found in the UK generally and in the social services department studied.

On the other hand, the public sector provided rather better conditions of service than the private sector, and at least on paper, better policies for working parents. It also provided a little more maternity pay than the national legislation and some entitlement to sick leave and annual leave. However, entitlement depended on length of service in the local authority. Paid parental leave was limited to six months – two months more than statutory leave. Leave for family emergencies or planned days off for children was limited to five days but, as we will show, few knew about it and, if they did, they had to negotiate it individually with managers. Most parents took annual leave or sick leave instead. Even the scheduling of annual leave was problematic for those delivering frontline services because of staff rotas and quotas. The consequences were different for higher- and lower-status employees, with social workers having greater autonomy over the organisation of their time compared with care workers working, for example, in elder care or disability. On the positive side, it was only at higher levels of management that people worked more than their contracted hours.

Manager perspectives and practices

Unlike in the UK insurance company that is the subject of Chapter Seven, in the social services department there was no deliberate strategy to change management style or management practices towards a more flexible person–oriented direction in spite of the challenges it faced, namely problems of retention and motivating employees. On the other hand, new-style managers were being brought in from other local authorities at a senior level. Significantly, all three of the senior managers who were interviewed were women and had young children themselves. What was striking was their positive attitude to family-friendly policies and practices.

However, these managers were only responsible for the next level down the hierarchy and did not manage those delivering frontline services.

> *I think it [management] could be a bit more imaginative, rather than being reactive and wait for you to go cap in hand to your manager. I think things like you have this sick dependants leave … you can have up to five days extra off around this caring responsibility. I think that's very forward looking. I'd like to look at much more flexible working around families' needs.* (Woman manager, mother of a young child)

Another female senior manager, also a mother of young children, was in favour of allowing staff to work from home occasionally and was critical of the discretionary nature of policies:

> *Even if a manager lets somebody work from home, if they make them feel they've done them a favour or begrudgingly they let them do it, I don't think it does any good at all.*

In contrast, the female head of human resources, an older woman who had no children and who had worked in the private sector, felt that the policies were 'more than generous' compared with the private sector. Another younger female member of staff in personnel confirmed the account given by employees that members of staff only learned about policies by word of mouth rather than being informed. The head of human resources suggested that this lack of information was not accidental:

> *As an employer you generally don't put on the website 'Did you know you get parental leave?'. Though you ought to, if you were totally responsible. But you generally put it up somewhere and hope not too many people read it.*

By contrast, the line managers of frontline employees in local centres and local areas said that they wanted to accommodate employees' work–family needs but were heavily constrained by the need to maintain 24-hour cover for a service that was run on a tight budget. Typically they were required to refer leave decisions to middle management, giving the local line managers little scope to respond positively to staff requests. Sometimes they turned a blind eye to their staff's arrangements while being officially obliged to scrutinise leave calendars and sick leave. An exception was a manager of a family centre[1] who allowed some of his staff to work out their own flexible arrangements. Significantly this was not a statutory service and the manager was employed part time and on a temporary contract.

Given the *scarcity* of resources in social services and the high pressure of client need in this metropolitan area, all managers expressed some concern that staff did not take "*undue advantage*" of any benefits available. In addition, other pressures contributed to managers' inflexibility. One was a culture of blame that existed at the top of the organisation, pushing the blame for inefficiency down the organisation. The other was the way in which family-friendly policies were defined as a "*women's issue*" in which the family responsibilities of fathers were systematically ignored. Thus, working parents (mothers) managed childcare responsibilities by working out informal arrangements with one another in the workplace. This practice was reported by a female middle manager who had no children. Seen by her staff as uncompromising, her 'story' was that staff did not approach her with requests for leave.

In contrast to the conditions and cultures that prevailed, managers sought to present their own individual practices in a good light. They considered themselves responsive to their own staff's family commitments while employees complained about managers' practices. However, where they had some latitude in decision making, managers described being caught in a double bind between being responsive to staff's family commitments and guarding the resources of the local authority and ensuring that the jobs got done. Senior managers who were mothers with young children held the most enlightened views but had no direct experience of managing those delivering social services, as already noted. They were able moreover to negotiate their own work–family responsibilities advantageously, a fact that was noted by employees at lower levels of the hierarchy.

Middle managers were caught in an 'intercalary position' situated between senior and line management: they had to meet the former's targets, which meant not acceding to the requests proposed by lower-level managers on behalf of their own staff. Managers at that local level had not only little leeway to respond to working parents' needs but also little scope in managing their own work–family responsibilities. Both middle and line managers described being caught in a tension between being "*too hard*" by ensuring that employees did the work they were paid to do and being "*too soft*" on employees who might exploit any discretionary support for meeting their family commitments.

Before moving on to exploring the experiences of employees as working parents, it is necessary first to make some comments about the focus group method and its possible implications for the themes that 'emerged' from the data analysis.

The application of focus groups in this organisational context

Focus groups enabled us to study a number of employees simultaneously within a workplace, an important consideration given the constraints on employees' time and, as it turned out in the social services studied, the relative rarity of employees with young children. Focus groups also allowed us to study employees who possibly knew one another and who shared the experience of being in the same workplace and in a setting under considerable pressure. The method thereby emphasised the shared aspects of the context. Moreover, it provided an interactive context (Morgan, 1996), capturing group processes in the workplace (Bloor et al, 2001).

In analysing and interpreting the focus group data, a number of considerations and caveats were important (Brannen and Pattman, 2005). First was the pre-existing nature of the groups. The focus group literature suggests that it is useful if participants share some styles of talking (Macnaghten and Myers, 2004). Thus, a workplace environment in which 'people skills' are important and in which the assumption is that it is 'good to talk', for example a social services environment, provided a conducive setting. On the other hand, issues of privacy and confidentiality arise when focus groups are carried out in pre-existing groups (Bloor et al, 2001): those in more senior positions in the organisation have the possibility to exploit any unguarded views or personal information volunteered in the course of the group by lower-status employees (to the latter's disadvantage). This power imbalance was unavoidable in some groups we conducted, for example when a manager of a care unit and one of her staff were the only employees in that setting who had young children. There were advantages as well as disadvantages to having members of the same organisation or work team in a group, namely their shared knowledge of the organisation, their shared position as employees and their shared parental status. While undoubtedly the fact that some members knew one another well helped the interaction, in some groups members were barely acquainted but interaction was often as intensive. The disadvantages of pre-existing bonds were compounded by difficulties of finding enough parents in what, in many cases, were relatively small offices and units at the local level.

A second related consideration was the small size (dyads) of most groups, a factor likely to detract from group interaction. However, this did not necessarily lead to less social interaction between participants and provided for considerable revelations of personal experience, although not via lengthy monologues. Not only was it easier for the participants to speak in dyads and small groups, it was easier for researchers to transcribe the groups and to attribute responses accurately to the participants (see Bloor et al, 2001).

A third consideration was the lack of within-group homogeneity, which methodology texts consider important. In the case study there was a mix of mothers and fathers, ethnicities and level of education. Given the lack of parents with younger children and the structuring of social services on the ground, this was inevitable. Such diversity had to be offset in part at least by the small size of the groups in which there was little opportunity for some participants to be silent.

Because of the large geographical spread of employees across this social services department, the rarity of parents with young children due to the character of the locality and the low public sector pay (as already described), it was necessary to conduct a larger number of groups than in the other case studies (11 groups, of which nine consisted of two people). The groups consisted of both higher-status workers, most of whom were social workers (although not all were fully qualified), and low-status workers (care workers; and administrative assistants who had no or low educational qualifications).

Employees' perspectives on being working parents in a social services department

Not surprisingly, the themes that emerged in the workplace groups considered by working parents to help or hinder the management of family responsibilities were workplace related. Their accounts focused on everyday life in the organisation, on management practices in particular. They tended not to mention issues relating to wider conditions such as difficulties relating to the high cost of housing in the area and metropolis, the high cost of (private) childcare and the financial problems of lone parenthood. However, these issues were identified for the individuals concerned in the methodological approach adopted in the biographical interviews that were conducted subsequently (Nilsen and Brannen, 2005).

Lack of knowledge about family-friendly policies

In several focus groups, mention was made of poor communication of workplace policies, notably concerning the entitlement to up to five days of 'dependants leave' provided by the local authority in question. Participants suggested that while the policy was applied at the discretion of management, it was also poorly disseminated (by human resources) and therefore applied inconsistently. (Mention has already been made of human resources management's strategy not to publicise policies.) However, in three instances it was during the focus group encounter that some employees first discovered the existence of the policy. The focus group thereby became a forum for information and advice. In one group comprising four female social workers and a male manager from different ethnic origins, the manager (who did not manage any of the group), Will, was knowledgeable about this policy and took it on himself to inform the group about it. He did so in response to the moderator's question about the existence of workplace policies.

Will:	*There's Special Leave, you get –*
	[Lots of voices – some saying they were not aware of this policy]
Zarina:	*If you have a rotten manager, then obviously they won't say 'Yes, yes!'. It entirely depends. It's a discretionary thing.*
Will:	*It's a certain period of time you are allowed the leave – five days – and after that it's down to the discretion of the manager.*
Zarina:	*You are allowed to take five days' leave??*
	[Sounds of surprise]
Will:	*Five days a year.*
Prue:	*I wasn't even aware of that to be quite honest.*
	(Parents with children of primary school age and younger)

Will, a father with a child aged 18 months, picked up on this issue at the end of the focus group when commenting on the 'learning points' of taking part in the research for the group:

> *Yes, it's been very useful, very interesting. It makes you think. Somebody's learned something about Special Leave.*

Overt criticisms of management practice and employee flexibility

In some groups, criticism was spontaneous and overt, with working parents describing line management as a "*lottery*" in terms of being responsive to employees' responsibilities, for example allowing them time off to attend their children's school meetings or medical appointments. However, 'the lottery' was shaped by employees' status since lower-status workers had much less work autonomy than higher-status workers. Many of the former were in frontline services that delivered 24-hour cover, were run on tight budgets and had little extra staff cover, leaving local managers little flexibility to accommodate staff needs. In one group consisting of four social workers (three women and one man, of different ethnicities), a deluge of criticisms followed the moderator's very first question in which participants were invited to make word associations with the concept of 'working parent'. Participants, especially the one very outspoken male, were 'setting the agenda' in a way that meant that subsequent contributions would tend to be critical. These interjections were not purely narrative accounts of individual experience, they also served to open up spaces for others to join in with similar anecdotes and may have *encouraged* the expression of criticism. The male social worker (Esa) went first, focusing on government's failure to support working parents, especially for people like himself. This prompted three female social workers to make similar remarks. A critical remark that provoked others' endorsement was the use of term 'management lottery' (by Ursula, see below). She evaluated managers according to whether or not they were accommodating and sympathetic towards employees' caring responsibilities. As can be noted, the remarks and reported experiences are woven together seamlessly without pauses and only minimal encouragement from the moderator.

> Ursula: *Here is called the manager lottery – if you have a good manager he can give you compassionate leave. If you have a terrible manager, sorry you're out of luck....*
>
> *I had cases where I had letters to show I needed to be at my child's school. The same manager said no. So it's not an even-handed thing. Depends on whether they like your face, you know, which I think is very unfair on mothers. There should be clear-cut policies and guidelines on compassionate leave and on the working parents. It's not very clear cut* [agreement from another member], *it's*

> *very messy, it should not be dependent on having to suck up to somebody. If your child is very ill you have to go.*

Moderator: *Have either of you tried to take compassionate leave at all?* [to Leila and Ann]

Leila: *My son, the little one, he was on like an operating theatre table, I was told to come in to work, even though explaining the situation that I couldn't leave him until he actually came out. But I was told to come and I was threatened that I would lose my job.*
[Esa joins in here and Leila resumes her complaint about lack of knowledge about special leave policies]

....

Ann: *I had to take some time off recently because my daughter, my youngest daughter got chicken pox.*

Moderator: *Right.*

Ann: *And I was dropping big hints to the manager that I wasn't happy having to take that off as annual leave 'cos it was –*

Moderator: *Yeah.*

Ann: *But he just said: 'Well what else are you supposed to take it as?'*

Moderator: *Really?*

Ursula: *This happened to me before, yes. I use up most of my annual leave because....*

Ann: *We get our 24 days' annual leave and then as a parent you have to say: 'Right, 10 of those days I'm going to leave aside for when my kids need time off' and that's what I do.*

Esa: *I had to do that with the previous manager – certain hours they call compassionate leave.*

Ann: *Our manager previously did not give you special leave for anything.*

Ursula: *No, she didn't.*

Esa: *I have to fight to have special leave. And I have to go and see the service manager and I have to put it in writing....*
(Parents with children of primary school age and younger)

A second example of overt criticism occurred in a 'group' of two black fathers employed as care workers. The men were critical of management's treatment of fathers in respect of access to family-friendly working practices. They were also critical of mothers (one was a lone father), expressing indignation about women who actively discouraged men from seeing and being fully involved with their children. The two participants acted as accomplices in setting the agenda, egging one another on by repeating each other's words and supporting one another's statements (Jacoby and Ochs, 1995):

Joseph: *And the same thing, I think the law don't really give all parents the chance. As he said, the law is always on the women's side. Women finish with the men, they take the children.*

Sid: *They take the child.*

Joseph: *There's a lot of men out there want to do their best for the children. [Sid: Yeah] Maybe I'm lucky [Sid: Yeah] because I'm allowed to be with my daughter and I'm in a relationship with the woman. So....*

Moderator: *Yeah.*

Joseph: *And he is very lucky because he can have his child.*

Sid: *That's right, yeah.*

Joseph: *A lot of women wouldn't give you that child.*
            (Fathers of children of primary school age or younger)

Whether the discussion and interaction in this all-male group would have been quite so lively had the moderator been a man or had women participants been present is debatable. The two men united in their masculinity and were complicit in expressing criticism – safe in the knowledge that no mothers were present to contest their views. The moderator was by definition non-judgemental in her moderator role and in the study's focus on gendered parenthood was alert to these responses. The two men were also complicit in the delight they took in their portrayal of opposed gendered ways of managing work–family boundaries. Elaborating on these to another man would have had less rhetorical effect and would not have generated so much humour. If other women participants had been present, these comments would have been seen as provocative. Indeed, the moderator offered the suggestion that men were more likely to separate work and home than women in a rather leading way. This provoked a strong response as, laughingly, the men did not hesitate to portray men as 'better' than women, in this context as meaning 'less emotional than women', emotionality being a quality that the two later in the discussion went on to portray as 'weakness'.

Moderator: *Do you think men are better than women at cutting off from their work when they get home? Or do you think that's just my stereotype view?* [laughter]

Joseph: *I would say this is more feminist or sexism idea.*

Moderator: *Yeah.* [laughter]

Sid: *I think* **yes, yeah!** [loudly] *Men are better, you know.* [laughter] *[inaudible] sorry.*

Joseph: *We tend to let things go.*

Sid: *Just go through our heads, you know.*

Joseph: *Within our work environment you see things that happen, you know, men are 'Oh yeah [inaudible]'* [Sid: Yeah yeah yeah yeah] *Women will see like –*

Moderator: *Why do you think men are so much better at it then?*

Sid:	*Because women are more emotional* [Joseph: *Emotional yeah*] *than men. You know. Or some men. So women are more – you know, listen, then think about it, then say 'Well hold on, this person's talking about me' or 'This person's doing this to me'. Bring it home and then, you know, confide in their partner. But a man will just let it go over his head, go home and just totally* –
Joseph:	*Have your pint and that's it.*

In this conversational play, the moderator was slightly mischievous in her questioning as she risked teasing the two young men by seeming to go along with them but through laughter implying she might not be so neutral. She also distanced herself a little from the question by referring to her view as "*just stereotypical*". The risk and tension involved in teasing is reduced here since teasing only has the effect of 'biting' when it takes place between intimates (see Boxer and Cortes-Conde, 1997). This was reinforced by the social distance between the moderator (older, female, white, an academic) and the participants (younger, male, black, care assistants). The laughter signified complicity between the two participants and also between participants and moderator, creating a temporary bond for the duration of the conversational interlude. Moreover, the tension inherent in a discourse of resistance – the raising of a 'taboo' that men might be discriminated against – was moreover smoothed away through laughter (see Griffiths, 1998, on humour as a modality of resistance).

Covert criticisms of management

In some groups, criticism of managers was tacit and disguised through laughter, as if a parent was fearful of being overtly critical. Two workers were interviewed together in a centre for adults with learning disabilities, a white male professional (Bob) and a black female lower-qualified administrative assistant (Samantha). The status imbalance was reflected in their differential autonomy in their power as parents of young children to negotiate time off for their children: Bob having greater freedom, and Samantha much less. The encounter was punctuated by lots of laughter, some of which centred on Samantha's manager. Samantha said she was fearful of asking her manager for time off and was reluctant to go on record with criticism of her manager who, it was hinted at by Bob as well as by Samantha, was unsympathetic and inflexible to her staff. The criticism was largely unspoken and implied through laughter. Laughter also created a bond of solidarity between the two, neither of whom had previously known each other. As the more senior colleague and as a man, Bob was careful that he did not draw too much attention to differences in their power nor break the boundaries that Samantha had set about communicating her criticism publicly.

Moderator: *Do you know what people do if they want to, you know, move to*
            part-time work?
Samantha: *I don't know what people do.*
Moderator: *Mmm.*
Samantha: *It's a thought that has crossed my mind occasionally, going part*
            time.
Moderator: *But you've never asked about it?*
Samantha: *I've never asked, so I wouldn't know who I would really approach.*
            I suppose personnel but – no, I wouldn't know the procedures to
            do that.
Bob: *Umm, I've never done it either but I guess I would just liaise with*
            my manager, umm, and then just say, you know, that I wanted to
            alter my contract.
Moderator: *Do you think managers would be sympathetic here?*
Bob: *Mine would be, I don't know about yours.*
Samantha: *I don't know about mine* [general laughter].
Moderator: *Right.*
Samantha: *I don't know about my manager.*
Bob: *Mine would be fine* [laughing].
Samantha: *Yes.*
            (Parents of children of primary school age or younger)

In this context, laughter alerts us to something serious being said (Driessen, 1997). As Mary Douglas (1975, cited in Driessen, 1997: 224) has suggested, 'something formal is attacked by something informal'. Laughter stands in for criticism, signalling the existence of something being withheld while retaining its disguise. Laughter also serves to create solidarity between the two participants even though Bob was not constrained from taking time off by his manager to the extent that Samantha was. However, Bob suggested that he was 'in the know' about the manager and joined in the laughter, thereby supporting the implied criticism. At the end of the focus group, Bob, as the employee with greater power in the organisation, sought to redress the inequity and strengthen Samantha's lonely position in his suggestion that employees should collectively try to improve conditions: *"to get together within teams"* so that those without children (like Samantha's manager) *"can understand where people [parents] are coming from"*.

Other types of criticism expressed in the groups were also accompanied by laughter, for example male partners' lack of participation in domestic work. In an all-female group, women criticised men by infantilising them, enabling them to attack men in ways that did not seriously question their investments in adult heterosexual relations.

One group consisting of mothers and one father from different ethnic backgrounds discussed whether fatherhood had changed since the participants were children. The group was much more comfortable talking about their own fathers than about their partners and portrayed their fathers in fairly cruel but humorous ways. However, one of the three mothers in the group, Judy, asserted that most fathers today have not changed by referring to *Wife Swap*, a popular and compelling 'reality TV' programme where wives swap families for a few days. There was laughter at this point also – clearly everyone in the room had seen the programme and knew what was being talked about. Then another mother agreed with her, which drew more laughter (solidarity) from the group. Next, the only father present piped up that this was an *"individual thing"*, suggesting that not all men were like this. There was no clear support for this view, with Alicia having the last laugh here, and thereby winning the argument (Sacks, 1992) at men's expense (*"If you **can** find the husband!"*). The male moderator then moved on to another topic and the father acquiesced rather weakly with the criticism.

Judy:	*That goes the same as me and my husband. We share the childcare, we share the jobs* [laughs]. *Umm, but my Dad, yeah, he went off to work and umm, came back and had his dinner on the table and fixed the washing machine and things like that.* [laughter]
Judy:	*[inaudible] quite traditional, really.*
Alicia:	*My Dad didn't even fix the washing machine!* [laughs]
Moderator:	*Do you agree with these changes for men?*
Alicia:	*The changes for men – definitely!* [laughter]
Judy:	*Yeah, I don't think, I don't think. I wouldn't say men overall have changed, I think some have, I don't think all of them have by any means. You only have to watch Wife Swap to see how many aren't doing anything.* [laughter]
Katherine:	*You know, there's still, both can … be working and both at – and the woman's still doing everything. I don't think it's changed **that** much, it's maybe cultural, it may be how you've been brought up or, or, you know, practical. But umm –*
Peter:	*I think, again, I think it's personal expectation as well –*
Katherine:	*Mmm.*
Peter:	*– as well as the cultural. And it's how much the actual, the man wants to get involved himself.*
Moderator:	*I mean, you see a lot of this in your own work, presumably?*
Katherine:	*Yep.*
Alicia:	*If you **can** find the husband* [laughs].
Peter:	*Yes, true.*
	(Parents of primary school-aged children or younger)

Emotions and supportive relations among working parents

As well as criticism of managers and complaints about lack of information, the workplace groups provided some positive insights into how employees with family responsibilities managed. The discussions themselves were emotionally engaged, reflecting the importance that participants attached to work–family issues and their keenness to take part in the study. The groups provided a forum for the expression of positive as well as negative emotions and, as indicated above, produced much joking and laughter. As well as generating feelings of solidarity and making the groups entertaining and enjoyable, such laughter also seemed to have a cathartic quality, 'allowing' people to vent their frustrations at the expense of people holding greater power, like managers and male partners, and also created a collective feeling that together they might do something to change the status quo.

This expression of emotion tells us much about the experience of working parenthood. Positive emotions and smiling accompanied mention of employees' children and positive aspects of the workplace, especially working with colleagues, a good atmosphere at work and high morale, whereas anger, despair and concern were expressed about difficulties of juggling so many responsibilities and about management.

The expression of positive emotions in the groups may reflect existing solidarities between employees who have worked together and have depended on each other in informal ways to solve the dilemmas of managing their family responsibilities in the face of manager inflexibility (see Chapter Four). However, not all employees knew one another despite working in the same type of job or part of the social services department. Thus, it is also likely that positive emotions and relations were a product of participating in the groups.

Conclusion

This presentation of social services has to be understood in *context*: the wider context of public policy, the general trends in the UK public sector and social services, and the specificities of the particular local authority. Indeed, the particular case study organisation and its setting influenced both the composition of the workforce, with relatively few parents of young children, as well as the experiences of the workers. Situated in an area with a long history of in-migration and a new wave of migrants in the context of present shortages of trained staff, this small-scale study reflected these characteristics. Most working parents were either second-generation migrants or new migrants – most of South Asian or African descent. Many lived outside the expensive housing area where the social services department was located.

The main discourses to emerge focused on criticism of management. Managers' approaches were important to working parents since there were few policies which employees felt they had an unequivocal right to draw on when they needed to take leave for family reasons or change their hours. Moreover, the implementation of any workplace family-friendly policies was discretionary. Line management was described as "*a lottery*" in which there were winners and losers. Manager flexibility that gave employees time off for care responsibilities, for example leave for childcare emergencies or routine appointments for young children, was highly prized. Managerial discretion was a source of great frustration and created a sense of inequity among staff. Women managers and those who had young children themselves were seen as generally more sympathetic towards staff needs.

A second theme concerned lack of information about what policies were available. In the absence of knowledge and clear communication of policies, many employees, notably those with little autonomy and who worked in frontline services where resources were scarce and line managers reported little scope for flexibility, had to resort to taking their annual leave or sick leave when care responsibilities called them away from work. Those more highly qualified workers, for example some social workers, typically suggested they had some autonomy in organising their work and thus to manage the boundaries between home and work.

A further theme related to the invisibility of fathers in the family-friendly discourse and a bias in favour of mothers.

The frustrations experienced by many, especially those in lower-status occupations, need to be understood in relation to their strong sense of commitment to the work (caring for people in need). Thus, the expressive rewards of the work were important; people went into the work for this reason rather than for the extrinsic rewards (money). An ethic of care was an ideal that many employees considered essential for the organisation to live up to in order to fulfil its duty to care for its clients but also for its employees. Social services as a supposedly caring organisation was found wanting in its care of working parents.

The discourses of working parents were supported by evidence from the managers in which managers at the most senior level were most in favour of flexibility for staff. But since they only managed other managers below them rather than frontline workers, they were limited in putting these beliefs into practice. Line managers felt most constrained about adopting a flexible approach to those with caring responsibilities. Middle managers were caught in the middle: accountable for employee performance to senior managers while seeking to be responsive to line managers who were obliged to refer employees' requests for flexibility and leave to them. Such management practices had greater negative impact on those staff in lower-status occupations who had less autonomy in their work and in the scheduling of their time.

There are some lessons to be learned from this case study. First, focus groups proved to be a form of action research giving a voice to employees' often unspoken concerns about organisational change, management practices and a culture that was not family friendly. Second, social services failed to develop a management strategy to match its goal for organisational change, which is to become a more efficient and effective deliverer of care services. In particular it continued to have a very hierarchical approach, with many tiers of management. This led to a lack of discretion on the front line of service delivery and management of staff. Because local line managers had little power in the devolution of resources (including staff), they had no leeway to respond to staff requests for working-time flexibility and needs relating to their children. Third, because workplace family-friendly policies were ineffectively advertised and subject to management discretion, this led to feelings of inequity in entitlement in the organisation. While senior managers were seen to negotiate flexibility for themselves, employees felt discriminated against. Fourth, in so far as existing work–family policy and practice existed, on the face of it the policies were gender neutral. However, in practice they were directed to mothers so that fathers with young children felt discriminated against. Finally, on a positive note, the case study suggested that the workplace is a context that generates feelings of solidarity between employees. If the employer were to build on this then greater benefits in terms of problem solving in the workplace might result.

Note

[1] A family centre offers services to families who need support but not services that the authority is mandated to deliver such as social worker support to children in care.

FOUR

Social service as human service: between loyalties; a Swedish case

Lars Plantin and Margareta Bäck-Wiklund

The aim of the case study on which this chapter is based was to capture the experiences of parents with young children working in a social service agency in one of Sweden's largest cities. In this chapter, we will focus on features that block or facilitate the balance between work and family as well as form social workers' career paths in a context of organisational change. The balance between work and family is often discussed with reference to the overspill from one area to another (Johansson, G., 2002). However, the study of work–family strategies is seldom related to the nature of work performed or to the character of the organisation in question. In this chapter, we will draw on these themes. Furthermore, we will discuss work–family strategies among young working parents. We will use the Transitions project's broad approach with multiple layers of information, and combine focus group discussions with information from biographical individual cases to further the context of work–family strategies (see Chapter Two and the Appendix). Our focus is especially on social workers who are working in face-to-face situations with individual client cases. The analysis is based on their accounts, sometimes contrasting these with those of employees in different positions in the organisation as well as with those of managers (see also Bäck-Wiklund and Plantin, 2007).

Against this background, we will provide an analytical picture of the organisation and of some individual career paths, with a focus on the following questions:

- What does the social agency look like from the perspective of social workers who are new parents?
- What strategies do managers adopt to meet their needs?
- What does the nature of work, notably working face to face with clients, mean in this context?
- What dilemmas and loyalties do the social workers in this case study face in relation to colleagues, clients and family?

Human service organisations: a theoretical approach

Social service organisations are *human service organisations* and, as such, they have certain characteristics. First, they work directly with and on people whose attributes they attempt to shape. In a sense, people are their raw material. Second, they are mandated – and this justifies their existence – to protect and promote the welfare of the people they serve (Hasenfeld, 1983).

Public sector organisations are financed via taxation, are politically mandated and are based on political values; and they are not driven by professional considerations or market demands as in the private sector. They are particularly sensitive to the *dominant cultural* and *value systems* in the community at large and are sometimes forced to change service delivery according to variations in the environment and/or claims made by civic groups. To analyse and understand internal factors such as *practices and workplace cultures* (Johansson, G., 2002) the neo-institutional approach (DiMaggio and Powell, 1991) with an emphasis on *dependence on the environment* is valuable. The neo-institutional approach also questions the idea about organisations as closed systems exercising rationality (Ahrne and Hedström, 1999). Instead, it views organisations as 'loosely coupled systems' (Perrow, 1986) with different teams and functions targeting groups with different needs. This loose system creates an uncertain lineage for decision making. In such organisations it is difficult to control staff and their encounters with clients and they are thus according to Lipsky (1980) termed 'street-level bureaucrats'. Social workers are engaged in power relations, and intervene in individual lives and thereby reveal the division of the private and the public sphere (Dominelli, 1997). This makes social work's role in society open to question and subject to scrutiny by both the media and the public. Social service agencies constitute an organisational context where the frontline workers have a great deal of *discretion* in their occupational practice. The work is difficult to perform routinely and social workers must be flexible, create instant solutions, as well as build longlasting relationships with their clients. To characterise the work as discretionary is a way to relate the organisation to the social workers' free choice of conduct. Discretion can be used in various ways, for example to promote the social workers' own relative autonomy and interests even if this is not always in accordance with the management. However, social workers are often seen as 'semi-professionals' as they do not fulfil the strong requirements for a profession (Brante, 2003; Dellgran and Höjer, 2005). Medical doctors and lawyers are considered the classic examples of occupations with full professional status with an established and exclusive knowledge base of their own and jurisdiction for independent practice and accordingly for discretion (Hellberg, 1978). Social workers often act with discretion but without fully recognised legitimacy. To solve this dilemma, social workers in most Western countries struggle to develop full professional status with academic status and better recognition.

National characteristics of social work and social policy

Following the theoretical perspective outlined above, in this section we will clarify various national characteristics that have special importance for organisational practices, workplace cultures, qualifications and education for social workers and gender policy in Sweden.

In Sweden, most social work is administered through social services. The Social Service is the central part of the *local welfare state*, with objectives laid down in the 1998 National Social Service Act, but also with some special legislation for disabled people, drug abusers and young people. The organisation is steered by a local political committee. In an international perspective, Swedish social workers are often in regular contact and have greater accountability to their political committee than in most other European countries (Bergmark and Lundström, 2005).

Social workers are trained at state universities (with the exception of one private university) for three and a half years, qualifying with a Bachelor of Social Work. The universities offer many possibilities for further specialised education as well as a Master's degree. Women are in the majority, comprising 88% of the students. Entry to the training is highly competitive. However, for the last few years, the number of places for training has increased, resulting in higher levels of unemployment among new graduates (SCB, 2005). The change has been especially dramatic over the last three years and a growing number of social workers today are forced to apply for less-qualified jobs.

Swedish social workers are seen as 'semi-professionals (Rigné, 2002; Wingfors, 2004), but have a long-desired goal to achieve a 'professional' status. In their everyday casework, they have contact with lawyers, doctors and psychologists, all of whom have a state licensure,[1] something that social workers have failed to achieve (Wingfors, 2004). Social work practice, education, qualifications and knowledge base are questions dealt with on different levels in society, from legislators to the individual frontline workers and their unions. The two top-managers of the agencies in the case study discussed in this chapter both highlight that access to further education is a means to steer and retain social workers. It is also used as a response both to legislative changes and to employees' requests to have their professional training recognised (Bäck-Wiklund and Plantin, 2004). In the most recent revision of the 1998 Social Service Act, an amendment was added regarding how to develop social work. Education is mentioned as a strategic factor in attaining competence in qualified social work practice: 'Interventions within the social services shall apply to good practices, conducted by personnel with adequate education and experiences' (Social Service Act, §7).

Sweden has a long history of welfare state development and gender policy. Regulations state that, in tandem with the welfare state, service delivery employers within the social services agencies are also responsible for developing gender equality and implementing a national policy for working parents. The most important tool is *parental leave*, which allows all Swedish parents up to 480 days' leave from work when their child is born. The compensation level for 390 days is 80% of previous salary (up to the same standard ceiling as for sick leave). For the remaining 90 days, parents receive a flat rate of €7 per day. Parents who were unemployed before the birth or adoption of their child receive a flat rate of €20 per day for the first 390 days of the insurance period, then the same €7 rate as everyone else. The parental leave is allocated on a quota basis, so that the mother and father each have 60 earmarked days, while the remaining days guaranteed by statute can be shared between them. In addition, the parental leave also includes a temporary benefit that allows parents to stay at home to care for a sick child (up to the age of 12) for up to 60 days per child and per year. Along with the parental insurance and child benefit systems, *childcare* is one of the mainstays of Swedish family welfare policy, covering almost 90% of all children over two years of age (Swedish National Agency for Education, 2005).

A gender policy with generous support for working parents and their work with clients calls for a flexible organisation with the potential to adapt to both internal and external demands. Most social work with clients in Sweden has historically sought to construct its professionalism on the casework method and, since the 1960s, a more psychoanalytic methodology (Pettersson, 2001). This approach emphasises structure and continuity in contact with clients and therefore offers a lower level of flexibility in relation to family life. Facing an emergency situation at home, for example having a sick child to care for, immediately creates a dilemma for these 'professional' social workers as they are not only absent from work but also seen to jeopardise their professional ethics by abandoning the client. However, as we shall see further into the analysis, these kinds of statements tend to be gendered, as men and women are subject to different preconceptions when handling clashes between work and family life.

The culture of continuous change

This case study involves two agencies under a shared central citywide administration. The main context for the case study is their department for individual and family care (IFC), whose objective is to support individuals and families in need. These agencies each have a different history of organisational change, one slow with staff involvement, and the other much more management driven with immediate implemented change. Contrary to a common ideology in the social services aiming at a 'comprehensive view of the client' with multifunctional units, actual development has led to organisations with a vide variety of service units, each with a special function and competence. This trend towards specialisation is similar for the whole country (Bergmark and Lundström, 2005).

The two agencies have a similar structure – a multifunctional 'horizontal organisation' with few layers of management and with several service units (9 units at the first agency and 10 units at the second) targeting special functions or groups. Both agencies have a unit for disabled people. They also have a special unit for immigrants, young people at risk, issues of long-term unemployment and homelessness. The IFC is led by a manager and deputy manager, and each separate unit (often divided into three or four subunits) has a unit manager. The subunits are spread out in the neighbourhood in order to give easy access to the people they are supposed to serve, while unit managers often are located in the central administrative building. These physical settings, where the employees are near the clients but far from the managers, also contribute to strengthening the relative autonomy and greater *discretion* to act that the social workers have.

Factors behind organisational change in the Swedish public sector have meant tightened budget restrictions and efforts to make costs more visible. These global trends seem to mainstream the structure and functions of human service organisations. The district councils in Sweden responsible for its social services have for the last two decades been in financial trouble and forced to find ways to be more effective and reduce costs. In spite of this, reduction in staff has been minimal. Notions and ideas from the private sector such as 'demand and supply' have been introduced as an interorganisational 'buy and sell' system (Bäck-Wiklund and Plantin, 2005). Seen from an international perspective, Sweden has been a forerunner to adapt to the 'new management trend' in public service organisations. Recent research in the area has explored the political debate, leaving out changes in or effects of service delivery and practices affecting clients (Johansson, 2005). However, the social services have been subjected to *continuous organisational change* for several decades and, as the saying goes, organisations come and go but the problems remain.

Both of the agencies in the case study have been subjected to organisational change as described above, units have been merged according to their functions, new units and projects have been added and unit managers have been appointed and/or changed. For example, projects have been created for the treatment of drug abusers, for young people at risk and for clients with long-term unemployment. With their strong dependence on the environment, the organisations adapt to fit societies, new technologies and growing social problems. One way this is done is through ad hoc projects targeted towards specific groups, as mentioned above. This gives the organisation a resemblance of a network and adheres to the principle of a loosely coupled system but also efficiency for easy solutions – when needed. The organisation takes on a web-like shape and employees as well as managers give different views of constraints and changes depending on their position in the organisation. An organisation always in flux can also create a sense of insecurity and ambivalence among staff, but in this case study is not experienced as a risk of being laid off or made redundant (confirmed in the focus groups). 'Change' is instead a part of the everyday discussion in the organisation.

The workplace: between state and family

As mentioned earlier, Sweden is known for its generous family policies, especially the parental leave system, which allows parents to stay at home for a long time. However, for those employed within local authorities, as in this case, there is extra compensation for parental leave, such as two days' paid time off to attend childbirth classes or medical examinations related to pregnancy. Additionally, employees receive support from the 1991 Equal Opportunities Act, as its purpose is to promote equal rights for women and men in matters relating to work. It means that the social workers in this study have access to both national and local support to combine work and family life. Nevertheless, policies are not always implemented in practice and, according to the managers interviewed, equal opportunities is a typical example of this. Therefore, even if all Swedish parents formally can benefit from extensive rights, the actual outcomes may vary among the parents as the rights are negotiated in the work environment, for example in relation to the employer, the organisational culture and the actual work situation.

The agencies in the case study prided themselves on *"looking after their employees"* and this opinion was presented at different levels within the organisation. But it was also made clear in all interviews with management that *"working parents"* was not a policy issue, as such. Instead, working parents were *"treated just like everybody else"*. On the theoretical/discussion level, everything seemed to work according to the rules; managers as well as employees confirmed this. It was considered easy to take leave in relation to family matters but when the idea of family loyalties turned into practice, the picture changed. Leave was seldom followed by reduced or restructured workloads; instead, it was up to the individual to find their own solutions, more often with the help of colleagues. This situation inevitably created tensions, with dependencies as well as loyalties among colleagues and team members.

Managers subscribed to the *dominant value systems* in society, with individual *autonomy* and *gender equality* as well as with locally produced workplace policies. There was also a general discussion about *caring organisations* and understanding managers – confirmed both in the focus groups and in managers' interviews in words but not in deeds. Policies are poorly implemented and there is a tendency to leave it to the workgroup to reorganise its workload. The gender-neutral policy of treating working mothers just like everybody else gives no support to easing the work–family balance. The national policy, with individual autonomy as an all-encompassing goal, has little support at the workplace level. Instead, an informal value system offers guidelines for negotiable outcomes for individual autonomy in situations of involuntary absence, caused by children or other family responsibilities.

> It appears that individual autonomy within a work-place context transforms itself into a family issue. To conclude, even in the Swedish case, negotiations surrounding work–family boundaries are still questions to be dealt with in a family context that is still characterised by a persistence of traditional gender roles. (Bäck-Wiklund and Plantin, 2005: 36)

In order to understand the relation between the nature of work and the organisation as a loosely coupled system, we will now compare different strategies to handle the work–family boundary.

Relying on colleagues

When we focused more specifically on the efforts of the organisation to create a pro-family workplace, it became obvious that there was a clear discrepancy between management's intentions and actual practices. On an official level, all managers talked in line with the general prevailing attitude in Sweden on equality and the 'caring organisation'. They viewed the workplace as providing generous possibilities for personnel to further their education and for teambuilding.

Talking more specifically about family-friendly initiatives, all managers claimed to be against a work culture where people did overtime and worked long hours. They also argued that it was important to get working fathers to take parental leave and they were generally positive in regard to requests for part-time working. Furthermore, they claimed to be tolerant and empathic when employees were absent due to family matters and positive in regard to the use of telephones at work for family matters. The managers were also *"in principle"* positive towards expanding possibilities for employees to work from home; and finally they saw themselves as more important for family friendliness than *"empty"* policy documents. This means that they provided support in individual cases rather than working to institutionalised, local family-friendly policies. This opinion is not unique to the managers in our study but is instead, according to previous research, a general attitude among employers in Sweden (Jämo, 1999; Haas and Hwang, 2000; Tyrkkö, 2001).

However, despite the managers' positive attitudes in supporting pro-family policies in the workplace, in practice they often delegated most of the questions in this regard further down in the organisational hierarchy, to be handled by each separate workgroup. If someone needed to leave work for family matters during the day or stay at home with a sick child, they were told to negotiate this with their colleagues and utilise flexible working hours. From the managers' point of view, this was said to be a way of reducing the bureaucracy and creating more flexibility for the individual employees. From another point of view, it could be seen as a way for the managers to diminish the importance of these questions in the daily life of the employees.

The fact that negotiations around the work–family boundary were most often handled in the periphery of the organisation, between employees and without interference from the manager, and that managers were unwilling to call in substitutes when someone was away for a short time, resulted in a general experience among the social workers where they felt *"neither support nor resistance from the managers"*. Instead, they pointed to support and empathy from fellow workers as central.

David, a working father with small children, voiced the dilemma as follows, arguing that he felt like he put his work on colleagues *"in a strained situation"* when he had to stay at home for different reasons:

> *It's really important to deal with your colleagues, as when you are away they are the ones who have to do your job, it's not the manager … so you try to not be away too much.*

The managers' unwillingness to call for substitutes and their way of pushing the responsibility for work–family issues further down the organisational hierarchy forced the employees to strike a balance between an individual and a collective responsibility. It clearly had a restraining effect on working parents' possibilities to stay at home due to family matters, as they knew that their absence would have a negative impact on their colleagues.

The managers' strategies also led to differences in family friendliness within the organisation. Some teams had extended agreements to cover for each other while others showed less solidarity if someone, in periods, often needed to stay at home due to family matters. Some said, for example, *"there is always some whimpering if you have to stay at home"*, while others, who work with other parents with small children, said, *"we are many working parents in my team so it's often easy to negotiate with the others"*. In the long run, this situation may lead to less mixed workgroups where parents, especially women, will only work in certain jobs and teams. The employers' way of delegating these matters to each team also strengthens the view of the organisation as a 'loosely coupled system' (Perrow, 1986) with lots of different units and a weak or reduced linkage between the different parts of the organisation. However, it also emphasises *discretion* as a potential source for conflict of loyalties between parenthood, colleagues and clients.

Handling work–family boundaries: shaping different strategies

Through the case study analysis, with a comparison of the biographical individual cases, it became obvious that, depending on the position in the organisation and the kind of work the employees performed, they tended to develop different work–family strategies and professional careers (Bäck-Wiklund and Plantin, 2005). Staff working in maintenance were able to establish a boundary between family and work while staff working face to face with clients were not.

The strategies to handle work and family life described in the 10 individual interviews can be categorised into three different groups: *permeable, semi-permeable* or *impermeable*. The criteria are based on whether the interviewees bring work home and/or keep going over a client case, mentally unable to disconnect themselves, even at home with their family. The typology only takes into account the kind of work performed and its related feelings. It leaves out all the talk about time pressure to complete everyday routines and feelings of guilt as well as there being no time left for partner, friends or leisure activities. It is striking that none of the low-status interviewees reported any major problems in separating work and family life according to the criteria stated above.[2] On the other hand, the six social workers working face to face with clients reported clear problems with this and half of them were therefore classified as 'permeable' and half of them 'semi–permeable'.

Patricia, a social worker who works 80% of full time and has two small children, serves as an example of a strategy with a *permeable* work–family boundary. She describes that her first child was not planned but she felt *"mature"* and ready to take on the challenge of becoming a mother. This is a well-known model for the transition to parenthood in Sweden where many first-time pregnancies are 'unconsciously planned' (Plantin, 2001).

Patricia's feelings about being a working mother show ambivalence, as she gets neither support nor resistance; she gets some understanding but also feels criticised for not being *"committed"* to work. She thinks that equal sharing of childcare and household duties between working parents is important but states that she has lone responsibility – no support from her husband, a source for family conflicts. She describes the return from parental leave as *"tough"* and a *"big difference"* from before and she is reflective about being a working mother:

> It is difficult to get all pieces together, spend time with your children, pursue your career, and find a strategy for self-fulfilment and things like that. Many expectations to live up to, just being a mum would have been easy but there is a lot more to it … for me it is self-evident to work and to have children, but it isn't easy. Different loyalties – work versus ill children…. But as time is precious you need to be efficient at home.

Patricia describes how family and work constantly affect each other. She says that her work with cases where she meets troubled children often spills over to home and that she then feels *"totally exhausted and worn out because some cases really get to you"*. She used to make work-related telephone calls from home and regularly brought paperwork home to do after the children had gone to bed. She was not happy with the situation and therefore asked her manager to give her a new position with assessments and paperwork instead of meeting clients:

> I hope it will open up new possibilities … it is really exciting. I might even consider expanding my working hours as I will have more freedom and maybe greater possibilities to work from home. It all depends … because it seems like I still have to keep parts of my present work.

The *semi-permeable* cases talk about keeping family and work apart but also give numerous examples of the overspill between the two spheres. For example, Anita, a 34-year-old social worker with two small children, reduced her working hours in order to get a better balance between family and work. Today she works part time – 60% – and says that *"it's much better, a real difference to what it was like before when I worked full time. I have a better balance today"*. Since she became a mother, she has also changed work tasks, as her previous job was too stressful and too emotionally demanding with long hours:

> *Before I worked as a social worker in 'the unit for children and youth' and I mainly worked with investigations and cases where the children needed to be taken into immediate custody. At the time when I got pregnant, I worked really intensively with 12 families with various but serious problems. It was too tough. So when I went on parental leave, I decided not to go back to the same job but instead try to work with something more preventive. Now I work with young girls at an ordinary school who have only minor social problems. I like that better.*

However, even if Anita has striven to find work that is more separate from family life, the boundaries are still permeable. She continues to work long hours from time to time, prepares meetings and reads work papers in the evenings at home, makes work-related telephone calls from home and *"talks a lot"* about her job when she is at home. She also feels that her job often affects her mood at home negatively:

> *If something happens at work and I get into a bad mood, there's a risk I bring that home with me. I mean if I have been nagging the girls at work [clients] the whole day, I often continue with that when I come home ... and nag my children. And I lose my patience so easily ... especially with my daughter; she is often exposed to my anger. And I get angry with myself for that. It's a hard situation ... it gives me a bad conscience.*

Unlike Patricia in the permeable case, Anita is not happy with the situation when she cannot separate work from family life and when the boundaries get too permeable. The fact that none of the professional social workers, unlike the lower-educated workers, managed to draw a distinct line between work and family life indicates that the character of the work itself matters. Working with individual cases and a large proportion of authoritative responsibilities, notably discretion, makes it harder, as one of the interviewees expressed it, *"to leave the job behind and really feel that you are at home"*.

However, looking more closely at this from a gender perspective, differences between men and women appear. It is clear from all of the interviews that the men most often were in a position where they got better back-up from their partner when they confronted clashes between work and family life. The reason for this is that the women adjusted their working life to their family life much more than men did. For example, almost all women reduced their work time when they had children, they took most of the temporary parental leave when the children were ill and they were the ones who most often picked up the children from daycare/school in the afternoons. Men involved in the leaving and picking up process tended, on the other hand, to take their 'responsibility' in the morning and take their children to daycare/school. This led to a situation where the women, despite their initiatives to gain a better balance between work and family life, often complained about a troubled conscience in relation to their work; that they always had to leave work for family matters and never got the chance, if needed, to stay longer and finish their job.

Feeling continually responsible for clients

An important and often-mentioned reason given by social workers as to why it is hard to draw a distinct line between work and family life, is a sense of responsibility to clients. Working in face-to-face situations with clients was described by many of the social workers as *"demanding"*, *"emotionally arduous"*, *"tough"* or *"problematic"*, as the clients' needs have a significant impact in the work situation. It sometimes made the work unpredictable and harder to adjust to the need for predictability and structure in family life. Anita, whom we met earlier, highlighted this when she described why she left the job she had had with vulnerable families during her pregnancy:

> *I was pregnant and the job was too tough. It was impossible to plan and structure the day as different acute situations occurred all the time … it was like that all the time. I was travelling around to different residential homes for youths and I never knew how the day would end … it was stressful not knowing if I would manage to be home at a certain time or so.*

Other issues put forward by interviewees in relation to difficulties in staying at home for family matters when working face to face with clients included the exclusiveness in the contact between the social worker and the client. One of the interviewed team managers at the social service agency put it this way:

> *I look upon this from a general point of view, not only from this particular workplace. We cannot deny that being a social worker is a pretty tough job. When working with people you realise that you are important and mean something to your client – you stand for continuity in their life. So, when you are forced to make a choice – to stay at home with our own child or break the continuity in the relation with a particular client – you are facing a difficult decision. Situations like that are creating a lot of stress in the balance between work and family life.*

The arguing of how *"important"* social workers are and how they *"stand for continuity"* in the client's life illustrates clearly the historical roots to the casework method and how professionalism is related to structure, continuity and 'being there' for the client. Being a social worker is seen as *"a pretty tough job"* and those who cannot handle the stress it creates in the balance between work and family life might risk serious consequences. For example, Pia, a 35-year-old social worker and single mother with two children, was on sick leave for burnout syndrome a long time before she finally changed job:

> *I used to work with clients – treatment and support – but now I spend most of the time in front of the computer. I can spend days without seeing a single client. The reason to that is I do not want direct contact with clients any longer. I used to work intensively with troubled families, but I couldn't handle it. It became too much for me. And as I did not feel well myself it wasn't fair to expose other people to my own troubled situation. So I changed job and now I'm more of a typist ... I also have better possibilities now to manage my own family situation, to combine work and family life.*

Even if Pia's situation is extreme in a way as she has been on sick leave for a long time, her story still shows many similarities with the experience of many of the other interviewees. Pia changed job, for example, just like Patricia, as she could not handle the stress of the balance between work and family life. However, many of the interviewees reported that not only do they feel guilty in relation to the clients when they have to be absent due to family matters, but that they also feel bad about their colleagues:

> *If you are in the middle of handling a difficult case, let's say a forced taking into custody of a child, it is hard to just leave it ... at least I don't feel it's OK. And you leave your colleagues with more work as they also have to do mine....You have it constantly in your mind. (Felix, 34-year-old social worker with two children)*

This feeling of letting down both clients and colleagues when absent from work, often expressed by the social workers as a 'double responsibility', is not merely the consequence of restricting professional ethics but also a result of a managerial strategy, an organisation structured as a loosely coupled system and professional discretion. In fact, the way this situation is handled by employers makes the employees dependent on their colleagues' willingness to cover for them in their absence.

Conclusions

The aim of this chapter was to analyse features that block or facilitate work–family balance for social workers in a context of organisational change. Our focus was on parents with small children who are experienced social workers and who work directly with individual client cases. It is important to bear in mind when analysing social services that women dominate all staff categories. Nine out of 10 of those employed are women, and gender equalisation in this area is proceeding very slowly (Hammare, 2004).

In line with the theory approach that highlights human service organisation and their dependence on the environment, the two social agencies are pictured as mainstreamed multifunctional organisations responding to budget restrictions, selected groups' special needs as well as comprehensive gender policy permeating throughout Swedish working life. The general discourse about the importance of a proper education for social workers also affects social work from the state level through law directives to the individual social worker's ambitions and practices. The analysis in this chapter, which built on the focus groups and manager interviews, shows that the actual workplace, on a discourse level 'a caring organisation', adapts to most of the external claims but at the same time has a poorly developed practice for implementation. With the special focus on working parents, this becomes evident as few local policies are developed; instead, both employers and employees lean on the generous state parental leave scheme. In this context, managers tend to leave clashes between family and work to be sorted out by employees. This reduces bureaucracy, creates both solidarity and dependence among the employees and emphasises the organisation as a loosely coupled system with weak lineage for making decisions. It also leaves to the individual social worker the discretion to take action and obtain a balance between family, work, colleagues and clients.

Through the analysis of individual cases, we noticed that none of the professional social workers, unlike the lower-educated workers in the study, managed to draw a distinct line between work and family life. This indicates that the nature of the work itself matters: working with individual cases coupled with having *discretion* in determining just how those cases are managed makes it harder to draw the line. An important reason for this is that professionalism in casework with clients is very much associated with ethics and a methodology that emphasise structure and continuity in the contact with clients. For example, *"always being there for the client"*, *"never to let the client down"* or *"to stand for the continuity in the client's life"* are common devices closely connected to being professional in this type of direct social work. It is regarded as *"tough"* and *"highly demanding"* as the social worker has to be flexible and let their own private needs take a back seat, otherwise they are caught in a loyalty conflict between the client's needs and their own/their family's needs.

The individual cases we have followed in the analysis indicate that both parenthood and gender strongly affect people's positions and situations in their working life. Working parents (read mothers) strive to change their work position as they become parents, moving away from clients and instead into paperwork. They are without doubt well qualified to handle clients but the transition to parenthood makes them feel uncomfortable and they take radical actions to change their situation. Most working mothers in our study have, for example, reduced their working time and changed working tasks after becoming a mother. The lack of pro-family policies in the work arena forces the working parents to strike a balance between an individual and a collective responsibility. It clearly has a restraining effect on the possibilities of staying at home due to family matters, as the employees know that their absence will have a negative impact on their colleagues. It is also clear that gender matters and that men have made much fewer changes in their work in accommodating family life compared with women, even if they often feel guilty about it (see also Connell, 1995; Bäck-Wiklund and Bergsten, 1997; Plantin et al, 2003).

What, then, are the consequences of this process whereby working parents, most often women, form a career path away from clients into paperwork or more structured work tasks? What happens when highly qualified and well-experienced social workers leave the front line and their position as 'street-level bureaucrats'? A great risk, as we have pointed out, is that we get segregated workplaces within the field of social work. Social workers with small children tend to be found in structured jobs with predictable routines while young and often inexperienced social workers are to be found in face-to-face work where they are expected to be flexible, create instant solutions and build longlasting relationships with their clients. This might have a negative effect on the quality of work with families in acute crisis, as many of the social workers are not parents themselves.

Notes

[1] A state licensure is an official certificate executed by the National Board of Public Health (not by universities), given to occupations such as doctors, dentists, veterinarians and psychologists, which gives them authority to practise and treat patients. The licensure is based on exams but also certain qualifications. It makes the individual responsible for their handling of patients, and in case of misuse or maltreatment, it can be withdrawn according to specific legal procedures.

[2] The low-status workers were mainly recruited from the maintenance service where they worked as porters, kitchen personnel, cleaners and so on.

FIVE

Organisational social capital and its role in the support of working parents: the case of a public social assistance agency in Bulgaria

Siyka Kovacheva

In Europe in recent years there has been a growing concern about the quality of integration between work and family life (Eurostat, 2001; Lewis, 2001; Rapoport et al, 2002; Webster, 2004). Fundamental changes in work organisations and in the nature of work have set new dilemmas for employees in achieving their career goals and managing their wider lives. One major route to the reconciliation of the conflicting demands from the workplace and the home is perceived in many European countries to be flexible working arrangements: most often reduced working hours, flexitime and home working (Lewis, 2003b; Peper et al, 2005). In contrast, the reconciliation of work and family life is not a pressing issue that is raised in the academic and policy debate in Bulgaria. While the declining birth rate is causing public concern, it is attributed to the rising poverty and job insecurity that accompany the market reforms. There is a very low rate of part-time work (about 5%) and a large informal 'shadow' sector where higher pay comes as a result of long working hours and low social protection (Kovacheva, 2002). How do young parents in Bulgaria manage to integrate paid work in the market economy with unpaid childcare at home in these conditions?

Social capital may be an important factor in the work and family equation in this context. This chapter therefore sets out to address this question by applying a social capital perspective to the analysis of social interactions in a specific workplace. Methodologically, the analysis builds on a case study of a public agency for social assistance in a large Bulgarian city. Like the other case studies discussed in this book, it was carried out in 2004–05. The chapter starts with a discussion of the concept of social capital as a tool for understanding the relationships of trust and support that allow individuals and communities to pursue their work and family goals more effectively. It then proceeds with a description of the organisational context for the formation and mobilisation of social capital in the case study organisation. The chapter examines the structural and value components of social capital in the workplace and ends with a discussion of how these are affected by organisational and social change.

The perspective of social capital

The concept of social capital was made popular in academic and particularly in policy debates by the groundbreaking research into institutional reforms in Italy by Robert Putnam (1993). According to Putnam (2000: 19), 'social capital refers to connections among individuals – social networks and the norms of reciprocity and trustworthiness that arise from them'. It is an indispensable condition for creating strong and effective representative institutions. Putnam is concerned with the decline in active political and civic engagement in modern societies, finding arguments in the weakening of formal structures linking citizens to each other and enabling them to pursue common goals more effectively. Coleman (1988), on the other hand, has a wider understanding of social capital and stresses the role of informal networks in the context of education. For Coleman, social capital is a resource within the family that arises from intergenerational relationships and which spills over into the community and fosters the creation of voluntary organisations. Another significant difference in the approaches of the two authors is that Putnam understands social capital as a primarily collective resource – 'a public good' – while Coleman perceives it as a resource that can be mobilised and built upon by the individual.

Furthermore, Putnam (2000) introduces an important distinction in the variation of social capital. 'Bridging' capital is an inclusive form of social connectedness, looking outward and linking people across diverse backgrounds. 'Bonding' capital is an exclusive form of social capital, inward looking and reinforcing specific identities in homogeneous groups. Bridging capital allows information diffusion and provides a linkage to external resources while bonding capital relies on solidarity within the group and mobilisation of in-group resources. A similar approach is used by Granovetter (1973) when explaining the role of different types of social capital in the search for jobs. For him, the weak ties formed between acquaintances moving in different social circles might be more instrumental for achieving individual goals than the strong ties that link relatives and intimate friends. However, these accounts tend to neglect the hierarchies of power along status, gender and generation lines (Edwards, 2004). Bourdieu (1983) offers an approach that introduces structural analysis of social, economic and cultural inequalities and relations of power into the concept of social capital. Whereas for Coleman and Putnam the amount of financial and cultural resources of the family is largely neutral in the creation of social capital, Bourdieu underlines the link between social and other forms of capital that underpin and perpetuate social inequalities.

Research on social capital has focused more on its role in families, communities and civil society as a whole (Wallace and Pichler, 2007) than on the study of work organisations. Organisational studies have commonly stressed the notion of human capital (educational qualifications and skills) and its effect for generating economic returns. Nevertheless, accounts of social capital in organisations highlight the role of social relationships based on trust and reciprocity that help individuals to access information and resources. In his analysis, Fukuyama (1995) regards trust as a collective asset in civil society and a major ingredient in the performance of organisations. The 'high-trust workplace' is a condition for creating prosperity. Cohen and Prusak (2001: 4) define organisational social capital as 'the stock of active connections among people: trust, mutual understanding, and shared values and behaviours that bind the members of human networks and communities and make cooperative action possible'. When listing the benefits of social capital in organisations, they take a narrow economic perspective: better knowledge sharing, lower transaction costs, lower turnover rates and greater coherence of action (Cohen and Prusak, 2001: 10). The advantages for employees' well-being or opportunities for reconciling work and family are not examined specifically as the authors focus only on the effect on business organisations and their competitiveness.

The concept of social capital has often been criticised as being gender blind (Stolle and Lewis, 2002; Edwards, 2004). In his later work, Putnam (2000: 95) recognises the particular role of women as 'more avid social capitalists than men' but also perceives a causal link between women's greater involvement in paid work and the decline in social capital. His argument stems from attributing social capital to the realm of civil society and political institutions but Putnam largely neglects the workplace and family life and hence the possibility that women can produce social capital there. Opposing the narrow understanding of social capital as inherent in formal organisations only, a gender perspective stresses the informal cooperation of women in civil society such as networks around childcare and neighbourhood issues, as well as their contribution to social capital in workplace organisations creating ties that allow the reconciliation of paid work and family life (Molyneux, 2002).

The following analysis applies the concept of social capital to social relationships in one work organisation – a public social assistance agency. The public social services sector is a particularly interesting case for investigation as its purpose is to deliver care to people in need. The analysis focuses on two major components of interactions in the workplace: structural, that is, networks and ties fostering cooperation; and cultural, that is, norms and values of trust and reciprocity. In organisations, social capital is an investment in reciprocal social relations that allows the sharing of skills, expertise, information and material resources. Social interaction in the workplace generates social capital when fostering a sense of belonging and creating networks of mutual obligation, care and concern. Workplace social capital brings benefits to the organisation and to individual employees. This chapter considers reports of social interactions and relationships at work not just in terms of the value of expected returns in the marketplace (Lin, 2001) but also from the perspective of the value employees place on it in relation to their well-being – allowing them as working parents to combine paid work for the organisation and unpaid childcare for the family.

The organisational context

The public organisation studied in Bulgaria is the Regional Agency for Social Assistance in a large city in Bulgaria, which is under the auspices of the Ministry of Labour and Social Policy. It has seven centres for social assistance in the territory of the city (responsible for the provision of poverty alleviation, and child and family benefits), one Centre for Home Patronage (providing food, home help and other services for older people in their private dwellings) and one Department for Child Protection (dealing with the prevention of domestic violence, placement of children in foster families or in specialised institutions, protection of homeless children and support for children with special needs). For the case study, managers were interviewed and focus groups were carried out with employees. Although the Transitions study approach was applied, a specific characteristic of the fieldwork in Bulgaria was that when asked for contacts with parents the managers pointed to mothers only and despite the efforts of the researchers only two young fathers came to the focus groups. This reflects the situation of a predominantly female workforce profile in the Agency (80% women) but also the cultural understanding of the informants in Bulgaria about who bears the responsibility for the care of young children.

The organisation has undergone many changes. Social care in Bulgaria, as in most communist countries, was not well developed before the start of the market reforms in 1989. After the establishment of the communist regime in the second half of the 1940s, it was expected that the state ownership of the main means of production would automatically cure all social ills and that there would be no strata in society in need of social support (Kovacheva, 2000). Although in the 1960s this strategy was changed and all state policies were declared 'social policies', in practice poverty was not recognised officially and hence, no adequate services were developed until the end of the regime (McAuley, 1993). The social services sector in post-communist Bulgaria began its institutionalisation in 1991 with the creation of public social care offices under the auspices of municipalities. In 1997, a new Regulation for Social Support was adopted, which accelerated the decentralisation of the system by strengthening the municipality centres for social care. Following the strategy to harmonise its legislation with that of the European Union, the Bulgarian Parliament adopted the Law for Social Support in 1998, which established three main forms of social support: allowances, social services and the placing of people in need in specialised care institutions of various kinds, funded by the state. The 2000 Child Protection Act established the National Agency for Child Protection, which started its activity on 1 January 2001. The latest structural reform was at the end of 2002.

In January 2003, all employees in the case study organisation received new temporary labour contracts for six months as the name of the organisation was changed from 'Offices for Social Care' to 'Agency for Social Assistance'. In July 2003, most employees of the organisation were given permanent contracts and somewhat higher salaries. These changes were accompanied by a small reduction in staff numbers (about 5%) and personnel reshuffles among high- and middle-level management. At the time of the focus groups, the situation had calmed down somewhat but employees at all levels had learned that *"there is no such a thing as a secure job in the state sector in Bulgaria"*, in the words of one of our participants.

The director of the Agency and the human resources manager explained that they had no problem with the recruitment or retention of personnel. Actually, the percentage of people who sought employment with the Agency was far greater than the number of vacancies in the different branches. Employees very rarely left their jobs and some of them had even returned to the Agency disappointed with working conditions elsewhere. Employees' contracts with the Agency were permanent, in line with the Bulgarian legislation and the requirements in state institutions. Temporary contracts were very rare and were used only for a probationary period of three or six months, after which the employer was obliged either to employ the person on a permanent contract or to release them from work. The normal working week was 40 hours. Part-time work in the Agency was very limited and was decided by the National Agency in Sofia. It would usually only be allowed in small centres where there was a small number of clients. Social workers and carers preferred to work full time, not only because this was expected by management, but also because pay was low and a reduced salary would be insufficient for a family with children. Similarly, there was no flexibility of working hours. The working day for social workers and the carers in the Centre for Home Patronage started at 09:00 and ended at 17:30. This schedule was decided by the National Agency in Sofia and was uniform for all divisions of the Agency in the country. In some branches there was evidence of shift working but this was an operational change within the normal working day – for example, the social workers who were on duty to accept emergency cases in the morning did the paperwork in the afternoon, and vice versa. Staying after working hours was a common practice. This overtime work was not paid; it was compensated with five days added to the annual leave. The policy of working at or from home was not known in the Agency. All employees worked in the offices and centres of the Agency. Although they might take extra work home, neither carers nor social workers were allowed officially to work permanently or on certain days from home.

The Agency as a whole does not offer its own family-friendly policy and follows the statutory provisions fixed in the National Labour Code (valid for all employment contracts in the country). Maternity leave is 135 days, of which the mother takes 45 days before the expected date of birth, paid at 90% of the mother's previous earnings. From then on until the end of the child's second year, employees are entitled to paid parental leave, which can be taken by the father, mother or one of the grandparents. The pay for this leave is a fixed sum equal to the national minimum wage. After two years, the employees can negotiate unpaid leave for one more year. This can be used by one of the partners or their own working parents. Additionally, employees can take leave to care for a sick family member. The maximum sick leave in a year is 60 days' full pay for sick children under 16 years. There is no workplace nursery in any of the branches of the Agency. The parents cover the childcare costs themselves and use public and private crèches and kindergartens run by the state and located in their communities. The Agency does not provide assistance with finding placements or funding childcare. Nevertheless, the fees in the public centres are very low. The organisation of childcare in the state crèches and kindergartens is as inflexible as the working schedule of the parents – a full day five days a week with fixed starting and ending hours. While the statutory provisions of leave for working parents seem generous, not all parents take all the entitlements, and as our research shows, this depends on the willingness of the manager, on the understanding of the colleagues and on the relations within the team – all intangible resources that are conceptualised here as the social capital in the organisation.

Social capital as a resource for working parents

In this section, the components of social capital that helped working parents in this organisation to achieve an effective balance between their work and family responsibilities are identified. The interplay of two major ingredients of social capital is highlighted: structural, in terms of formal and informal ties between the employees of the organisation; and cultural, in terms of values and norms that foster solidarity and cooperative action among them.

Structural components of social capital in the Agency

Analysts of social capital distinguish between the formal organisational ties and informal networks among members of a community. Our study provides information about both formal and informal social ties that exist within the case study organisation. The formal associational structure representing the interests of employees in the Agency is the trade union 'Podkrepa' [Support]. This is the second largest syndicate in Bulgaria, created from the basis of a dissident organisation that sprang up in the last years of the communist regime in the country. Trade union membership in the country fell significantly from the obligatory membership during the communist regime to about 8% of the workforce at the beginning of the 21st century (Mikhailov, 2005: 28).

The focus group discussions showed that the employees of the Agency did not use the union as a source of social capital. Active members of the union were few, while in some of branches of the Agency there were no trade union members. When asked specifically whether they received support from the trade union, the employees denied any impact and voiced an opinion that *"membership in a union is totally useless"*, in the words of Natalia, a care worker and focus group participant. It was difficult for the researchers to find out who the head of the union was, as people were not sure who was acting in this capacity. It turned out that the union leader was one of the social workers in the Agency. She shared the opinion of her co-workers about the lack of influence of the union over Agency policies — *"my hands are tied; I can't change anything"*. Pay bargaining, parental leaves and working hours were all decided at the national level. Two years before the fieldwork of our study when the employees of the Agency collected signatures against the dismissal of the director of the Agency, their protest was ignored by the top management in Sofia.

While the social workers in the Agency did not use the formal organisation (the trade union) to achieve a better work–life balance, they were more successful in generating social capital by developing informal networks of solidarity and support in the workplace. These were formed within the units of the Agency – the offices with 7-15 employees. Social capital was created in the process of teamwork; the practice of covering for each other's absences in cases of family emergencies (see also Chapter Eleven); the informal sharing of information and advice on family problems; and various celebrations.

Both interviewed managers and employees participating in the focus groups felt positive about working in a team. The head of one of the city offices considered teamwork as a way of managing the constant change of regulations for providing social benefits. According to her, collaborative work helped employees learn from each other and fill in gaps in their knowledge. This was particularly helpful for young mothers coming back from a long period of parental leave, as well as for those who were often absent from work to care for sick children. The manager of the Department for Child Protection pointed to the role that teamwork played in discussing and solving problematic cases. This largely informal mutuality created ties between colleagues that allowed them to solve problems efficiently. The line manager in another city office responsible for delivering poverty benefits explained:

> When I first came here, each employee was working on their own files and when they were on a leave to care for a sick child for example, nobody could open their files. But sometimes the leave was prolonged — there were cases of such leave more than a week long and the files waited and the clients complained.... Now working in a team they share the information and can cover for each other's absences.

Thus, both employees and clients benefit. Employees largely shared this appraisal of teamworking and gave examples of informal support by colleagues to help them to learn quickly the new regulations that had been introduced while they were on parental or child sick leave. The sharing of work and responsibilities helped social workers discover mistakes in documentation promptly before they had serious consequences. At the same time, however, working parents felt pressured not to take the leave to which they were entitled by law, feeling concerned about colleagues who would be overburdened with their work given the heavy workloads that were the norm. Iglika (a social worker and focus group participant) said that *"sometimes, especially at the end of the month, I end my sick leave earlier in order to go and help my colleagues. I feel uneasy"*.

Whether or not the employees made full use of the policies for which they were eligible depended on the informal atmosphere and ties of mutuality created in the workplace. Rosa, a care worker in the Centre for Home Patronage and focus group participant, claimed that they all took the full amount of the leave since most of the employees were mothers of young children and considered it normal to cover for each other in such cases. However, Nelly, a social worker in the Department for Child Protection and focus group participant, had to return from parental leave when her daughter was only six months old, as her job was threatened because of restructuring in the department. As the crèches only accepted children above the age of eight months, she had to take her daughter to her grandmother who lived some 600 kilometres away. In this case the working mother made use of the tradition of strong intergenerational support in the extended family, which is another widely used form of social capital in Bulgaria.

The web of mutual obligations among co-workers in the social sector was strengthened by the practices established in cases of family emergencies. Since working-time schedules were extremely inflexible, the social workers could not officially negotiate coming to work an hour later and compensate by staying an hour longer. What they did was talk to the manager and ask for informal permission to do so. Both managers and employees accepted this practice instead of trying to change the regulations officially or using the channels of trade union negotiations.

> When my child was little, I took him to medical consultations on Fridays, each month. The consultations started at 9 o'clock, and I asked for permission to come an hour later to work. There was no problem, permission was always granted. Once, my boss was absent, and I had to make a call [to the middle manager], because some tests had to be made on my child, and still there was no problem. (Marusja, social worker, focus group participant)

The role of line managers in creating and maintaining these informal networks was very important as they were the people with whom the leave had to be negotiated. Interviewees considered that the gender of the managers was less important than their collegial aptitude for *"understanding"* and creating an atmosphere of tolerance towards young parents. The focus group participants agreed that employees tried to reciprocate by staying later at work to deal with heavy workloads.

The group discussions clearly showed that it was mothers who most often experienced conflicting demands and loyalties. The two fathers participating in the focus groups, Angel and Milan, said that they had never used parental or child sick leave, because their wives took care of their child. It was not a problem for them to stay after working hours or travel on a business trip. For working mothers, however, child sickness was a grave problem as kindergartens did not accept sick children and they had to take leave. Mothers commonly voiced an opinion that they could not rely on the father; as men they were perceived as not competent to perform medical tasks such as applying nose or ear drops or taking the child's temperature. While both parents have equal rights in terms of the law, the real practices of childcare are strongly gendered, underpinned by cultural understandings of traditional gender roles.

Another informal practice that created a family-friendly work culture in the Agency was the taking up of annual leave in a flexible way; instead of 20 full-time days, some working mothers requested to take these days as 40 half-time days. For example, Ivanka, a social worker, did this when her son started school for the first time and she wanted to be at home with him for longer. Instead of applying for permission to work part time from the headquarters of the Agency in Sofia, which, first, was very difficult to get, and second, would reduce her pay by half, Ivanka, like other parents, negotiated with her line manager. This practice was also informal and not recorded in any official document and was made possible by abiding by norms of trust and mutual obligations.

Social capital functioned inside the units also as informal channels of information flow. In three of the focus groups it was reported that in the workplace employees informally discussed expected structural changes, personnel cuts and replacement of top managers. Two of the interviewed line managers complained that organisational change was announced post facto and sometimes they even learned it first from the mass media. The dissatisfaction with the way change was communicated from the top management in Sofia, however, created a feeling of solidarity among employees in the local units. Focus group participants often used 'we' to identify with colleagues in their department/centre and contrasted it with 'they', which they used to refer to the higher levels of the organisation. These alliances were not so much to oppose the organisational changes (for discussion of employees' perceptions of change, see Kovacheva et al, 2004) but were strategies for adapting to the changes.

The informal ties among colleagues served as sources of advice about children and family life. Employees knew the family situations of their immediate colleagues in the department and so did their managers. They often shared information about their children, the problems they had concerning their health, food, clothing and education. Managers not only allowed this practice as a safety valve for the work tension but they themselves took part in the talks. The focus group participants pointed to the fact that women were usually more talkative about their children than men. This gendered practice was not only due to the fact that men were a minority in the departments but also that the two male participants in the focus groups considered it more appropriate for men to maintain a clear border between work and family. Angel, a male social worker in one of the city centres, claimed: *"I have never transferred problems from work to home or vice versa. It is an unnecessary strain"*. In contrast, in the focus group conducted in the Centre for Home Patronage, the care worker Rosa noted: *"Look at us here. We are all young mothers working here. I look forward to coming here in the morning and enjoy laughing and talking with them"*. The status of motherhood created a bond of solidarity but it could easily exclude the working fathers.

Although rare, socialising after work was another practice creating ties and solidarity among employees and contributing to their well-being. However, parents of young children were often in a hurry to pick up their children from kindergartens or to do domestic work. In recognition of their responsibilities, employees organised celebrations in the office during lunchtime. The resources for such celebrations were very limited but were still appreciated by social workers. Tinka noted:

> *Of course not all of us could gather at one and the same time, because some of us should work with clients even during the celebration. Yet, this is important for us to get together and talk about life outside.* (Focus group participant)

Participants in one of the focus groups pointed to the social connections that were established among employees from different offices during training sessions. While training courses provided by employers were rarer in the Agency than in the private financial sector (Kovacheva et al, 2004), these were organised more often during working time and thus eased the task of working parents to manage professional and family responsibilities.

The value components of social capital

The informal ties of support between the employees in the local offices of the Agency fostered the creation and strengthening of social capital through the norms of reciprocity, solidarity and trust. The participants in the focus groups made it explicit that they trusted the employer to comply with the protective state legislation and treat them fairly as employees and as parents. Positive feelings were most strongly expressed when comparing this organisation with companies in the private sector. Milan, a car driver in the municipal Agency, explained his preference for his job in the Agency to work in private companies where the pay is much higher:

> *…'cause in the Social Care Agency there is honesty, which the private employer lacks – the private employer usually exploits his subordinates in respect to leave, payment, work time.* (Focus group participant)

Tinka, a social worker in one of the city offices, had started working in a small business company but was dissatisfied with the treatment of working parents and when she could, she moved to the state Agency. She trusted her new employer to follow the social protection legislation:

> *[A] private employer might exploit me and demand to work more than eight hours a day. Usually at first you start at eight hours [working time per day], but then there is work to be done, and you stay until it's done. They don't care*

*about leave, and if [private] employers find out that the applicant for the position
has a small child, they don't even hire him.* (Focus group participant)

Although the language that the social workers used in the focus group discussions
is reminiscent of the official communist ideology that linked private ownership to
exploitation, it was from their personal experiences with small private companies
that these parents made their conclusions rather than just repeating ideological
stereotypes. The perspective of the managers was very similar. They also stressed
that the organisation was a good employer because it complied with the National
Labour Code, which was very protective of working parents. Our analysis, however,
discovered a significant difference in managerial discourses. The line managers who
were managing offices and departments of up to 15 people were people centred
and accepted the rhetoric of the ethics of care. They stressed that they understood
the problems of working parents and tried to support them as best they could
without neglecting work efficiency. The higher-level managers, however, focused
on the new business ethics. The head of the city agency who managed the staff
in all the branches in the city considered that caring for one's employees was a
thing of the past. The new market economy had changed that.

> *We are supposed to care for our clients in need, not for our staff. It is enough
> that we as a budget structure [public organisation] keep to the legislation.*

It is not surprising, then, that in the focus groups parents expressed trust in the
line managers whom they knew personally and who helped them balance work
and care. Participants were more sceptical about middle and particularly top
management. Similarly, the line managers identified with the teams they worked
with and distanced themselves from the top levels. The line managers interviewed
were pleased that an atmosphere of trust prevailed in their offices. Liljana said:

> *They [team members] always come to me in case of problems. If they have
> made a mistake, they tell me, so I can fix it. They don't hide their mistakes.
> The aim of revealing the mistake is not to incriminate the employee, but as
> I've always said, to correct it, so that it won't reach a higher level. And if they
> have problems in the family, they share with colleagues in order to receive
> sympathy and attention.*

Most of all, however, employees trusted their co-workers. In the focus groups
they described a climate of trust and mutual understanding in their departments
as they thought that this is important, *"otherwise things just won't work"* (Margarita,
focus group participant). In the focus groups, there was a lot of evidence of the
identification of the interviewees with one another. When discussing workplace
practices, or atmosphere, it was sufficient for one employee to give an example,
and then the others added many more stories reinforcing the argument of the

first one (see Chapter Three). The focus group participants expressed feelings of pride and belonging to a team with a good reputation.

> Nina: *My contacts with other specialists in social work have enriched me.*
>
> Zina: *...something we usually forget but I think it's important. It is just that our colleagues are very sophisticated. It is normal that in other European countries people with a secondary school diploma or with even lower educational level do our job. But here you can rarely come across people with only a secondary school diploma. This influences our contacts and the communication between us.*

Identification with the organisation and the feeling of belonging were higher among social workers with qualifications in social work, such as Nina and Zina. These seemed lower among those social workers with qualifications in other fields such as economics or engineering, many of whom saw themselves primarily as mothers who held jobs mostly in order to contribute to the family income. In the focus groups the care workers demonstrated identification with the collective rather than with the organisation or the social sector in general. Angel and Milan, the two male participants, also said that they enjoyed going to work, and got along well with their colleagues. However, they did not participate in the talk about family problems and both persisted in establishing strict boundaries between work and home.

Overall, the ties of mutual understanding and support established between the employees in the agency tended to be strong ties, creating a form of bonding social capital. This did not create bridging between the departments and particularly between the different levels of the organisational hierarchy.

Conclusions

The analysis of the data from the focus groups with working parents and individual interviews with managers in the public social assistance agency in Bulgaria showed that long parental leave policies and state-funded childcare were not enough for a satisfactory work–life balance. In cases of child sicknesses and other family emergencies or heavy workloads and staying on after work hours, employees who were also parents of young children had to search for additional support in order to meet their responsibilities. While the extended family – the partner (especially women partners) and grandparents – were a most significant source of such help, organisational social capital also played an important role. Establishing ties of trust and understanding with managers and colleagues allowed working parents to manage inflexible working schedules and inflexible public childcare in the face of work intensification and demanding family life. However, this social capital at the workplace was being threatened by the organisational change towards more efficiency-focused senior management practices.

The inquiry into the structural and value components of the social capital in the case study organisation revealed several important characteristics. First, working parents tended not to trust the formal associational structure in the organisation – the trade union. Rather, they relied on informal ties with colleagues and managers in the workplace. Second, these ties, which served as social capital for the working parents, did not encompass the Agency as a whole but were formed in the local unit – the office, centre or department. Employees relied on strong ties with a close circle of colleagues they knew personally rather than on a wide network including colleagues at different levels of the organisation.

Our results are congruent with forms of social capital established in society as a whole. Large-scale comparative surveys (Raiser et al, 2001; UNDP, 2001; Mikhailov, 2005) have measured low accumulation of social capital among the Bulgarian public in terms of general trust (in strangers), trust in political institutions and low membership of formal civic organisations. The legacy of distrust among citizens during communism still persists in post-communist societies and undermines the population's readiness to participate in collective action (Sztompka, 1996; Mikhailov, 2005). At the same time, norms of reciprocity, trust and support that were widespread among extended families during communism were further strengthened with the reduction of state intervention in the economy and public life. Studies have highlighted the role of families in creating social capital during young people's transitions from education to employment and to independent housing (Kovacheva, 2006), and in women's fertility decisions (Buehler and Philipov, 2005). When trying to ease their offspring's labour market integration, families in Bulgaria rely mostly on strong ties within the extended family and close circles of friends. In the same way, reliance on family support increases the probability of having children because the intergenerational exchange of money and services reduces the costs of having children and stabilises the economic situation of the young household.

The formation of social capital in the case study organisation – the Agency for Social Assistance – was thus influenced by the very low prevalence of norms of generalised trust and reciprocity among society as a whole and the lack of support for and membership of voluntary associations and political organisations. At the same time, there was a high degree of accumulation of social capital within the families and close circles of friends. As in society at large, in the case study organisation, the social capital was closed in the local unit and did not spill over into the organisation as a whole, that is, it did not become organisational social capital as envisaged by Fukuyama (1995) and Cohen and Prusak (2001). There were examples of social capital being created in the organisation and spilling over into the community. Social workers and carers did counselling and filling in documents for their relatives, friends and neighbours. However, it was not the organisation as a whole that helped the community and carried out common projects with civic organisations. The process happened through the personal contacts of employees with their clients whom they served personally and not through the organisation, but these activities remained limited in scope and did not generate rich community capital.

Organisational change directed towards restructuring and work intensification was making such social capital even more necessary for working parents while at the same time undermining the effect of investing in such collaborative activity, and destabilising trust and norms of reciprocity within workplaces. The management of the Agency could profit from encouraging the formation of social capital in the organisation instead of exploiting, as it currently does, a labour market situation of a high supply of qualified labour. In particular, the organisation could make efforts to become more open about prospective changes and encourage trust among all levels of the Agency.

The role of managers in the public social sector agency was strongly influenced by organisational and wider social change. They had to negotiate employees' requests for more flexible work–family boundaries while balancing these against issues of costs and efficiency. Line managers seemed to be person centred, and closer to practising the care ethic while higher-level management perceived the new style as more task oriented. As a result, social benefits once organised by the enterprise (under communism) such as opportunities for family holidays, free workplace canteens, health and childcare were considered a thing of the past. Subsidies covering transport expenses and work clothes had also been withdrawn. Part-time work, job sharing and working from home were perceived as not (yet) applicable in the new Bulgaria due to the low living standards and poor standard of technological equipment in the workplace. What worked best according to social services workers in Bulgaria were the informal practices of flexibilisation of working time and place, and giving and receiving informal support in the workplace; and also traditional intergenerational support from extended families, often not voiced in the focus groups but nonetheless important as the backcloth of state institutional support (see Brannen et al, 2002).

Building social capital in the organisation in Bulgaria was a gendered experience. Women invested much more in such collaborative activities than did men. They also needed social ties in the workplace more than men did, as the responsibilities for combining paid work and family care were largely theirs. While women and men in Bulgaria both work full time, they do not share childcare and domestic work. These are seen as primarily women's responsibilities while men would normally 'help'.

The use of a social capital framework for the analysis of relationships in the workplace has the advantage of highlighting the interplay between structures and values in the case study organisation. The fact that informal ties were more important for working parents in Bulgaria to achieve a better work–life balance than formal structures and policies was due to the type of trust prevailing among them. The solidarity that was created in the public sector organisation was one based on personal ties and mutual help rather than on generalised trust. The values underpinning the social capital in the organisation were in congruence with the values predominant in the wider society. This lens allowed us to bring into the analysis the different layers of context: organisational, family, social (Nilsen and Brannen, 2005). However, what we could not elucidate sufficiently was the role of the state, which remained in the background as provider of policies and services. In social capital literature the state is more often regarded as a source of influence (positive or negative) over civil society and for the creation of social capital. Focusing on the workplace rather than on political institutions and those of civil society has relegated the role of the state to the background.

Finally, the social capital concept has been traditionally used in quantitative studies measuring high and low levels of social capital. Applying it in a qualitative study of one organisation shows that besides high and low levels of social capital across communities, regions and nations there are also different forms of social capital that have implications for research and practice.

Part Two
Private sector organisations

SIX

Old rights in new times: the experiences of parents in a Slovenian organisation

Nevenka Černigoj Sadar

Introduction and background

At the macro level, two processes contributed to change in organisations in Slovenia. The first was Slovenia's separation from Yugoslavia in 1991 and its transformation into an independent state, with its own political and economic systems. After the separation, Slovenia lost most of the Yugoslav market and had to replace it with exports to Western European and other countries. During the first phase of the transition to a social market economy, there was a drastic fall in economic activity and in the standard of living, extreme market instability and growing unemployment. In the middle of 1993, the economy bottomed out of the recession and entered a period of intensive restructuring of production and consumption. The second phase of transition involved intensive ownership, financial and managerial restructuring (Hanžek et al, 1998).

The privatisation process in Slovenia has created a high level of involvement by both employees and managers (Kanjuo-Mrčela, 2003). However, in the second phase of privatisation, share ownership in Slovenian companies grew (Simoneti et al, 2001). As Kanjuo-Mrčela (2003: 1) notes, the 'involvement of non-managerial internal owners and state funds is decreasing while the share of investment funds and managers is increasing'. Nevertheless, in the first five years of the 21st century, various state and para-state funds/associations still held a significant share in about half of the big Slovenian enterprises. These ownership changes were accompanied by structural and functional modifications in enterprises. Workers' self-management was abolished and the new Law on the Participation of Employees in the Management of Organisations provided some co-decision-making rights. The old trades unions were re-formed while some new ones were founded. They gained significant bargaining power and defended the interests of employees (Svetlik, 2005). Due to the drastic political and economic changes over the past two decades and the challenges brought by preparations for European Union and NATO membership (which happened in 2004), organisations in Slovenia were encountering constant change.

Coping with multiple societal and organisational changes is especially difficult for parents with young children. During the second half of the 20th century, Slovenia successfully developed public policies to enable parents to balance their work and family lives. Since firms were relatively well endowed with staff and various support services (large firms especially have social workers, psychologists, doctors or other professionals), parents' needs were not high on the management's agenda. However, with the introduction of a market economy, flexibilisation of the labour market and precarious work, experienced mostly by the young generation in Slovenia, the problems of young parents have increased.

This chapter explores the rights that existed under the former communist regime that applied to parenthood and how they have played out in changing contexts at different levels. It explores Slovenian public policy in relation to working parents and the key features dealing with work–family issues within organisations. This is followed by the presentation of a specific case study of a financial organisation in which working parents' experiences of their rights and employment conditions and the implementation of policies are examined, together with the role played by managers in organisational practices. In particular, the chapter examines whether rights that derive from public policy are largely supported or undermined in this particular changing context.

Public social policy discourses

Slovenian public policies to support working parents appear similar in some ways to those in social democratic countries. With regard to public services for children and other family members, it is close to the Swedish model. In the mid-1970s fully paid parental leave was introduced and the proportion of pre-school children has been steadily increasing as a proportion of all children from 41.2% in 1981/82 to 55.2% in 2001/02 respectively (Statistical Yearbook of Slovenia, 2002, 2003). Some forms of social assistance for families and family members and benefits regarding shorter working hours for parents were introduced anew, even while we were conducting our Transitions project, for example paternity leave. However, societal and organisational responsiveness to and acceptance of these measures depends on the way that basic social policy terms are conceptualised.

Taking into account Tronto's (1993) and Sevenhuijsen's (2003) understanding of the ethics of care not only as a moral but also as a political concept can explain why the same social policy measures are implemented in different ways in different social contexts and have varying impacts on different social groups. In Tronto's words (1993: 9), 'care can serve as both a moral value and as a basis for the political achievement of a good society'. Tronto and Sevenhuijsen see the person as a relational being who is involved in relations of interdependence. Relationality is also present in institutions and among public and private spheres of life. In this conceptual frame, the concept of care, which is a key aspect of social policy, is not only the role of some specific social groups or institutions, for example family, it is also relevant to overcoming the unequal treatment in organisations and different life spheres. The explicit or implicit conceptualisation of basic social policy terms in national policy documents significantly contribute to the interpretation of its measures and also to the creation of dominant public discourses that are decisive in determining how various social groups in different contexts accept and implement social policy measures. The social policy contexts are not gender neutral but are embedded in the system of gender relations (Walby, 1997; Pfau-Effinger, 1998) in which care is mainly attributed to families and women. However, if we understand care as an integral part of citizen rights (Knijn and Kremer, 1997), then we extend the conception of work to the unpaid work in the household and family, which has a status equal to that of gainful employment.

Drawing on the ethics of care perspective, it can be argued that 'care' is conceptualised in a narrow way in Slovenian policy making: focusing on childcare, but neglecting gender relations and self-care. In Slovenian social policy, individuals are treated in a binary way: either as being self-sufficient, autonomous and independent or as people who need help, support or care, that is, 'dependent'. In Slovenian family policy documents, care is mainly about childcare. 'Family policies do not take into account the need for mutual care between healthy adults nor do they acknowledge the need for care of the self' (Švab, 2004: 51). Care of older people was mainly covered by the 2007 Social Security Act and National Social Protection Plan until 2005 (Official Gazette of RS, 2000). In addition, policies related to parenthood are primarily focused on caring for children and not on the promotion of equal opportunities for both sexes that should encompass the division of labour in various private and public spheres of life, unlike in the Scandinavian contexts. Moreover, the concern with family issues has never been as strong as work issues.

The dual-breadwinning model where both partners are employed full time has been the main pattern for Slovenian parents for half a century. However, the division of tasks within the family has been, and still is, largely traditional (influenced by the strong Catholic tradition in Slovenia despite its suppression during the communist period). Although gender equality in paid work was reflected in values expressed in recent public opinion surveys (Toš, 2004), the contradictions regarding attitudes and aspirations related to the gender division of labour slowly diminished but did not disappear by the beginning of this century (Toš et al, 1994, 2003). A family survey (Toš et al, 2003) indicated that most respondents in a representative sample (89.6%) agreed that a husband and wife both have to contribute to family income. However, at the same time they thought that women with preschool children should stay at home (28.8%) or work part time (45.7%). Thus, attitudes and aspirations regarding women in Slovenia are similar to those in Western Europe (Crompton, 2002) and in some aspects they are even more advanced (Fagnani et al, 2004) but accompanied with more contradictions. As a result, at the end of the 20th century, the dominant public discourse was still about dual-earner families in which promotion in paid work was mainly achieved by men and rarely by women. Even the most recent Equal Opportunities Act for Women and Men (2004) underlines the integration of women into the public sphere through their participation in the labour market and in politics, while changes in the private sphere are rather neglected. The strong public support for women in paid work is reflected in a relatively low gender pay gap (7% in 2007). However, Slovenia has a greater gender division of labour in the private sphere compared to 'old' EU countries (Kanjuo-Mrčela and Černigoj Sadar, 2006).

Most social policy measures related to parenthood are based on an active labour market policy, which is supposed to guarantee independence and self-sustainability. With rare exceptions, in the latest Employment Relationships Act (2002), the employer's role regarding work–family issues is not defined and therefore the managing of these two spheres of life is left to private initiative and to state support, which employers are obliged to implement. During the Socialist period, the state was the main initiator of social change and the provider of social provisions such as parental leave, childcare and daycare centres that were accessible and affordable for most parents. The role of the state was strong and paternalistic and care provision for parents with young children was considered a public matter. In the post-socialist period, the state has become the promoter of neoliberal, market-oriented social relations and a pluralist welfare system. At the same time, it is trying to transfer care away from its own responsibility to the private sphere, namely, as empirical studies have indicated, to women (Jogan, 2001).

However, public policies enhancing women's labour market participation and work–life balance have limited positive effects due to the very narrow definition of care in Slovenia (Švab, 2003, 2004). While equal opportunity rights are mainly focused on the public sphere (Humer, 2004), in the public discourse, care is a term that applies to the private sphere. In people's ways of thinking, care is segregated from their working life. Besides, during the Socialist period of full employment or even quite often over-employment, the implementation of parenthood rights, which in reality meant mothers' rights, was never in question. With political and organisational change, increased globalised competition and employment insecurity, tensions regarding the implementation of parenthood rights in organisations are growing alongside the greater labour market discrimination against women. Among long-term unemployed first-time jobseekers there are more women than men, and among newcomers to the labour market, more women are temporarily employed compared to men while, in addition, highly qualified women have problems getting their first job (Černigoj Sadar and Verša, 2002; Kanjuo-Mrčela and Černigoj Sadar, 2006).

In Slovenia, especially in private organisations, management formally implements public policy measures but also puts subtle pressures on parents who take advantage of these. There is, moreover, very weak monitoring of public policy measures. In most organisations, parents with small children are in a minority and do not act as a relevant pressure group. Therefore, the management of organisations has no decisive push to introduce additional family-friendly measures or attend to implementation and practice. Taking care of customers and employees now does not rank as high as increasing shareholder value. According to the latest comparative research (Ignjatovič and Svetlik, 2005), Slovenian organisations have a non-intensive human resources management model, which means that policies that are crucial for improving parents' quality of life are weak. For example, there are no working-time flexibility policies in many organisations. Human resource management mainly serves to give administrative support to (top) management and decision making in organisations is highly centralised (Ignjatovič and Svetlik, 2005: 42-3). However, compared to other countries in the EU, organisations in Slovenia are considered 'ahead of others in terms of flexible work arrangements with potentially negative impacts on employees and are behind others in work arrangements with potentially positive impacts on employees' (Černigoj Sadar and Vladimirov, 2002: 11).

Management as an agent of change is mainly occupied with organisational changes to adapt to the new demands of the globalised market and the problems of communicating these changes to their subordinates. To understand the process of change in Slovenian organisations it is important to know that employees do not participate on equal terms in organisational decision-making processes. They 'primarily carry out managers' instructions' (Svetlik, 2005: 19).

Although Slovenia has a relatively long tradition of research into work–family issues (Boh et al, 1989; Černigoj Sadar, 1985, 1989, 2000; Černigoj Sadar and Lewis, 1996), only recently has this topic become part of public discourse, but still not in relation to employer responsibilities. The discourse about social responsibility of enterprises in Slovenia is mostly about ecological matters, donations for humanitarian purposes and the development of the professional skills and knowledge of employees, but not about the importance of work–private life relations.

Case study of 'Sava': organisational changes

The continued definition of work and family as separate spheres, and narrowly defined care concerns as women's rather than parents' issues, is illustrated in the case study of a finance sector organisation to which the researchers gave the pseudonym 'Sava'.

The case study also illustrates how the legacy of paternalism from the former Socialist regime contributes to the continued construction of work and family issues as individual but also state responsibilities rather than as employer concerns or business issues.

Sava is partly owned by the state and is partly private. With about 1,000 employees, it is one of the biggest financial organisations in Slovenia and has a predominantly female workforce, which is also characteristic of other organisations in the financial service sector in Slovenia. Most of its employees (95.7%) have permanent contracts. Fixed-term contracts are used mainly in cases of temporary replacement, when employees go on maternity/parental leave, for example. According to the collective agreement, employees have to work 40 hours a week (a half-hour daily break is included). The working week usually lasts five days, while for those employed in the branch network the working week might also include Saturday work. Younger generations have 'front-office' posts, while middle-aged people mainly occupy 'back-office' posts. Most employees participating in the case study (all but two) worked full time and had a work contract according to the collective agreement. Four managers had an individual employment contract.

Flexible work schedules were introduced in the 1990s. In most support functions of Sava, working time is flexible at the start of the day from 07:30 to 08:00 and at the end of the day from 15:30 until 16:00. However, the most drastic work-time changes for parents were introduced in the branch network during the early years of the 21st century. Branch units changed from two shifts, when they were open the whole day long, to one fixed split-shift. This means that opening times are from 09:00 until 12:00 and from 14:00 to 17:00, which means a longer working day and can create problems for parents of young children.

The transformation of the planned economy into a market economy as well as privatisation processes have had an impact on organisational and labour force changes at Sava. A drastic reduction of the workforce was achieved by so-called soft measures such as early retirement, ending the extension of fixed-term contracts or limiting new employment opportunities except in management positions. Compared to smaller private organisations in the financial sector, employees with a permanent work contract had secure job positions but relatively average salaries.

The development of information technology (IT) changed working conditions in all functions of the organisation. It enabled quicker communication and the introduction of various new services. In addition to a positive effect, it also contributed to the intensification of work. As new services were introduced and *quality* improvements in already existing services occurred, this demanded from employees greater knowledge, constant learning and greater responsibility.

In 2000, there were also changes in wages policy that took the business efficiency of a particular branch unit into account. There were also changes in management; each function and the departments gained more autonomy. Due to rapid financial growth, there was also an enlargement of the management. In recent years, one significant economic event improved Sava's position in the market yet this also increased work intensification.

Since the organisation became autonomous (no longer part of a big Yugoslav financial organisation) and has changed its ownership status, the employees reported reduced influence on the organisation's business decisions:

> Now the management board is in charge, they don't have to listen to us employees. I used to [in the period of the self-management system] sit as a shop steward in front of the general director. And as a trade union representative I told him what was wrong. (Man, low-level manager, aged around 50, child aged over 20)

It was also felt that the introduction of structural, functional and technological changes and the expansion of services were not accompanied by positive changes in organisational culture, especially in terms of communication. Direct personal communication was rare between the various hierarchical levels and there were also signs of communication gaps. Individual initiative was taken for granted with the implicit message 'try to find the best way yourself':

> *We [line managers] were informed only that document X had been passed, the document was published somewhere there, and who examined it ... I? I wasn't even asked by the managers to examine the Act and explain it to the workers. Further, every manager has not enough time ... I think that the office that is concerned with the change should do it ... write an e-mail and explain....* (Woman, manager, aged around 40, two children aged four and eight)

Workplace policies in Sava relating to parents

The reconciliation of work and family/private life is strongly supported by the generous statutory regulations concerning parental and sick leave.[1] However, the problem lies in its implementation: the subtle pressure put on those who take it, together with the fact that parents and managers expect the state to resolve most of the problems:

> *It is clear that it is the state that somehow regulates and implements all this legislation. A lot of things have been written and sound good ... but then what is going on in reality and how is it going on, this is not being checked, nobody is interested in it.* (Man, aged 30, two children aged two and four, focus group participant)

Expectations of employer support tended to be low:

> *I think that the state should take care of this [supporting parenthood] so that an employer would not be deprived [not have any loss] and afterwards the employer would agree to consider such demands.* (Woman, aged 37, child aged six, focus group participant)

State policies and laws determine the organisational policies that refer to family matters. Since the public policies in place were regarded as quite generous from the employer's point of view, there were no special or additional organisational policies for working parents at Sava. However, the solidarity of workers played an important role in planning annual leave for example.[2] Workers with small or school-aged children were informally given priority over other employees.

Due to its long tradition, fully paid maternity/parental leave was taken for granted by managers as well as by parents. Yet not a single interviewee mentioned the father taking parental leave. Also at the national level, the share of fathers taking parental leave during the last 10 years is about 1%; recently this rose to about 2% (Office for Equal Opportunities, 2007).

Changes in the working lives of parents after the birth of a child

The employment pattern of women in Slovenia is similar to that of men. Due to social policy measures and for economic reasons, most women do not interrupt their professional careers when having a child. Also, among Sava's sample of parents who participated in focus groups, only a minority introduced changes after the birth of a child, namely not working extra hours, not travelling or cutting down on work-related travel and reducing hours of work. Only two parents gave up activities that enhanced their professional promotion such as going on a training course. However, it was mothers who mentioned most of these strategies. Nobody in the focus groups mentioned downward mobility when returning to work after parental leave. Yet that did not mean that coping with work–family demands was proceeding smoothly. In the focus groups the experience of *"being a working parent"* was often described as coloured by painful experiences, for example separation from a small child and the experience of fatigue and even exhaustion.

Problems perceived by parents

Mothers usually came back to work when their child was about one year old and this was the most critical period for both working parents. The most common problems making it difficult for parents to balance their work and family lives were described as:

• vaguely defined organisational policies;
• the limited flexibility and the rigidity of working-time schedules;
• the intensification of work; and
• the parent's fear of failing to meet their co-workers' and their superiors' expectations.

Parents tried to resolve most of these problems with their immediate colleagues. They mainly used individual strategies and gave up trying to communicate their needs to their superiors. Most of them did not expect managers/the employer to be responsive to their needs:

> *It doesn't matter for him [the employer] that you are a parent. He expects you to work, he pays for it, and he expects results.* (Man, aged 26, child aged four, focus group participant)

We are not used to it [to speak about parental problems].... And then you do not expect it.... [that the manager will be responsive to problems]. (Woman, aged 34, two children aged one and four, focus group participant)

Due to a lack of communication between management at various hierarchical levels, parents had practically no chance of making their problems more visible and of expecting organisational strategies to solve their problems.

Working time

In Slovenia, unlike many other European countries, part-time work is rare and the majority of employees in Sava did not even think of this as a possibility. Some employees and managers thought this was due to the lowering of living standards because salaries were too low for employees to afford it.

The majority of participants mentioned that limited flexibility and, in some cases, the rigidity of working-time policy created considerable difficulties for parents:

I come home every day at 5pm, the kindergarten is open till 4pm. Thank God my husband can pick them up.... But he has a private company at home ... and then things are not working there.... (Woman, aged in her late thirties, two children aged two and three, focus group participant)

A change towards more flexible working time was only possible by special request and depended on individual managers and sometimes the human resources department. Employees could arrange very slight deviations regarding their working time on rare occasions, for example when driving to work from another town/place far away from the office (in 'SLO town') and/or because of parent responsibilities for small children. However, the participants mentioned that the process of making these changes was long and drawn out, since it demanded many written applications and requests before the demands were approved. Line managers as well as the human resources department were important when deciding to change an individual's working time but there was no formal policy on these issues:

If you are not from here [SLO town], you have to be able to pick up a child at 4pm at the kindergarten ... but they are not interested in this.... When you ask them, you're told your request will be granted but then they make you wait for six months and still nothing comes out of it. (Woman, aged 34, two children aged one and four, focus group participant)

In the branch network, working time created a lot of problems for parents with small children due to the split-shift and its inflexibility. In one worker's view, routine family responsibilities could be met by changing the split-shift work practice since it would make their absence from home shorter. But for the time being this was just parents' wishful thinking:

> *It is very hard for me because every day I work from 9am till 5pm, very, very hard. My superiors are not interested in these problems....* (Woman, aged in her late thirties, two children aged two and three, focus group participant)

Only participants from the IT department, where mostly men were employed, were satisfied with their working times. Due to greater flexibility in working hours, no problems were mentioned regarding the negotiation of work–family boundaries.

Work intensification/work pressure – it seems to be without end

The organisational changes that took place in Sava since the second half of the 1990s involved continuous intensification of work. In spite of this, overtime at Sava was not a regular practice although it was manifest in subtle ways. For example, some employees brought their work home or did not take a lunch break. Instead, they ate snacks while they worked. This was their strategy for managing their everyday obligations and avoiding having to work long hours in the office.

Experiences of working in Sava varied, particularly in relation to specific jobs and occupations. Some, such as the men working in IT, were highly satisfied while others reported extremely negative feelings. Work satisfaction depended on the particular job. Usually the participants did not speak about their work in general but only about certain aspects of their work, with the associated evaluations varying greatly. The majority of criticism related to feeling overburdened, rigid working-time policies and consequently time pressures in the workplace and in their families.

> *[Y]ou come home late and I have a headache and it is terrible.... I am completely drained....You get things late but you still have to do it today ... and these are not things that you do every day, routine things, but an exacting piece of work.* (Woman, aged 32, two children aged three and seven, focus group participant)

Nevertheless, there were some, especially men, who said that they thrived on the great volume of work involved:

> *Yes, there is a lot of work but the good thing is when you look at the clock it is 11am and the second time 'Wow I have to go home'....And there is so much work still to be done. This time passes really quickly. The week ends ... and*

there is the weekend again ... that's fine.... (Man, aged 30, two children aged two and four, low-level manager)

Working time in the branch network was the most problematic:

The work itself is very good; the job is also very good, only the working time involved is curtailing the free time I could devote to my child. Because I come home relatively late (at 6pm). (Man, aged 26, child aged four, focus group participant)

[I]t is suicidal ... you come home ... like worn out clothes. It would be much easier if you would work with a spade all day long because you are so emotionally tired ... but we are the least paid.... (Woman, aged 36, three children aged four, nine and 10, focus group participant)

In general, extremely negative experiences of work were quite rare. However, some employees working in the branch network found that work intensification had an extremely negative impact on their health and created a relatively gloomy vision of their future.

If one gets sick ... this sick one is no longer needed; it is a burden for them.... They have to get rid of him.... And where is this hitting us? ... in our psyche ... here you are physically and psychologically exhausted, at the counter we are on the front line ... customers all the time ... there is so much work, you go to eat very quickly or you don't eat at all. (Woman, aged mid- to late thirties, two children aged two and three, focus group participant)

Particularly mothers with small children were very emotionally engaged in explaining their work and family burdens but, at the same time, they were very proud to manage it all. However, managing work and family demands also meant that they were pushing themselves to the limit and jeopardising their health.

Leave to care for sick children – to take it or not to take it?

Formally speaking, child sick leave policy was implemented according to the rules. However, informally, employees felt pressured by their superiors. Therefore, it often happened that parents took sick leave only for the first few days of their child's sickness or opted to use their annual holiday time instead. Some workers reported that they could take sick leave for childcare whenever necessary but it made them feel uneasy so they preferred to apply for annual leave, even though their superiors might be very understanding. If you applied for sick leave too often, said the participants, your fellow workers and superiors gradually stopped relying on you because they had to take on your work. So you had a feeling of responsibility intertwined with a feeling of guilt. The frequent taking of sick child leave sometimes led to a reduction of trust among co-workers. It seemed that there were implicit expectations that hindered the implementation of national policies and turned them into family-unfriendly organisational practices:

> *When I was on sick leave for a week, because both of them were sick, I had a really bad feeling when going back to work on Monday, one sick leave day after another.... How can I be trusted at all?* (Woman, aged 33, two children aged two and three, focus group participant)

> *I used up most of my annual leave for my child except for 14 days. Sometimes I had to leave work earlier to attend a parents' meeting, on another occasion I had to see a doctor myself or I was just feeling so low that I had to take a couple of days off and before I became aware of it all my annual holiday time was gone.* (Woman, aged around 40, three children aged four, 11 and 16, focus group participant)

However, not all experiences of taking sick leave were negative:

> *It depends on what kind of person your superior is. You may apply for sick leave because you have a sick child at home and you won't hear a word of criticism from him and all your work will be done. My experience is positive.* (Woman, aged 33, child aged five, focus group participant)

Factors that were equally important with regard to sick leave and how it was experienced also included the specific department and the amount of work. In general, employees were trying their best not to take too many days off because frequent absences could jeopardise their chances of promotion.

There were great gender differences regarding the taking of sick leave. It was mostly mothers who still took sick leave when their child was ill because:

> *[I]t seems right to be at home at that time.* (Woman, aged 34 years, two children aged one and four, focus group participant)

or

> *[O]nly a mother can really comfort a small sick child, the father can care for the sick child but it is never the same as the mother's care.* (Man, aged 30, two children aged two and four, focus group participant)

Mothers and fathers still therefore saw the mother as the primary nursing parent, having a stronger emotional attachment to the child and implicitly also offering better care.

The role of managers and their perceptions of problems

The majority of managers were aware of the decisive role they played in the implementation of workplace policies. They decided on leave and short-term absences and assessed the work effectiveness of their subordinates. They had a great impact on practices not formally defined as organisational policies. A higher-level manager (woman, aged about 55) explained that middle- and low-level managers organised all work processes in their work units and that the human resources department had no other role but to ensure that all procedures were implemented in accordance with the regulations.

There was a widely shared perception that some managers were more or less supportive of the needs of parents and other employees. It was also a widely accepted opinion that managers' own family situations made a difference when it came to supporting staff with young children and influenced the meaning the managers attributed to the problems parents had to cope with. Some managers who were parents themselves said that:

> [E]xperiences of your own parenthood are definitely positive; until you become a parent you don't know what that means. (Man, low-level manager, aged about 36, one preschool child)

> It is about feelings of what a certain event means to me, or if a child is sick that you are present with the child. You know how to appreciate these values [family] more. (Woman, low-level manager, aged about 45, one child aged around 20)

Generally, managers thought that there was no need for additional family-friendly organisational policies due to the small number of young parents in the organisation and because the existing organisational policies did not violate the laws. They also mentioned that, according to the 2002 Employment Relationships Act, organisations were obliged to implement laws that helped in the coordination of work and family life. However, most of them did not see themselves playing a more active role in helping parents with young children.

In the main, there were no formal obstacles to taking parental leave but the managers' comments on this varied from benevolent opinions through to clear descriptions of management problems in the case of unexpected parental leave. Managers were responsible for the smooth running of work processes and for paying attention in the case of increased absenteeism so as not to overburden the rest of the workforce. Managers could find themselves in an extremely unfavourable situation due to the unpredictable long-term absence of mothers, for example in cases when they hired a new employee to cover someone on maternity leave and where after six months this new person took maternity leave too.

Most managers were reluctant to permit part-time work. Some managers were indifferent to or hesitant about part-time work, others were very negative.

According to the managers, working-time directives were very strictly and clearly set due to the nature of the work, such as relatively strict time limits, work tasks and official business hours for customers (in the branch network). Thus, working time was a core business decision:

> *Work is work of course. Anyone who has made a work contract knows that this means working on the counter, he has to consider it ... or he can find some other job. The most difficult condition is in fact the working time ... the work has to be done, ... we are here for the sake of customers and customers aren't there for our sake.* (Woman, middle-level manager, aged over 50, two children aged around 20)

Managers tended to be critical also about split-shift work times. Managers at different levels (all women) considered that the introduction of split-shift work time in the branch network negatively influenced employed parents because they spent most of the day at work and had only a short period at home when their children were awake. For parents' part, it made it difficult to negotiate work–family boundaries and above all influenced the amount of time they could spend with their families.

Conclusions

Sava had undergone organisational, technological and ownership changes. It had also experienced the intensification of work like all the other organisations discussed in this book, but had retained a relatively committed workforce. In terms of human resource management, it did not mobilise all the human potential available to it, especially that created by social networking between different organisational levels. Employees in working groups created social capital mostly at the informal level, for example in one branch unit employees said that they experienced the work group as a family, they shared new knowledge and took over extra work when one colleague was absent for illness reasons. In the meantime, a communication gap between employees and various levels of management had developed. This presented a great hurdle to be overcome, requiring long-term positive organisational change that would also consider parental rights as part of strategic business goals (see Lewis and Smithson, Chapter Seven, this volume).

The management at Sava respected the law by implementing public parent-friendly policies at the organisational level but did not make any additional effort to make work–life balance a possibility. Managers played a decisive role in implementing formal organisational policies and informal workplace practices related to parents' needs. Although they were aware of parents' problems in negotiating work and family boundaries, they treated parents as a minority group that did not need special attention. The introduction of more flexible work practices and additional supports were mainly viewed as increasing labour costs.

Hence, time and place flexibility in favour of parents was not implemented to the extent permitted by law.

Working-time rigidity, the strong orientation towards productivity and high-quality services combined with very limited considerations about parents' needs and rights, and parents' fears of not meeting their colleagues' and superiors' expectations, constituted the main barriers to the development of organisational practices that would make the balancing of work and out-of-work demands easier.

Recent legislative changes in Slovenia that were stimulated also by accession to the EU were in favour of gender equality, especially regarding fathers' involvement in parenting. However, the implementation of new policies had not been evaluated in organisations. Besides, the narrow approach to care evident in public policy documents and the dominant public discourse created segregation between paid work and family life in the minds of most parents as well as in their managers' minds. Therefore, no one expected a more active organisational role in implementing parents' rights. The long arm of the former paternalistic role of the state and the constant organisational changes undermined parents' rights and diminished the potential positive effects of implementing parent-friendly public policies in the organisation. The management of work and family life continued to be significantly gendered and was still treated as a woman's issue. The relatively generous public policies enabled the mothers of young children relatively successfully to deal with work–family demands. Yet they did not prevent stressful situations that could endanger parental health and mothers' increasing discrimination in the labour market. In this context, young parents, especially mothers, bear the brunt of political and organisational changes associated with a market economy and increased globalised competition. It could be concluded that both the old and the new rights relating to parenthood are constrained by organisational practices.

Notes

[1] Various laws define leave policies for employed parents. The 2001 Parenthood Protection and Family Benefit Act regulates parents' rights related to giving birth and nursing and caring for a child (see Chapter One, Table 1.1).

In relation to sick leave and care for sick children, the compulsory health insurance scheme (1992 Health Care and Health Insurance Act) covers all Slovenian citizens and their family members, as well as non-citizens who are economically active residents of Slovenia, and foreign students.

[2] The 2002 Employment Relationships Act and the collective agreement govern annual leave; its minimum duration is 21 working days. The length of annual leave depends on work demands (related to the required level of professional education), length of employment, working conditions, work efficiency, special social and health conditions of the employee, and the age of the employee. The

length of annual leave is prolonged by one extra day for sole parents and each child under the age of 15 years.

[3] However, note that some positive change has occurred during the last two years with the introduction of the basic 'Family friendly enterprise certificate' into 32 organisations in Slovenia (Černigoj Sadar, 2007).

SEVEN

Work–life initiatives and organisational change in a UK private sector company: a transformational approach?

Suzan Lewis and Janet Smithson

Introduction

There is now abundant evidence that work–family policies without systemic change in work structures, cultures and practices have limited impact on employees or organisations (Lewis, 1997, 2001; Rapoport et al, 2002). Contemporary organisations are undergoing dramatic changes in response to new forms of competition in the global context and technological developments (White et al, 2003). Yet despite the pervasiveness of change, employers often adopt a relatively *minimal approach* in response to changing demographics and the work–family needs of employees. A minimal approach might involve ignoring this issue altogether, or taking token actions, for example developing policies to support equality of opportunities but paying little attention to the implementation process and the deeper changes needed for policies to be effective (Lewis, 1997, 2001).

Some employers genuinely aim to transform workplaces to benefit both employees and the organisation and to keep ahead of contemporary economic and social trends – a *transformational approach* (Lee et al, 2000), although they may encounter many barriers along the way (Lewis and Cooper, 2005). While a minimal approach seeks quick fixes and has only short-term effects, a transformational approach has the potential to harness change in positive ways and to contribute to innovation and long-term benefits. We refer to a transformational approach rather than good practice, family friendliness or flexibility in order to emphasise a dynamic ongoing process in response to or anticipation of changing needs. The search for 'good practices' in relation to work–family arrangements assumes that there are once-and-for-all solutions to work–life issues – that once good practices are in place, employees' work–family problems are taken care of. This obscures the need to keep work–life issues constantly in mind as things change, 'mainstreaming' them into organisational decision making.

In this chapter we consider aspects of a potentially transformational approach to work–life issues in the rapidly changing contemporary context. We consider how this may be conceptualised, what would be the criteria for a transformational approach and what the barriers to transformational change are, drawing on one case study of a finance sector organisation in the UK, from the Transitions study.

In conceptualising a transformational approach, we draw on theories of organisational learning (Senge, 1990; Senge et al, 1999; Lee et al, 2000) including the learning resulting from a particular form of action research that focuses on systemic change to meet the dual agendas of gender equity and workplace effectiveness (Rapoport et al, 2002; Bailyn and Harrington, 2004). All organisations have to learn and adapt to changes that are all around them – but some do so faster and more effectively than others. These have been described as 'learning organisations', that is, organisations in which people are collectively and continually expanding their knowledge to create their future (Senge, 1990). Organisational learning theory suggests that organisations respond to changes in the external environment or challenges to the status quo in variable ways. Work–family or personal life issues are a significant part of the context that has to be taken into account in creating this learning.

One change to which organisations may have to adapt, and could potentially learn from, involves employee requests for reduced working hours. These are particularly challenging if they come from senior staff. This is because such requests challenge the assumption that good or ideal managers or professionals should be present whenever subordinates are working. This is an outdated assumption in the context of growing flexibility of working time and place and contemporary workforce demographics and needs, but nevertheless a view that is often deeply ingrained in organisational cultures and resistant to change. The role of organisational learning in response to such challenges was explored by Lee et al (2000) in a qualitative study of managers and professionals voluntarily working on what the authors term a reduced load basis (defined as anything less than full-time work, with reduced compensation) within specific organisational contexts. To focus on the organisational rather than individual level of analysis, Lee at al (2000) used a case study approach. This involved generating multiple perspectives on each example of reduced work arrangements by interviewing target managers/professionals (with reduced load) plus four additional stakeholders per case, namely their senior manager, a peer-level co-worker, a human resources representative and where applicable a spouse or partner. The interview focus was not just on the present but also on changing employment relationships and career structures that might emerge in organisations due to demographic changes in the workforce. Based on an in-depth analysis of data from 82 cases of reduced work load (the target workers and four stakeholders) from 42 firms, it was possible to compare organisations systematically in organisational learning terms. This led to an emergent theoretical framework capturing important organisational-level variation in response to employee requests for reduced load working and to the identification of what are described as three organisational paradigms of implementation and interpretation of reduced load work: accommodation, elaboration and transformation. The three terms were chosen to represent organisational differences in response to an external stimulus and different modes of learning.

Accommodation involved minimal adjustments in response to requests from managers or professionals to work less than full time. Requests were accommodated reluctantly and were more easily acceded to if the employee was a highly valued manager or professional. However, moving to a reduced load working arrangement tended to be regarded as a career-limiting move, as ideal role incumbents were still regarded as those who worked full time and long hours. In this paradigm, the employer posture was to contain and limit reduced hours working so that other employees would not try to follow suit.

The subset of organisations that were subsumed under the *elaboration* paradigm tended to have more formal policies to support non-standard ways of working, usually based on a recognition that this could benefit the organisation as well as individual employees – for example by reducing turnover. Stakeholders had mixed opinions about the potential impact of reduced load status on individual careers but the assumption that full-time employees would be advantaged over those working less than full time persisted. In this paradigm, the employers' posture was to control and systemise procedures for these 'experiments'.

In the *transformational* organisational paradigm, reduced load work arrangements were accepted with or without formal policies in place. There was a greater willingness to embrace change and learn from opportunities presented by employees working in this way. This was viewed as a normal reaction to the need to retain managers and professionals and an opportunity to learn about how to be more flexible in changing contexts. The focus here was not on hours worked by managers but on, for example, developing people and preparing them for future leadership roles in the long term. The employer stance was not to limit or formalise but to experiment and learn. Transformation as it is used here involved learning, trust and a willingness to listen to employee needs and question taken-for-granted assumptions about ideal workers.

The surfacing and questioning of taken-for-granted assumptions about the nature of work and ideal workers, which are not necessarily articulated, but are powerful in sustaining the status quo, are also central to the dual agenda approach used in action research by Rapoport, Bailyn and colleagues (Rapoport et al, 2002; Bailyn and Harrington, 2004). Their action research process, which they term 'collaborative interactive action research' (CIAR), addresses a 'dual agenda' for change. The dual agenda refers to the mutually reinforcing goals of supporting both work–life integration and other aspects of gender equity on the one hand, and enhancing or at least sustaining workplace effectiveness on the other hand. Rapoport et al (2002) argue that both agendas must be kept in mind at all times for optimum and sustainable change. The goal of the dual agenda is systemic change, that is, changes in workplace structures, cultures and practices, which are achieved through a process of experiential, collaborative and ongoing iterative learning (Rapoport et al, 2002; Bailyn and Harrington, 2004). This approach also stresses the importance of collaborating with work teams to find innovative solutions to dual agenda issues. While CIAR is usually carried out by external action researchers in collaboration with management and work groups, the dual agenda approach can also be used by internal change agents.

Both the organisational learning and dual agenda approaches imply an ongoing dynamic process. Work–life initiatives are often developed by human resources departments but have to be implemented by line managers. Research on the impact of work–life initiatives on employees' experiences has identified a prevailing implementation gap between policy (organisational and social) and practice in most organisations (Hochschild, 1997; Lewis, 1997, 2001; Brandth and Kvande, 2001, 2002; Crompton et al, 2003; Gambles et al, 2006), a gap that was also evident in all the organisational case studies in the Transitions study. It also indicates that perceived organisational supportiveness and particularly the supportive role of line managers are crucial for the effectiveness of policies and practices (Thompson et al, 1999, 2004; Allen, 2001). Transformational approaches would thus pay attention not just to policy but also to implementation in practice. They would work towards systemic change that narrows the implementation gap, encourages consistency and supportiveness among managers and promotes a culture in which work–life needs are respected and supported.

To summarise, we argue, based on these two approaches to organisational learning and change, that the criteria of a transformational approach include moving beyond the mere development of work–life policies and requiring management at all levels to:

- recognise changing workforce needs and treat these as strategic challenges and opportunities to learn and innovate in changing contexts;
- address business needs and employee needs: a dual agenda;
- listen to and collaborate with the workforce;
- actively work towards achieving consistency between espoused values and actual practice (narrowing the implementation gap) by paying attention to implementation issues, including the role of line managers and the need to build support and trust;
- be willing to question deeply ingrained assumptions about ideal workers and the nature of particular jobs;
- monitor changes for continuous, ongoing learning.

In the remainder of this chapter we draw on the case study of 'Peak Insurance',[1] a private sector company in the UK, to explore the complexities and pitfalls of a change approach that attempted to move beyond policies to support work and family, in a transformational direction.

The UK context of work and parenting

As described in Chapter One, parents in the UK in general receive relatively little formal support for combining paid work and parenthood. Childcare is expensive, and often difficult to arrange and coordinate with working schedules, which was reflected in concerns about working flexibility and childcare provision among the parents at Peak. In Peak, as in many private sector companies, there was a lack of awareness among employees of their rights, such as entitlement to unpaid leave if a child is sick and the right to request flexible working (see Chapter One). Moreover, there was considerable inconsistency among managers in the interpretation and implementation of policies. Parents' experiences therefore tended to be heavily dependent on line managers.

Nevertheless, the UK context has changed in recent years. Developments in paternity and parental leave as well as entitlements to request flexible working arrangements, although driven by European agendas, are also part of a government-led campaign on 'work–life balance', which strongly advocates organisational support for parents and other carers, within a business case framework. The term 'work–life balance' has become a hot topic in employer and union discussions (DfEE, 2000; DTI, 2001; TUC, 2001; Hooker et al, 2007), in the media and in everyday language. Although it has been argued that this discourse trivialises the issues and obscures more fundamental problems associated with unbridled capitalism (Fleetwood, 2007; Lewis et al, 2007), the popularity of the debate may have influenced, to some extent, employee expectations of support for reconciling paid work and family.

The case study organisation: Peak Insurance

Peak is a large national insurance company. The case study took place in one location – the offices of Peak, in 'Peaktown', which has been the company's main national site for 16 years. This office handles mainly personal insurance policies, which are sold directly. Approximately 450 people worked in the Peaktown offices, mostly in the servicing side of the organisation. Some had worked there a long time, while others had come more recently, often as a consequence of mergers. Other employees (sales staff, mostly men) were based around the country. There was, at the time of the case study, a 15-17% turnover rate in the Peaktown workplace, which the human resources team considered average for the sector.

As discussed in Chapter One, the Transitions study examined the impact of workplace policies and practices introduced to support new working parents, in the context of wider changes occurring in European workplaces. The broader changes forming the background to the study represent responses to changing environments and technologies and new forms of competition in the global market for private sector organisations. The changes at Peak were taking place in the context of a national situation for the insurance industry, where mergers, downsizing, reorganisation and introduction of new regulations, structures and technology were the norm. Insurance companies faced competition with supermarkets and other bodies selling insurance as well as the aftermath of pension miss-selling scandals. There was an increase in auditing of insurance work, which was putting pressure on managers and employees at Peak, and many new government regulations affecting their work. There was also an increase in call-centre work – albeit not currently as big an issue as in other financial sector industries such as banking. Computerisation of the industry was ongoing.

Organisational change was regarded as a fact of life at Peak, following mergers, takeovers and restructuring, and was widely accepted as inevitable in the face of business imperatives and changes or anticipated shifts in regulation. Downsizing and reorganisation were associated with increasing job insecurity and intensification of work for those who survived redundancies. The mergers and take overs had dramatically changed the company over the previous few years, although the impact was uneven. There had been many redundancies but some departments remained relatively unchanged. For example, customer services, which had always been based at Peaktown, were known for being efficient so when mergers occurred, this team took over the other customer services offices. Other teams and departments had experienced constant change and relocation. A few focus group participants and managers had been relocated from London and the South, although most people in those locations tended to stay there and look for new jobs, while new local people were recruited to the Peaktown office. In the UK overall, at the time of the Peak case study, there was high employment, albeit with high levels of changes. Despite numerous rounds of redundancies in this organisation, participants talked about how those made redundant found new jobs fairly easily, and often on higher salaries. This contrasted with many of the experiences of case study participants in other Transitions countries, and affected the Peak participants' perceptions of the labour market and their own security within it.

Other changes resulting from the mergers and restructuring included changing terms and conditions of work, partly as an attempt to standardise these across the merged company. A subsidised workplace nursery on site first moved to another location and then became a private nursery, as part of financial changes due to the mergers. There was also a shift from formal (key-based) flexitime to informal 'trust-based' flexitime. The national provision for requesting leave arrangements is based on formal policy with formalised procedures. Peak's move away from formalised to informal trust-based flexitime was therefore a shift in the opposite direction, which the company saw as a more modern approach – influenced more by 'new management theory'. There was also an increased emphasis on autonomous, self-managing teams, as in many of the other case studies.

Flexibility was a buzz word at Peak. There was a drive for flexibility: numerical flexibility (mostly through the use of agency workers but also some staff on temporary contracts); functional flexibility (via multiskilling); and flexibility of working time, via policies and pursuing culture change primarily through management training, as discussed below.

The experience of work intensification that occurs often in the face of downsizing and 'efficiency' drives, together with changes in the organisation of work, put more onus on individuals to manage demanding tasks and schedules (Burchell et al, 2002). This was reported at Peak, as in the other Transitions case studies.

> *I do think there's an awful lot more expected of people. Nowadays. I mean if you look at like the basic, the lowest job, which is like the lowest-ranked job now, to what it was when I started here, which was only nine years ago, what's expected of them now is so much more than what we expected then. I think they're expected to do a lot more work for the money.* (Mother, child aged one, focus group participant)

In this context there had been a strategic drive to develop a distinctive culture for the new merged company. Managerial discourses sought to create a less task-oriented and more people-focused culture, based on trust, mutual flexibility, autonomy and self-management at all levels, non-hierarchical relationships and collaboration and mutual responsibility. Developments such as the shift from a clock-based to an informal flexitime system negotiated with management meant that increased emphasis was placed on autonomous, self-managing teams. Employees' experiences of these changes, however, were varied, as we will discuss.

So how did the approach to change, including the support offered to employees with family commitments within the new 'trust-based' culture, measure up against our criteria for a transformational approach? Below we discuss each of the criteria set out earlier.

Recognising changing workforce needs and treating these as strategic challenges and opportunities to learn and innovate

The managers' accounts indicated that the most recent merger was accompanied by a decision to attend to staff well-being. They made deliberate attempts to develop policy and practice and to create a culture change through greater flexibility of working hours. According to the managers interviewed, the recognition of employees' needs for flexibility and the potential mutual benefit of this were central to these strategic shifts. Traditional ways of working were being challenged and there was a prevailing discourse of the value of two-way flexibility. Potentially, this represented a move beyond the accommodation and elaboration approaches to a transformational strategy, in that there was recognition of the need to move beyond policies to focus on implementation and to view employees' flexibility needs as an opportunity – in this case, to forge a new post-merger culture and identity. In practice, however, change was uneven across the company and the move from formal to informal flexibility and trust was perceived as double edged.

Some work–family policies, such as the replacement of the workplace nursery with childcare vouchers and changes in the flexitime system, were viewed by parents, if not by management, as a deterioration of conditions. Employees tended to construe the changes in the flexitime system as a way of taking away 'their' flexidays: whereas under the old, formal system, time off was automatic, under the new system, people could take up to 13 flexidays in lieu but this had to be negotiated with managers. Therefore it was seen by employees as a 'favour' rather than a 'right'. The scepticism of some of the parents partly reflected a view held by many employees that these changes had been imposed for money-saving reasons, and without proper negotiation with employees.

Addressing business needs and employee needs: a dual agenda

There was an implicit dual agenda in the management discourse of pursuing business priorities by meeting staff's need for flexibility, or at least a recognition that for business needs to be achieved it would be necessary to address employees' needs:

> They've [the company] had all the um you know the stock market things and everything so they've had to all get a little bit more business focused. But, in becoming more business focused what they've done is focus on the employees and asked them, you know, what is it that you want, what can we do for you and, no, no longer do people want to work well, ... a percentage of people no longer want to work just nine till five. They want to work sort of 10 till six or ... [more flexibility]... (Manager, father of teenaged children)

> It's a different kind of, the old adage that a happy workforce is a productive workforce, isn't it. So if you can ... you know if you start challenging well, why are we working nine to five, because, you know, customers do ring after five o'clock so why not leave it open till six when there's people willing to work till six? So, why are we saying no to people? It's just about challenging some of the preconceptions that were there.... And I think we're changing the culture in a positive way erm ... because we do recognise that, you know, we're only successful if our people are happy. (Manager, mother of two school-aged children)

Meeting the needs of employees was regarded as essential to deal with the consequences of the demands of intensive market competition, such as the stress that arose from the intensification and insecurity of work:

> We're putting a lot of pressure on existing people, so, now there's more emphasis on people who are here, um, introduction of bonus schemes, um, flexible working hours.... So you perhaps want to keep people happy, they'll realise that it's a good employer. (Manager, male, no children)

However, a dual agenda approach, according to Rapoport et al (2002), involves listening to and collaborating with employees to ensure that both sets of needs are met. In the Peak case study, this did not occur: the lack of collaboration and consultation, at least as perceived by the employees, led to frustration by both some managers (who perceived the employees as resistant to change per se) and some employees (who perceived management as only interested in saving money).

Management's willingness to listen to and collaborate with the workforce

Managers talked about listening to employees, taking on board the need for flexibility in working hours and developing mutual trust. However, this was a strategy developed by management rather than the consequence of collaboration with staff. This can be illustrated by the changes in flexitime defined by management as a more trust-based system. Moreover, it was communicated top down from managers to staff, and it was introduced without taking account of the views of staff, who saw it as a way of controlling workers and taking away benefits. Indeed, it was clear from some of the managers' accounts that the changes were about control as well as trust, although the manager quoted below did not see these as incompatible:

> They weren't actually doing any more work, they were just clocking in 10 minutes early a day. So, from a business perspective it doesn't really gain the business. But then they were taking half a day off ... it makes it actually very difficult to resource. And plus we wanted to get to a culture where, you know, there's trust in the environment ... clocking in and clocking out was felt to be, um, quite a factory mentality and we want people to be um, you know, think about things flexibly rather than, um, very stringent and dogmatic. So that's what, part of the reason why we took it [the clock-based flexikey system] out. (Manager, mother of two school-aged children)

Consequently, many employees resented and in some cases resisted changes:

> When they took flexitime, see flexitime was a big thing to me, so when they took that, I was one of the ones who, who fought to the end to keep flexitime, as such. (Single father, of three school-aged children, focus group participant)

A transformational approach would involve managers and work groups thinking collaboratively about how best to meet the needs of employees and workplace effectiveness, generating support at multiple levels. Failure to collaborate undermined the changes because, although purporting to address a dual agenda, the changes were perceived by many employees as prioritising the business case and hence failed to keep the entire workforce engaged and committed to the changes.

Actively working towards achieving consistency between espoused values and practice by paying attention to implementation issues: management training

Management training and development were regarded as a crucial component of the change strategy. Managers, as the agents of change, had undergone training and development to inculcate new values and new management styles. Managers discussed the ways in which management training was used to shift the culture and help supervisors and managers to deal with resistance among staff. They talked about experiences of training and development focusing on self-management as well as team management, that is, on people – rather than a task-oriented focus – in bringing about change:

> Manager: *There's a big emphasis, last year, on managing departments, managing people, social skills, um, you know there was designated manager training, ongoing, um which is still ongoing … you know, I do other people's preferences, looking at people, understanding their reactions against a given change, um recognising my own preferences, that kind of thing.*
>
> Interviewer: *Do you think it made you a better manager, going on these courses?*
>
> Manager: *Yes, without a doubt. We've also, there was nothing about targets, production, you know, day-to-day activities, just managing people, getting the best out of people, but also understanding why you can't go far wrong, and they took away the old-style management when you were told you will do this, you will do that.* (Manager, father of one child, aged two, expecting a second child)

A distinction was made by both managers and staff between 'new–style managers' who endorse and promote the new culture and 'old–style managers' who failed to do so and persisted in adopting more autocratic and task-oriented styles. The ideal manager was now one who was adaptable, flexible, non-directive and collaborative. All the managers whom we interviewed described themselves as new style and endorsed the new culture drive somewhat uncritically. Old-style managers were viewed as generally resistant to change. This was seen by senior management as a temporary hurdle as they gradually learned new management styles or left the organisation. Sometimes this occurred through retirement or through voluntary moves. But there were also hints that managers who were seen as not being flexible, adaptable and new style got moved on or out in other ways (see also Linstead and Thomas, 2002).

There was a perception among staff that management had been told to be flexible and supportive to staff with family commitments, as part of the culture change:

> *Managers are told to be supportive, aren't they?* (Father, two children aged six and nine, focus group participant)

Nevertheless, at the time of the case study (2003–05), employees expressed mixed feelings towards management support for employees with family obligations. Employees with new-style supportive managers were very satisfied with the enhanced level of trust, autonomy and flexibility, but those with old-style managers were resentful:

> *I think it depends on the manager, to be honest. It really does. My previous boss was brilliant. And the thing is I can honestly say I gave more, I worked harder. I, you know, this is like confidential, he was a fantastic boss and if you needed anything, it was just a very open, two-way relationship that I had with him so I could be completely honest, tell the truth, and I'd make the time up and I used to make sure that I made it up. You know, there was no way that he was going to be a minute out from my time. Whereas I think when you're working for someone who is completely inflexible, and has no respect for your problems, you sort it out but you don't give 100%. You sort it out to the bare minimum, if you like, rather than making sure that you give that extra.* (Mother, child aged 18 months, focus group participant)

The new values and discourses of empowerment, particularly in the wider context of prevailing work–life balance discourses, raised expectations of support. Nor was lack of change restricted to line managers. Some human resources managers too had yet to practise the new values. The comment below was made by a former manager who had struggled to be allowed to change to part-time work and eventually had to accept a demotion to temporary project work to be able to work less than full time. She was later made redundant and when we interviewed her a year later was working for another company. She felt that human resources and some line managers were undermining the otherwise good intentions of the company:

> *I think Peak tried to be supportive. [Human resources] tried, but they're very rigid and what they're scared of doing is making a decision, a new decision, because they're scared that everybody'll want it. But in reality, everybody doesn't want the same things because everybody's circumstances are different.* (Former Peak manager, mother, child aged five)

This view that human resources was reluctant to make a decision about reduced hours work *"because they're scared that everybody'll want it"* resembles the accommodation and elaboration strategies described by Lee et al (2000), rather than a transformational approach. However, this does not necessarily characterise the entire organisation. One criticism of the notion of organisational learning is that it can imply a cross-organisational consistency that is rarely achieved. Workplace cultures are often uneven and fragmented and it appears that, while some Peak managers were keen to push for or buy into a more transformational approach to culture change, other line managers and human resources managers remained stuck in more cautious thinking. Thus, in Peak at this stage, as in many other organisations, despite undergoing drives for culture change, employees' experiences of flexibility and support for work–life needs, still depended largely on their managers (Hochschild, 1997; Lewis, 1997, 2001), although colleagues were also increasingly influential, as discussed later.

Willingness to question deeply ingrained assumptions about ideal workers and and the nature of particular jobs

The drive for a shift in culture and the changes in structures and practices that this was intended to bring about incorporated a deliberate questioning of some deeply ingrained assumptions about ideal workers, defined as those who work full time and according to rigid schedules. The process used to try to accomplish this, as discussed earlier, involved training and development in people management skills and new management theory about the business benefits of a more people- and less task-oriented style and about the benefits of trust and autonomy in, for example, self-managing teams. Training was inevitably a largely one-way process where trainers or consultants imparted 'knowledge' rather than a process whereby knowledge was mutually and collaboratively constructed. This approach failed to engage and work with resistance, which is an issue that a dual agenda approach addresses (Rapoport et al, 2002). Rather, old-style managers who resisted change had to feign commitment to new styles but manifest resistance in practice, or the company found ways if getting rid of them. Meanwhile, key assumptions that undermined the intended changes remained largely unchallenged. For example, at Peak, while there was growing flexibility and autonomy at some levels, there was still a widely held, albeit not unanimous, view that management roles required employees' full-time presence and the need to work longer than contracted hours. This was particularly evident from the biographical interviews with parents, in the second phase of the research. Some of the new mothers whom we interviewed had worked in managerial or supervisory positions prior to having their first child. Their experiences of returning to work after maternity leave were mixed; again some of their own managers were more flexible and supportive than others. Most had tried to reduce their (excessive) working hours and were moved to non-managerial roles, that is, demoted. The one exception was a mother who not only had a supportive manager, but also worked in a senior position that involved more technical skills rather than people management. The experiences of the mothers in managerial or supervisory roles quoted next were more typical:

> I went back to work full time when Cilla was five months old and I found that too much, because I was commuting two and a half hours a day. And full time, I just didn't have any time with her at all. And everything was fine, career-wise, until that point. And the minute that I asked to go part time, everything changed and my career just went downhill. (Manager, mother, child aged one year)

> *I'm going back [after maternity leave] part time but not as a supervisor, I've taken a drop in level.... Just so that I can work the hours that I wanted to work.* (New mother, formerly a supervisor)

The failure to question deeply held assumptions about the nature of jobs involving people management and the lack of trust implied in these assumptions, despite the high-profile drive for a trust-based culture shift, prevented Peak management from treating employees' requests as opportunities for learning and innovating.

Monitoring changes for continuous, ongoing learning

We have argued that a transformational approach involves continuous organisational learning about the impact of new practices in the context of ongoing internal and external changes. The importance of this can be illustrated by looking at the relationships within autonomous work teams in managing work–family boundaries at Peak. Autonomous work teams, self-rostering and other strategies for devolving responsibility for working time from managers to teams could be regarded as good practice as they are thought to provide the individual with control and autonomy that can reduce work–family conflict (Thomas and Ganster, 1995). However, our findings at Peak, and indeed in the other case studies in private and public sector organisations across Europe, suggest that in the context of an intensification of work and tight staffing, team members were reluctant to take time off or work flexibly because they knew that their already overburdened colleagues would have to cover for them. Colleagues within work teams, as well as providing support, could act as agents of social control, whether intentionally or unintentionally, limiting rather than expanding opportunities for flexibility:

> *I feel guilty sometimes because of, not so much my boss, but my, my colleagues and some colleagues who don't understand what, what I go through, what I have to do and one guy who's particularly keen about the clock, and has to be there at nine o'clock and you know, somebody will walk in at 10 past and you can see him look at the clock or his watch, laughter, and so I feel so much more, more as though I have to justify myself to him than, than my, you know, my manager.* (Single mother, child aged five, focus group participant)

Thus, 'good practices' shifted with changing conditions. Autonomy and teamwork in a context of intense workloads shift responsibility from managers to individuals and teams. In this context, it was not the presence of supportive or unsupportive managers that made a difference. Rather, it was individual feelings of responsibility towards the team that became a barrier to adopting flexible practices and thereby managing work–family boundaries. Of course, if the short-term business case is prioritised, this is viewed as a successful strategy. The organisation is seen to provide opportunities for flexibility and autonomy, yet employees apparently 'choose' not to use them. However, it creates new pressures for employees managing work and family commitments and if account is taken of the impacts at other levels of society, such as families and communities, this is unlikely to be socially sustainable in the long term (Webster, 2004). A transformational approach, as defined in this chapter, would involve recognising and learning from these issues, which would become a catalyst for further collaborative learning, problem solving and change. This involves keeping work–life issues constantly in mind as things change, 'mainstreaming' them into organisational decision making, and not losing sight of the personal side of the dual agenda.

Discussion

We began this chapter by proposing a framework for transformational workplace change to support employees' work–family needs, based on two different but complementary approaches to organisational learning: the learning paradigms identified by Lee et al (2000) and organisational learning resulting from the dual agenda approach to action research and change (Rapoport et al, 2002). On the positive side, at Peak, management understood the need to go beyond policies to focus on implementation and strove for more systemic change, that is, changes in culture, structures and practice. This approach was used strategically as a way of pursuing business aims in a rapidly changing and competitive environment. There was a concerted effort by senior management to train and develop managers as agents of change and to work towards putting espoused organisational values into practice. These strategies had achieved a certain measure of success, both in terms of workplace effectiveness and of satisfying the personal needs of some employees, but this was limited and uneven across the organisation. Management had engaged in some 'listening' to employees, although this fell far short of a collaborative approach in determining how to respond to workplace and employee needs (the dual agenda). Above all, however, there was limited questioning at a senior management level of assumptions about ideal workers, and a persisting belief that managers in particular must work full time and long hours. Moreover, at the point in time when the case study took place, the longer-term impacts of the changing practices had not been monitored in terms of the dual agenda.

So what was holding back transformational change at Peak? In a transformational approach, requests to work flexibly or less than full time are regarded as opportunities for learning and innovation. The drive for change at Peak was based on the notion that a more flexible, trust-based management style provided an opportunity for forging a new identity and culture change in the new merged company. However, not all managers bought into this. As with any large organisation, multiple workplace subcultures co-existed and organisational learning was patchy. The study by Lee et al (2000) identified the different learning paradigms based on a number of individual cases of reduced load work among managers and professionals. Although the methods used in the Transitions organisational case studies did not permit us to make similar types of observations, the interview and focus group data suggest that there may be limited examples of transformational learning in some departments and of accommodation as evidenced by a desire to contain and restrict flexible working in others. However, the trend to demote managers who request part-time work suggests that, at best, adaptation or accommodation appeared to be the normative responses in these cases. Women managers who requested part-time work were accommodated, often reluctantly, but this was career limiting and there was no openness to learning about new models of management. Thus, there appeared to be some initial movement towards a transformational approach in Peak, evidenced by a focus on culture change, not just the implementation of policy. However, progress was uneven at the time of the case study, varying across departments and according to the status of the employees wishing to work more flexibly.

Wider implications of the case study

A case study approach does not permit generalisation of findings, as such, to other organisations but it does illustrate aspects of processes of learning and change. There is considerable consensus from previous research that the development of work–life policies to support working parents, without attention to implementation and practice, is rarely effective. We have learned from this analysis of Peak's case that moving beyond policy to a focus on culture change has the potential to support working parents, but that this obviously depends on the details of how this is approached. At Peak, sustainable culture change involved a questioning of underlying assumptions and taken-for-granted beliefs about, for example, ideal workers and the value of part-time or full-time work. Without very explicit and strategic attention to the challenges of these highly gendered assumptions, culture change is, by definition, limited and likely to be, at best, patchy across large organisations. Moreover, management training and development as a culture change tool, in this respect, is again of limited effectiveness, if it results in top-down change rather than taking account of employee voices and interests, and engaging the workforce in collaborative efforts to meet the needs of both workers and the organisation.

Note
[1] 'Peak Insurance' is a pseudonym.

EIGHT

Work–family policies in a contradictory culture: a Dutch financial sector corporation

Bram Peper, Laura den Dulk and Anneke van Doorne-Huiskes

Introduction

In the Netherlands, support for 'work–family balance' is a responsibility shared between government, employers and working parents. The idea of shared responsibility is expressed in the Act on Childcare, which came into force in January 2005 and is based on the notion of tripartite funding split between the government, employers and parents. Parents pay the costs in advance, then receive an allowance from the government based on their income and on the cost of care used. Employers also contribute to the cost of childcare by paying their employees an allowance. The employers' contributions were voluntary until 2007, but have now become obligatory. With respect to leave arrangements (see Chapter One, Table 1.1), the government expects the social partners (that is, the employers' associations and trades unions) to extend this legal entitlement by offering additional support under collective agreements. Most Dutch employers nowadays offer at least one work–life policy that supplements the statutory provisions (Remery et al, 2002; van der Lippe, 2004). Employers in the Netherlands are generally not inclined to be frontrunners or champions with respect to work–family policies. Instead, they adapt to changing circumstances, and not primarily because they believe that setting up work–family arrangements is the best thing to do in terms of business or strategic planning. In fact, for many companies, *employee satisfaction* is the primary reason for introducing such provisions (for example, Remery et al, 2003).

There is some doubt as to whether work–family policies are being incorporated into company strategic thinking and, if they are not, whether they can produce any real changes within organisations. There is evidence that many employees are not taking advantage of existing policies in the Netherlands (SCP, 2004; den Dulk and de Ruijter, 2005), similar to the situation elsewhere in Europe (Haas and Hwang, 1995; Lewis, 2001) and beyond (Grover and Crooker, 1995; Hochschild, 1997; Lobel and Googins, 1999; Thompson et al, 1999; Williams, 2000; Anderson et al, 2002; Eaton, 2003). Formal policies are therefore no guarantee that work–family facilities will be used. Practical or financial reasons and an unsupportive culture in the workplace may deter people from using such policies.

Financial firms throughout the world have been through major organisational restructuring operations in recent years. In this chapter we discuss a case study conducted in a Dutch banking and insurance company, referred to here as BIC. We examine how formal work–family policies were implemented and utilised at BIC within the context of a changing organisational environment, doing so from the perspective of both managers and working parents. We address the following question: how do work–family policies play out in a contradictory and ambivalent organisational culture? We begin by discussing two theoretical perspectives on the utilisation or non-utilisation of work–family policies. We then introduce BIC, an organisation going through a process of organisational change, before explaining the research design. This is followed by an analysis of how work–family policies are implemented at BIC, and how managers and working parents perceive these policies.

Theoretical lenses for exploring participation (or not) in work–family policy schemes

Research into work–family policies in organisations has focused largely on whether the relevant facilities or provisions in fact exist (for example, den Dulk, 2001). There has been less interest in whether such facilities or provisions meet employee needs or whether employees actually utilise them. Having the facilities in place is not the same as their actually being used (Haas and Hwang, 1995, 1999; Lewis, 2001). Employers tend to report many more facilities than their employees do (Evans, 2001; Appelbaum et al, 2005). Explanations for the 'gap between policy and practice' tend to refer to different features and background factors: gender, industrial sector, occupational profile, household characteristics and organisational conditions, particularly organisational culture (for example, Haas and Hwang, 1995, 1999; Forth et al, 1997; Rostgaard et al, 1999; Thompson et al, 1999; Grootscholte et al, 2000; Lewis, 2001; Crompton, 2006). This chapter focuses on two theories explaining the widely reported implementation gap associated with work–family initiatives: institutional theory and the concept of 'sense of entitlement'.

Much of the research examining how and why employers decide to provide work–family benefits to their employees takes an institutional perspective, based on the assumption that there are growing institutional pressures in society to develop rules and regulations and in workplaces to develop work–family policies (den Dulk, 2001). Changes in the workforce, for example the growing share of working mothers and dual-earner families, have made these issues more salient. In addition, public interest in combining work and family life and emerging state regulations making this combination possible have heightened the pressure on employers to respond to work–family issues.

Institutional theory emphasises that policies may be adopted for symbolic rather than substantive reasons and thus may fail to produce any real changes in organisational structure or behaviour: companies may gain external legitimacy as desirable employers but may, intentionally or unintentionally, discourage employees from ever using these benefits. Blair-Loy and Wharton (2002) argue that institutional theory explains implementation gaps between policy and practice. They suggest that when work–family policies are in the early stages of adoption, before they are taken for granted, they are not yet embedded in organisational practices and structures and may hence conflict with organisational norms related to time and career demands. 'When organisational policies are controversial or ambiguous, intra-organisational interests and politics may shape policy outcomes' (Blair-Loy and Wharton, 2002: 816).

The institutional approach highlights the role of management discretion in organisations. When organisational policies are controversial or ambiguous, the associated meanings and expectations may vary widely across the organisation and be fixed locally by supervisors and work groups. Blair-Loy and Wharton (2002) argue that successful institutionalisation of contested policies generally depends on the political action and relative power of 'core constituencies'. In this case, these are working parents (mothers) with family responsibilities. The institutionalisation of policies and actual participation in policy schemes are also influenced by organisational processes such as communication. For example, Kirby and Krone (2002) argue that the way people talk about work–family policies and their utilisation influences whether employees will participate in these schemes in future. The way supervisors and even co-workers talk about work–family practices can undermine or reinforce formal policies. Actual participation in work–family policy schemes is thus influenced by a number of organisational and social processes. These in turn influence employees' beliefs about and perceptions of these policies and the consequences of utilising or asking to use them.

The second theoretical approach concerns the 'sense of entitlement' concept, derived from social justice theory (Lewis, 1996; Lewis and Smithson, 2001; Lewis and Haas, 2005). Work–family policies may be regarded as entitlements or rights, or viewed as favours that have to be negotiated and/or reciprocated. Lewis and Haas (2005: 353) define sense of entitlement as 'a set of beliefs and feelings about rights and entitlements, or legitimate expectations, based on what is perceived to be fair and equitable'. Sense of entitlement is the result of social comparison processes, and is shaped by the social context in which people operate. It is influenced by social, normative and feasibility comparisons (Lewis and Haas, 2005). For example, when participation in a formal policy scheme such as parental leave is not considered feasible or normative because few parents, especially fathers, participate and it is not clear how it will work, employees – especially men – are reluctant to utilise it. When people make social comparisons, they usually do so with people who are similar to themselves; for example, women compare themselves to other women and men to other men. Sense of entitlement therefore tends to be highly gendered (Lewis and Smithson, 2001), with women making more use of work–family provisions (den Dulk and Peper, 2007). Men, on the other hand, are more likely to reduce their involvement in childcare in favour of their careers. Lewis (1996) suggests that there are three factors influencing an employee's 'sense of entitlement' to work–family support: gender, the sociopolitical context and the organisational culture. In this case study, we focus on gender and organisational culture within the Dutch sociopolitical context.

Organisational cultures

The internal culture of the organisation influences the extent to which employees feel entitled to utilise or claim work–life provisions (Lewis, 1996). According to Thompson et al (1999: 394), 'A supportive work–family culture has been defined as the shared assumptions, beliefs, and values regarding the extent to which for women and for men an organisation supports and values the integration of work–family lives'. The literature distinguishes between various dimensions of work–family culture. Thompson et al (1999) differentiate between the time investment that employees are expected to make (which may conflict with duties at home), the career consequences of utilising work–family policies, and the support that managers offer with respect to the combination of work and family life. Allen (2001) distinguishes between perceived supervisory support and perceived support from the organisation as whole. Organisations may profile themselves to the outside world as 'family friendly' even though their internal culture does not actually support work–life balance other than at the expense of career progress. This is related to the still widespread assumption that employees can only demonstrate their organisational commitment by working full time or long hours (see, for example, Rapoport et al, 2002). The time requirements set by the organisation can also affect participation in work–family schemes. Fried (1999) shows that in an American company with a typical 'overwork culture' – where putting in long days is a sign of productivity and dedication – submitting claims for work–life provisions goes against the grain. Another dimension of organisational culture is the extent to which co-workers are supportive of employees who wish to combine working and family life (Dikkers et al, 2004).

A distinction can be made between the supportive dimension of work–family culture (that is, organisational, supervisory and colleague support for the combination of work and family life) and barriers, consisting of time and career demands (that is, the extent to which employees perceive negative career consequences and organisational time demands that thwart them from utilising work–family arrangements and managing their work–life balance). Based on the two dimensions of support and barriers, we can identify four different types of work–life organisational culture (Table 8.1). In a favourable or approving work–family culture, employees perceive a high level of support and few barriers; in a conflicting culture, a low level of support and many barriers; in a contradictory culture, a high level of support and many barriers; and finally, in an indifferent culture, a low level of support and few barriers (see also den Dulk and de Ruijter,

2005; den Dulk and Peper, 2007).The employees' sense of entitlement to support is likely to differ in these diverse types of context.

Table 8.1:Typology of work–life organisational cultures

		Support	
		Low level	High level
Barriers	Low	Indifferent culture	Approving culture
	High	Conflicting culture	Contradicting culture

Source: den Dulk and Peper (2007), based on den Dulk and de Ruijter (2005) and Dikkers et al (2007)

A contradictory culture? BIC in the context of organisational change

BIC has a workforce of over 30,000 people in the Netherlands, of which 37% are women and 63% are men. Although BIC has branches and offices in other countries, the case study is restricted to the Dutch division, which has its own human resources policies. The average age of the workforce is 40 years. At BIC, women are under-represented in upper-level positions. Indeed, the percentage of women in upper-level positions is low compared to other companies in the Dutch financial sector (internal human resources document). Only 2% of female employees are paid at the highest salary scales, compared to 10% of male employees. Female employees are more likely to have a part-time job: 5% of male and 48% of female employees work part time. In total, the percentage of part-timers is 21.5%, which is below average in the Netherlands.

Like other financial firms, BIC is known for its good working conditions. Specific to the Dutch banking sector is the introduction of the 36-hour working week in 1996. This provides various opportunities for flexibility, for example working four nine-hour days a week; working five eight-hour days one week and four eight-hour days the next week; or working nine five-day weeks and having the 10th week off. By and large, BIC follows the statutory provisions regarding leave arrangements, and it also has a flexible benefit system enabling employees to choose from a combination of benefits.[1] It is therefore possible to tailor working conditions to personal wishes, within certain limits. Although BIC does not present itself as a frontrunner regarding work and family arrangements, the organisation does offer initiatives that go beyond government policies. For instance, it has an additional, although limited, budget to buy childcare places for its employees at private daycare centres.

At the time of this study, major changes had taken place in BIC's organisational structure. Previously, separate banking and insurance activities had been merged into various divisions, with the aim of achieving more synergy in the organisation. The human resources department had been downsized, with more human resources tasks being allocated to the line managers. Employees no longer contacted a human resources officer first when they wanted to use a policy; they went straight to their own manager. BIC was also experimenting with output management and flexible reward systems. BIC's overall aim was to become a more businesslike, commercial organisation in order to improve its efficiency and performance management (BIC social annual report). The organisational change processes had increased insecurity and work pressure among its employees. On the other hand, as a large financial firm, BIC was – and still is – considered an attractive employer. It was a stable company that had long offered a reasonable level of job security. The salaries were good and there was a range of formal work–family policies.

Other issues played a role at BIC, however. Efficiency was becoming an increasingly important factor in the way work was organised. The need for efficiency was constantly being stressed. BIC had recently launched a drive for what it called a 'winning performance culture', one in which the company's shared values, behaviours and practices would create and sustain superior business performances (BIC's annual reports). Transparency and accountability were regarded as important elements of this cultural discourse. Employees were increasingly called to account for what they had actually contributed to the company's results. It had become harder for them to keep a low profile. Like many private organisations in the Western world, BIC was feeling the tension between the need to be a good employer, reflected in its excellent formal work–family provisions, and the need to create a winning culture in a very competitive environment. Rather than seeing these goals as mutually reinforcing, it evidently gave lower priority to work–family issues. This did not mean that the organisation neglected the rules in this respect. On the contrary, BIC tried hard to be a decent and caring organisation; that is the picture that emerges from company documents, interviews with managers, and the focus groups. These aspects of BIC appeared to be widely shared in the organisation. However, work–family issues were not seen as relevant when it came to modernising the company and preparing it for a challenging future. Work–family issues were not discussed in the boardroom when important strategic issues were at stake. They were not seen as a part of the company's transformation process that had to be dealt with in order to prepare the organisation for the near future. Work–family issues had no strategic relevance, so to speak. They were, rather, seen as relating to changes in society that – for that very reason – needed to be properly regulated, and as something that could potentially threaten the aim of creating a winning performance culture. Strategically speaking, work–family issues were more often placed on the debit side of the organisation than on the credit side. It was very interesting to explore how work–family policies played out in this contradictory and ambivalent organisational culture. Let us focus on what employees and managers had to say. First, however, we have a few remarks about our case study methods.

Methods and data collection

In addition to the data collection methods used in the Transitions study (see Chapter Two), we also conducted a survey among a representative sample of BIC employees (*N*=521) in order to measure the actual participation in work–family policy schemes by employees and to assess the 'work–family friendliness' of the organisational culture (van Doorne-Huiskes et al, 2005; den Dulk and Peper, 2007).

The data from the two research projects enabled us, first, to discuss actual participation in work–family policy arrangements at BIC and to define its organisational culture. Second, the focus groups and interviews with managers allowed us to investigate how work–family policies worked out in practice.

Use of work–family policies and the work–family culture

Table 8.2 shows participation in existing policy schemes based on the survey data (den Dulk and Peper, 2007). The most popular policies were those that enabled employees to be flexible in managing work and family life. A majority of employees had flexible starting and finishing times (69%). The utilisation rate for the flexible benefit system and the compressed working week was also relatively high (around 40%). Where the job allows, flexible starting and finishing times have become quite standard in the Netherlands over the past decade, something that also applies for the compressed working week in the Dutch financial sector. The participation rate for leave arrangements was much lower, between 11% and 6% of employees. It was also gendered: female employees were more likely to work part time and utilise childcare support and leave arrangements, whereas male employees more often used the flexible benefit system and the compressed working week. As long as flexibility did not include reducing working hours, most male employees felt entitled to use this.

Table 8.2: Participation in work–family policy schemes in 2003 (N=521)

	% of employees	% of women	% of men
Flexible starting and finishing times	69	38	62
Flexible benefit system	41	34*	66*
Compressed working week (four nine-hour days)	37	31*	69*
Part-time work	22	78*	22*
Childcare support	17	62*	38*
Emergency leave	11	44	56
Parental leave	10	63*	37*
Short-term family leave	8	55*	45*
Saving hours for sabbatical leave	6	43	57

Note: *=significant p=0.01.
Source: van Doorne-Huiskes et al (2005); den Dulk and Peper (2007)

Work–family policies are mostly framed as a women's issue in the Netherlands, despite recent government campaigns that stress fathers' caring roles. Traditional role expectations, which are deeply embedded in Dutch culture, remain influential (den Dulk et al, 2005). Women are still seen as the main carers, although fathers are becoming more involved. Fathers like the compressed working week because it allows them to shoulder care responsibilities on weekdays, although they realise that their manager will probably dislike their being absent one day a week. Women more often opt for part-time employment (less than 36 hours), as is reflected in the high part-time rate among women in the Netherlands. The questionnaire revealed the respondents' perception of the work–life culture in their organisation by having them respond to 17 items asking them how they saw the organisation's overall support for the work–life balance, their manager's support, their co-workers' support, the demands made on their time, and the consequences that utilising work–life policies would have for their careers (Dikkers et al, 2004; den Dulk and de Ruijter, 2005; den Dulk and Peper, 2007).

The outcomes of this questionnaire suggest a contradictory culture at BIC, in which the presence of formal work–family policies and support for combining work and family life are accompanied by career and time demands that make it difficult for employees to participate in work–family policy schemes. Such a situation can create inconsistency and differences in implementation within an organisation. A contradictory culture also means that the organisation is sending mixed messages about work–family support; on the one hand it is saying that work–family policies are open to employees, but on the other hand it is suggesting role models whereby employees are always available and prepared to work long hours (see also Kirby and Krone, 2002). Let us see how the contradictory culture at BIC shaped the perceptions of both managers and working parents in relation to work–family policies.

Perceptions of managers and working parents

According to national surveys among students and young professionals, BIC ranks among the top 10 – or sometimes top five – employers in the Netherlands.[2] Its reputation is based primarily on its generous salaries, numerous employee training facilities and excellent fringe benefits. It is also known to offer job security, although that may be less the case today than in the recent past. So far, however, BIC's reputation as a good and reliable employer seems untainted. Indeed, at first glance, working parents at BIC seemed to be quite content with the work–family policies available to them. However, a more detailed analysis of the focus group discussions with working parents and managers' interviews revealed contradictions and inconsistencies.

BIC: a decent and caring organisation

Discussions in the focus group confirmed the perception of BIC as a very good employer. Some participants suggested that the quality of the employment terms was precisely what discouraged BIC employees from seeking work elsewhere. They regarded it as a stable company offering a reasonable level of job security; they would not lose their jobs unexpectedly, salaries were good, and the work–family facilities were explained in the personnel manual. Managers confirmed this opinion. BIC cared about its employees. Managers felt that BIC was a good employer for parents of young children. They pointed out that it offered flexible working hours, the option of working part time, and teleworking, although they felt that it could do better on the last of these. They presented BIC as an employer with a social conscience, although its policy had become somewhat less generous in recent years.

Gendered expectations and participation in policy schemes

Did managers feel that BIC is a caring, decent organisation for women who want to move up the career ladder? Yes, some responded, BIC had a clearly defined policy of supporting women on the road to senior-level positions. If they decided to downshift while their children are small, they were allowed to do so. According to one manager, BIC was in fact more tolerant towards women than men in that respect. Men who expressed the wish to claim parental leave were viewed with more scepticism than women submitting the same request, reflecting traditional assumptions about male and female responsibilities. Such assumptions are seldom explicitly expressed and discussed, but they do have an impact on women's career opportunities or, to be more precise, on the career opportunities of mothers. The manager quoted below expressed stereotypical views of women's roles and commitments:

> [I]n general women have children. They start working part time, find their career less important, don't have ambitions and their career stagnates. You can't blame the organisation for this. (Man, manager, aged 37, no children)

One of the focus group participants noticed a strange inconsistency in the part-time policy of BIC:

> There are part-timers working in the company, but part-timers are never hired. Vacancies for job positions [on the internal job market] are seldom offered part time, always full time. (Woman, two children, focus group participant)

Career consequences as a trade-off

While many employees felt entitled to claim parental leave and work part time, they did not have a sense of entitlement about also sustaining their careers; accepting negative career consequences was the trade-off for individual choice. This is illustrated by the following quote:

> *I only have nice experiences. But at our department if you want to work fewer hours, and this is mostly done by women, you are moved back to square one. You can forget about building a career.* (Woman, two children aged one and five, focus group participant)

'Choices' are always socially embedded, however (Lewis et al, 2007; Crompton et al, 2007). There seemed to be a lot of leeway on paper, but in reality employees were asked to 'be sensible' and to 'think about their careers' when asking for leave or a sabbatical or to work part time. While the company permitted a great deal of flexibility in working time, the employee had to bear a large part of the risk.

Lack of awareness

Not all work–family policies were widely known in the organisation. There was a particular lack of awareness among managers concerning relatively new statutory policies, for example arrangements allowing employees to take 10 days of leave each year to care for a sick child or relative. Few parents claimed short-term care leave; they first tried to solve crises of this kind by asking their partner or other family members to care for the sick child. When this was not possible, they used their holiday entitlement. Only when they had no holiday entitlement left did they turn to short-term care leave. Hence, short-term leave was evidently regarded as a last resort, and not as the first option when a child fell ill. Quite a few respondents went on annual holiday leave to care for a sick child instead of using the relevant short-term statutory leave.

> *When I cannot arrange a childminder and I cannot make up for lost time, then I will claim short-term leave. Or I use up my holiday leave, which I did in the beginning, but I stopped, I lost all my days of holiday. And you are at home, not so nice with a sick child, it is not as if you can go out and have some fun.* (Woman, aged 30, one child, focus group participant)

The key role of the line manager

One of the elements that emerged repeatedly in our research was the key position of the manager or supervisor. As in the other case studies in this volume, it was the manager who actually decided whether or not an employee could utilise work–family policies. Although supervisory support was generally rated positively, managers differed as to how much they promoted good work–family practices. The contradictory culture left room for managerial discretion and the impact of other factors, such as individual convictions and specific circumstances within departments. Managers were responsible for meeting the targets set for their work units, and allowing employees to participate in policy schemes made that more complicated (Powell and Maniero, 1999). For instance, if the department was small and several employees were taking maternity and/or parental leave at the same time, managers encountered scheduling problems if no additional resources were available. Overall, the attitude and practices of managers were inconsistent; working parents reported both positive and negative responses.

> *If managers are inflexible and don't have kids themselves, they tend to say 'Well that's your problem, solve it yourself, the company can't help you and isn't responsible'.* (Man, aged 40, expectant father, focus group participant)

Although these complaints did not dominate in the employee focus groups, they were certainly expressed. It was managers who made the difference when it came to being flexible about the company's work–family facilities. *"If the manager objects to something, then everything comes to a halt."* Not all managers supported the different forms of work–life policies in the same way. It was therefore important for employees to know their supervisor.

> *Some female managers overreact and act as super macho, but generally women seem to understand more. Older managers are less understanding, because times change and they have different standards. They demand more of themselves; they see their tasks differently.* (Man, manager, aged 42, two children)

In terms of manager attitudes, sex was hardly relevant, with examples of supportive as well as unsupportive female managers being mentioned. There was more agreement about generational differences between managers, that is, older managers were perceived as less understanding and supportive than younger ones. There were still situations where the manager used their position of power, and in which employees felt that they had little voice:

> *It is always [presented as] in mutual consultation, but there is no mutual consultation, there always is a relative power situation. Then there is no mutual consultation in principle.* (Man, aged 36, two children, focus group participant)

Some parents felt that manager decisions were arbitrary. Uncertainty about managers' willingness to grant certain requests sometimes led to strategic or calculating behaviour on the part of employees:

> *I know that I postponed my request for parental leave until my appointment*
> *was final. I did this deliberately. And my boss said when I put forward my*
> *request, oh well if I had known beforehand I would not have appointed you.*
> (Woman, aged 32, one child, focus group participant)

Manager predicaments and limited resources

The lack of strategic embedding of work–family policies was also reflected in
the way BIC facilitated participation in schemes. On an operational level, BIC
paid only scant attention to the consequences for the available manpower within
departments. There appeared to be no standard replacement policy when people
went on leave, and no possibility of hiring additional workers when employees
reduced their working hours or went on leave. As a result, when parents asserted
their legal entitlement to leave, managers ran into operational difficulties and the
workload increased for co-workers. In the excerpt below, two employees discuss
the legal entitlement to parental leave and its implications. They discuss taking
one day of parental leave a week for a year.

> *[W]e do not have enough manpower. But I have a legal right to parental leave,*
> *and the manpower shortage is not my fault. So, I just stopped working, which*
> *probably will not be seen in a very positive light.* (Man, aged 36 years, two
> children, focus group participant)

> *I think you're right. The only thing is, BIC does not solve that problem.* (Man,
> aged 35, two children, focus group participant)

> *No, exactly. So, if they want to discuss it with me, I will turn the question back*
> *on them.* (Man, aged 36, two children, focus group participant)

Despite expecting a negative response or pressure from managers and co-workers,
the first father insisted on his legal right, implying a strong sense of entitlement
and a belief that this should be feasible. When employees used family leave
policies, it increased the pressure on their manager to find a solution while they
were absent:

> *We have a team with six people; one is on four months' leave, the other has*
> *maternity leave, so you lose a great part of your manpower. And to replace*
> *them is a lot of hassle, you end up with trainees who finally start to get it after*
> *three months. Looking at this situation as a manager, I think it has been very*
> *badly handled by the organisation.* (Man, aged 35, two children, focus
> group participant)

In general, managers tended to approve actual employee requests, even though they
would advise against it and warn the employee about the career consequences.

Managers also noted that they found it difficult to manage a large number of part-timers or people taking leave. Not everything theoretically possible was considered to be feasible in everyday practice.

> *We have all the options, from parental leave to sabbatical leave, and it's all possible. But in practice your decisions have to be well grounded and taken with care, because they can harm your career, unfortunately. It's the same for all these policies: it is possible, but take care, it's at your own risk, because it is not as ideal as you might expect.* (Man, manager, aged 42, two children)

When managers did approve employee leave, the pressure on the co-workers often increased. The managers lacked the resources to replace employees and were unable to change the output targets instantaneously. They therefore left the problem to be solved on the shop floor.

> *It does not work that way at [BIC]. You cannot change goals and targets in a flash. That's why you cannot instantly arrange a replacement. That's why there is a problem, and your colleagues must fix that. Fix it. That's the way it works.* (Man, aged 33, one child, focus group participant)

This practice added to the employees' already increasing workload. It also showed how difficult the manager's position could become: caught between the wish to meet employee needs but not having the resources to replace them, thereby increasing the workload for the others. This in turn put pressure on the solidarity between co-workers.

Solidarity between co-workers

Because there was no standard replacement procedure on an operational level, the actual utilisation of work–family policies posed a threat to the solidarity among co-workers.

> *You cannot replace somebody in no time. There is a problem your colleagues will have to solve. That's the way it works.* (Man, aged 33, one child, focus group participant)

Colleagues in the workplace often had to take over the work of the employee who was on leave or working fewer hours. Although the parents among the employees were highly supportive of one another, this was less the case for employees without children:

> *Parents need to take care of their children, that's very logical, but it has consequences for non-parents.* (Man, aged 41, expectant father, focus group participant)

Increasing pace of work

The general feeling was that BIC demanded a lot of its employees. The company was determined to transform itself from a 'sleepy' organisation into a world-class commercial enterprise. That meant retrenchment, stricter control of budgets and targets, and doing more with fewer people. *"Reorganising appears to have become our core business,"* according to some of the employees. Many of the barriers to utilising work–family policies encountered by parents were related to these changes and the subsequent lack of resources for successful implementation.

Conclusion

How did work–family policies work out in the contradictory culture of this Dutch financial sector organisation? Let us return to our two theoretical approaches. From the institutional perspective, the results suggest that work–family policies were in many cases not fully embedded and taken for granted at BIC. In fact, they often conflicted with the organisational culture and practices. This created scope for managerial discretion and was likely to lower the employees' sense of entitlement to work–family policies and the extent to which they used them. Many felt legally entitled to claim work–family provisions, but at the same time accepted the associated negative career consequences. Such consequences were taken for granted and, among women, accepted as the trade-off for individual choice. 'Choices' must be understood within the societal context of supports and constraints, however. Real choice implies that an alternative 'choice' is available (to be supported by one's employer and spouse in juggling a full-time career and childcare while achieving career progress; Lewis and Giullari, 2005). Thus, it was also predominantly women who worked part time and made use of parental leave. This fact also reflects parenthood norms in the Netherlands, where mothers are still seen as the main carers and fathers as the main breadwinners (den Dulk et al, 2005).

The ambivalence surrounding participation in work and family arrangements can be traced to two sources. First, BIC sent mixed signals about its policies. For instance, while it was possible to work part time, internal job offers were never for part-time positions, and so part-time work was not considered ideal. Second, and most importantly, managers differed in the way they granted employee requests. Their discretionary scope was quite considerable, which sometimes led to employees feeling that they had been treated unfairly. Managers were in a sticky situation, however; they had to respond to the formal organisational policies on leave arrangements, but were not always able to replace employees during their leave; the increased workload on the other employees in turn threatened co-worker solidarity. There was therefore a downside to letting managers and their employees sort things out instead of the organisation adhering to a strict policy on how and when to grant employee requests and on how to replace absent employees. Hence, because work–family policies were not fully institutionalised within BIC in a strategic sense, a contradictory culture persisted. The experiences of working parents and managers reflect this contradictory culture. Working parents were caught between the need to use policies and the career consequences if they did so. Managers were caught between the wish to be responsive and the need to meet organisational targets.

Managers generally recognised the necessity of offering work–family provisions. But the reality of the need for work–family policies seemed to be viewed as 'unconnected' with the reality of the requirements of modern, highly competitive organisations.

From the theoretical perspective of sense of entitlement, it is important to realise that BIC regarded work–family policies more as a cost than a benefit. As a result, employees did not really think it was feasible to participate in schemes while sustaining their careers, and had fewer opportunities for positive social comparisons. They therefore hesitated to utilise policies or would delay doing so until they were more certain about their position in the organisation. In terms of work–family provisions, a sense of entitlement to support was clearly gendered for employees. For historic reasons, women felt less burdened by the threat of having their commitment called into question when actually using work–family facilities. For the same historic reasons, managers thought such behaviour to be more obvious for female employees than for male employees. They showed more tolerance towards women than men when it came to actually utilising work–family policies. This tolerance came at a price, however. Women still constituted only a small percentage of the senior ranks within BIC. The higher the position the less likely that it was filled by a woman. Fathers were less prepared to miss out on career opportunities, while mothers seemed more willing to give up their careers for family life, something directly related to the persistent ideology of motherhood in the Netherlands (OECD, 2002; den Dulk et al, 2005). The wider societal context therefore reinforced and was reinforced by the organisational processes.

As long as work–family policies are not fully embedded in organisations, they will not provide an efficient means of achieving a satisfied workforce able to combine careers and family life equitably. On the contrary, the perverse effects found in this study – feelings of unfairness due to managerial inconsistencies, pressure on solidarity within the workplace, and gender inequality – have a negative impact on the organisation's performance and, moreover, will reduce the likelihood of such policies being institutionalised in the near future. The challenge for the near future is, therefore, how large companies such as BIC can make the concept of valuing and supporting work–family or work–life integration an integral part of their strategies. In other words: how can it become a concept that is raised in company boardrooms and is at the very heart of strategic discussions?

Notes

[1] The flexible benefit system makes it possible for employees to save up hours for three months of fully paid sabbatical leave. Employees who need extra days off can buy additional leisure time in exchange for salary (a maximum of one normal working week). On the other hand, employees can also sell annual leave or buy a computer in exchange for gross salary.

[2] The survey is conducted annually by *Intermediair*, a large weekly Dutch magazine aimed at university graduates between 20 and 45 years of age.

Part Three
Comparisons

Conclusions

Parents and organisational change: a cross-sector comparison of two Norwegian organisations

Ann Nilsen, Sevil Sümer and Lise Granlund

Introduction

Based on a case study of a Norwegian multinational company (NMC) in the private sector and a public sector social services organisation in Norway, this chapter seeks to explore and compare how employees who are parents of young children experience and talk about organisational change. An overview of similarities and differences between the two is the backcloth against which we develop our discussion. Comparing across sectors makes for a context-sensitive analysis that can highlight aspects of effects on employees' lives of organisational change that single case studies could not provide.

The wider context characterising the period during which the case studies were carried out (early 2003) was one of economic growth with low unemployment. The importance of oil to the economy enabled Norway to avoid the economic recession and major cuts in welfare benefits that other Scandinavian countries experienced during the 1990s. Political consensus on the subject of public responsibility for basic welfare provision continued throughout the period (Eitrheim and Kuhnle, 2000). During the 1990s, the institutional features of the welfare state were strengthened regarding labour market, gender equality and work–family reconciliation policies (see Chapter One). Norway's large public sector and the state's active labour market policies notwithstanding, now neoliberal ideas have become more influential. Privatisation and New Public Management (NPM) ideologies have become important in the 'modernisation' of the public sector of the economy (Christensen and Lægreid, 2002, 2007).

The gender segregation of the Norwegian labour market is persistent. More men occupy positions in the higher echelons of the occupational structure; many occupations are 'gender typed' in the sense that they are either male or female dominated. As in most welfare states, there is a large public sector of the economy that includes a range of teaching and caring occupations. In Norway, women comprise 70% of the employees in the public sector of the economy, where the part-time rate is very high. In the private sector, there are 63% men. Around 50% of managers in the public sector are women. In the private sector,

74% of managers are men (www.ssb.no/vis/emner/06/01/yrkeaku/main.html). Promotion opportunities are different in the two sectors as the occupational hierarchies differ, and the wage level is higher in the private sector (Tronstad, 2007).

The wider national policies and economic situation form one layer of context in which the case studies are embedded. In order to address the level of organisations, an overview of some main trends in recent organisation studies is useful.

Themes and concepts in recent organisational studies

The term 'new organisations'[1] is often used in international and national research. It is usually described in terms of non-hierarchical organisations that provide freedom and flexibility to employees, where work is said to be so interesting that little structural enforcement is needed in order for employees to work hard and put in long working hours (Coser, 1974; Hochschild, 1997; Sørensen, 1998; Brandth and Kvande, 2001; Ellingsæter and Solheim, 2002; Engan and Kvande, 2005). Concepts that have been used to characterise these types of new organisations include the catchwords 'greedy and seductive organisations' or 'greedy institutions' (for example, Coser, 1974; Kvande, 1998; Sørensen, 1998). The time regimes in the 'new organisations' are sometimes called 'time cultures without boundaries' while the more traditional ways of organising the working day are called 'time cultures with boundaries'. The former is said to give employees more flexibility in how to organise their day.

It has been argued that the current theoretical focus in organisational research stems from studies in knowledge production organisations rather than service production and care where women form the majority of the workforce (Ellingsæter and Solheim, 2002; Engan and Kvande, 2005). In a study of care and service organisations, Vike et al (2002) concluded that employees in welfare state occupations are likely to work more than they are obliged to according to their formal work contracts. Reasons for this were concluded to be associated with their values and norms and not structural enforcement. Thus, there is a contrast between what motivates employees in 'new organisations', which is said to be self-development and personal interest, and care workers who are driven by a feeling of responsibility for clients and patients.

Studies on sector differences show that a shared worker–carer family model is easier to combine with structures and cultures in the public sector (Ellingsæter, 1999). In female-dominated occupations in the public sector, normal working hours are flexible and shorter than in male-dominated occupations where the norm is full time or more (Abrahamsen, 2002). Women in male-dominated workplaces tend to leave their jobs if working hours are inflexible (Bø, 2001). It is, however, difficult to argue a case for a completely different logic in the private and public sectors, as studies focusing on NPM demonstrate how this logic is spreading from private businesses to public sector organisations, including hospitals and other care work institutions (Sørensen, 1998; Christensen and Lægreid, 2002, 2007), in Norway as elsewhere.

Our study in some respects reflects the findings in organisational studies at a more general level. The private sector NMC had policies and practices that coincided with the characteristics of 'greedy organisations', while the changes that were taking place in the social services were motivated by a NPM logic – providing client services at cost-efficient terms (Nilsen et al, 2004).[2] The ideologies behind organisational change may differ for the two sectors but among the questions we will look into in this chapter is how organisational change is experienced by working parents *in practice*.

Approach to the analysis[3]

The analysis in this chapter was carried out using a context-sensitive approach where insights from grounded theory as formulated by Glaser and Strauss (1967) and the closely related exploratory logic (Blumer, 1969; Stebbins, 2001) were applied. Qualitative data, in this instance from focus groups, are typically analysed by reading and rereading transcripts, and sometimes going back to listen to the tapes, yet all the while interpreting the voices in focus groups and manager interviews within a multilayered contextual framework. Depending on the focus of analysis, which might vary depending on what particular set of questions one seeks to explore, different meanings and dimensions might be identified. For this chapter the questions are related to *how parents experience and discuss organisational change*. When examining the data with such questions in mind, the different layers of context in which employees were embedded were taken into consideration. Hence, interpretations of both the private sector organisation and the social services took the overall situation for the respective groups of employees into consideration. All focus group participants were parents and parenthood is therefore an important contextual feature that affects the way employees experience and talk about their work situation.

The grounded approach involved developing concepts and categories in the process of analysis since preconstructed concepts would not meet the criterion of being context sensitive. Context-sensitive types or categories[4] are helpful for analysing and conceptualising different types of organisations yet at the same time making meaningful comparisons across diverse settings. The purpose of comparison is precisely to both understand the distinctiveness of one type of organisation as well as identify dimensions where there are similarities that cut across the two organisational settings. Ways in which employees and managers express and talk about their experiences of organisational change have been categorised as *types of approaches to change*. These vary across the organisations since changes are different in the respective settings. The context-sensitive types demonstrate how the different layers of context interplay to form specific patterns of approaches.

A brief description of the main differences between the two organisations will give some necessary background for understanding the different types of expressed experiences of organisational change.

Case studies: contexts and organisational change

The main difference between the two cases was that NMC operated on a for-profit basis and on principles of cost-efficiency whereas the social services, at least in principle, operated according to the logic of providing quality services for clients. The NMC thus made its policy decisions based on *principles of the market*, whereas decisions regarding social services were made by *political authorities* that were democratically elected bodies. These differences are important for understanding the context of the changes in the organisations, and also their policies.

The general trend in the NMC was towards a greater flexibility in working hours and the possibility of working from home. In some cases the latter was interpreted as a demand to be available for the employer at all hours, and for this reason quite a few of the employees did not make use of the option to get free internet access and a mobile phone since they thought that this blurred the boundary between work and home. Employees in the social services could not bring work files home for confidentiality reasons. They did, however, have flexible working hours, which helped in organising their daily lives with children. Most employees in both organisations had permanent work contracts. However, during the phase of changes in the public sector when the case study was carried out, there was an increase in temporary contracts since the overall need for staff had become uncertain because of mergers. The sick leave rate was high in the social services, and when employees were on long-term sick leave, replacements were needed. These were frequently contract workers or people on temporary contracts. The NMC also made use of contract workers; however, apart from cleaners these were mainly in other branches of the company than the one where we carried out our study.

Parenthood is gendered. In both organisations, motherhood and fatherhood brought different demands and called for variations in adjustment patterns between work and family. In the NMC and social services alike, most fathers made use of the one-month paternity leave to which they were entitled. There were a few instances of mothers employed in the higher echelons of the NMC who returned to work before the whole maternity leave period was up. Working part time to have more time for children was a women's strategy in both organisations. Part-time work had both positive and negative sides for employees. On the positive side, some mothers thought it important to be able to spend more time with very young children. This was the case in both organisations, although the part-time rate was higher in the social services than in the NMC. In the latter, a 'long hours part-time adjustment' (80% of full time) for a few years after maternity leave was not uncommon. The social services had more women employees working part time for longer time spans. The negative sides of part-time work included a feeling of not being perceived as committed to wage work. Such impressions were more common in the social services than in the NMC, partly because so few worked part time in the latter organisation.

Both organisations had gone through recent phases of reorganisation, but for different reasons. The main changes in the NMC happened because the company expanded and was sensitive to fluctuations on the world market. The social services were at the time of the study just embarking on a process of change that was ongoing and was motivated by political aims of restructuring the public sector as a whole. This overall 'modernisation'[5] of the public sector for the social services involved extensive reorganisations and merging of units and branches.

Organisational change in the NMC

The NMC had business operations in a number of countries. The company was involved in many lines of production and financial operations. Ten years before our study, the rate and speed of change was higher than at the time of the case study. The main changes had involved centralisation of certain operations, job cuts and other efficiency measures. Many employees had to move to other cities or branches while others were offered benefit packages to encourage them to leave their jobs. Branches and sections of the company merged both nationally and internationally. Changes and reorganisation were motivated by a need for cost-efficiency and increased profit.

Our analyses identified four broad types or categories of ways in which change was experienced and talked about in this organisation. These were all framed in *individualistic* terms in that they focused on how organisational change affected the opportunity structure for the individual employee. The 'business approach' was expressed when the financial and efficiency sides of reorganisation were prominent. Only top managers took this perspective on organisational change, focusing on the 'good of the company' with little attention to individual employees. The 'opportunity approach' was one where change was experienced as creating opportunities for development of skills and personal growth. A third type could broadly be characterised as the 'insecurity approach' and emphasised feelings of insecurity among many of the employees in phases where there was talk about merging of branches, which could lead to relocation of a branch and where people would not only have to change their occupational position, but also move house. The fourth was the 'ambiguity approach', which was mainly expressed by employees who had been with the company for a shorter time and who had not personally experienced the rather extensive reorganisation that took place in an earlier phase. Viewpoints matching this category were mainly found in the focus groups with employees rather than among managers.

The business approach

This approach was expressed in the account of one male manager in that the cost-efficiency reasons behind mergers and relocations were prominent:

> *About 10 years ago there were major changes. At that time there were parallel branches in two cities, then a third similar branch was suggested established in a city further north. Then we saw that this would be wrong somehow. One can't have all those parallel functions, we had to try and locate this function in one place to create advantages from having a larger unit. At that time many people were asked to relocate and to change their positions in the organisation.*

The quote expresses the overall concern of the company; profit reasons for changes were given priority and reorganisation was seen as inevitable if the company was to survive in a tough climate of competition on the market. Top managers frequently talked about change in this way. Most top managers were in a lifecourse phase that did not involve the care of young children; however, this group was supposed to look out for the overall interests of the company so their emphasis on this perspective on organisational change was what the shareholders in the company expected.

The opportunity approach

Some employees approached the topic of organisational change from the viewpoint of the opportunities such change presented for personal development and learning new skills on the job:

> *There have been major changes but I did not personally need to move, I was allowed to stay here all the time. Even though I had new managers and was placed in different departments I worked with the same tasks all the time. And these have been only positive experiences. I am all for changes, I think it is nice when something happens. I think we soon should have a new reorganisation! [laughs] That is what characterises [NMC], we change a lot, at least seen from outside. I think these changes have been positive. That we make changes both in the management and among the employees and that we replace those who hold the same positions for too long.... You do not fire people in [NMC], we don't have that American model, we keep people and take care of them and this is of course very positive. Through reorganisations we change people's positions within the organisation.* (Manager, mother)

The opportunity approach was strongly individualistic and resonated with the current rhetoric in management literature as well as in the overall climate of business (Coser, 1974; Kvande, 1998; Sørensen, 1998). It is an approach that is in keeping with a 'top-down' viewpoint on this topic. This manager did, however, also voice other perspectives when describing some of the reactions among employees.

Experiences of change that involved opportunities were voiced by some of the focus group participants, particularly with regard to moving to another city or abroad:

> *I have travelled a lot, and moved a lot, particularly abroad. I think it's a fantastic opportunity. Moving in itself is exciting, and in spite of having lived in this town for 20 years I'm not very attached to it.... But of course there are downsides, my wife would need a new job, the children are so young yet so for them it's not a problem.* (Father, focus group participant)

This man did not have school-age children so during the current phase in his family's life he still considered himself mobile. Organisational changes were thus seen in terms of personal opportunities. When taking his wife and children into consideration he did, however, see that what he currently thought of as opportunities could become a problem at a later phase in the family life.

The uncertainty approach

From the viewpoint of employees, what affected them most was when branches relocated and they were expected to move to a new city, or to a different area of the city in which they lived. The latter also frequently involved having to move house because of the commuting distance between work and home. One manager addressed this in her account. She stressed that attitudes towards changes in the company were influenced by lifecourse phase and personality:

> *We are a company that often reorganises. There are those who look upon changes as a threat, and then you have those who see it as an opportunity. And of course, if you are 30 I think you always look for the opportunities. But now and then this has led to insecurity and uneasiness among some people.... But it's clear that this focus on cost-efficiency and improvement and higher speed, it does something to people. And that could be both good and bad.* (Manager, mother)

This quote is indicative of a viewpoint that took all four approaches we have identified into consideration. She addressed changes from the company's perspective while still tried to take into account the perspective of employees with a variety of different personal circumstances.

Although most employees talked about their jobs as secure, there was an impression among them that the security had conditions attached to it:

> *From outside we might be considered employees in a 'protected' environment so I guess we're very privileged. I think most employees feel that way apart from during periods when there is a huge focus on savings campaigns, everyone becomes a bit wary then … but over the 20-year period I've been with this company I've never feared to be made redundant but I've had to be prepared to change my job or move. If they for instance close down a branch in one city they will not tell you that you're redundant, they will say that you have to go where the job opportunities are and that means moving to a different city, so it's up to you to take up the offer. I don't really know what they call this practice.* (Mother, focus group participant)

Bureaucratic procedures in this company involved dialogues between personnel managers and individual employees about their work situation and career plans. Sometimes forms were sent out for employees to fill in in advance of such dialogues:

> *A couple of years ago you had to fill in a form where one of the questions was whether or not you were prepared to move to another city in this country or abroad. This form is there still. If you say yes to one or the other you might be asked to move.* (Father, focus group participant)

A lone mother in one of the focus groups also raised concerns about the prospects of having to move because of the phase her family was in:

> *I am not prepared to relocate, I'd rather leave my job than move. That's to do with my children's situation. I am a lone mother and we have already moved. To uproot them again and again I don't think that's good for children. I'd rather sacrifice my job than sacrifice my children for me to have a future with this company.* (Mother, focus group participant)

This woman had made use of opportunities to further her career by relocating from a different city before. Her children were now at an age where she considered it would be better for them to continue to live in the same place.

One manager talked about changes that occurred a decade previously in order to give examples of how periods of change affected employees. At that time, two branches were merged and relocated, which involved moving personnel between two cities:

> *At that time, it was a pretty big reorganisation and people felt insecure. Do we have to move? This was of particular concern. There was a lot of talk in the corridors; what happens, who's moving, and who is not?* (Manager, father)

What came across in this quote was that in a period of uncertainty when there were more rumours than facts to relate to, people tended to feel insecure since the predictability they were used to was lacking. This may have been more important for some than for others. Parents with young children who operated on a tight time schedule in their everyday lives could be more heavily affected by organisational changes that involved relocation.

One manager gave an account of this when he talked about relocating a branch from one end of the city to the other. This move meant considerable commuting distance for employees who had bought a home near where the workplace was before it was relocated:

> *There was a lot of dissatisfaction about it at the time, and of course there are some who maybe have to travel one more hour to get to work.... So if you are supposed to combine this with kids and family, then it's hard.... I think the management took it into consideration. Those who lived furthest away, those who had a very long way to travel to work, or didn't manage to combine the long trip with picking up kids in the nursery, and I think it was considered. But there were some who were very dissatisfied. They got the opportunity to take early retirement.... I know that some who were affected by the long way to [new base] applied for this, and said that if they could have worked here, they would have stayed.* (Manager, father)

This account provided an example of how insecurity and dissatisfaction among employees were dealt with by the company. It also demonstrated how businesses in this sector of the labour market that have the financial means to do so could buy off employees who no longer wished to stay with them when conditions changed, or in situations where employees' skills and competence could be easily replaced.

The ambiguity approach

One of the focus group participants claimed that there were differences in the way employees thought about the organisation, depending on whether they had experienced extensive organisational change or not:

> *I have a feeling that those of us who have recently joined the company have a somewhat different outlook on the company than those who've been here for longer. They have been through several phases of reorganisations and I do think they like it here, but perhaps they have more diversified viewpoints on being a [NMC] employee. Those of us who haven't been here very long tend to be more wholeheartedly positive.* (Mother, focus group participant)

This participant thought that those who have been in the company longer were more reserved in their attitudes than employees who had recently joined the company.

The internationalisation of the company was also considered both positively and negatively. On the one hand it could be seen as an advantage that brought fresh opportunities and challenges. On the other hand it could be seen as a disadvantage, bringing in new practices and ways of doing things that put pressure on the employees:

> *In my line of work the company has become more international, and that's the way the trend moves. Abroad there are other working hours than here, and different holidays. We have to be available more of the time here....*
>
> *There's introduced a culture that allows things to be done in a different way from what has been traditional here.... There will be less activity in our territories and more elsewhere in the world. That demands that you either move to where the action is, or you have to be available for the people who are in a different part of the world. And this company has always had ambitions to become big abroad. That will have more of an effect on some than on others, someone will have to work with the international activity. There will be more of that, and of course this will have consequences.* (Father, focus group participant)

The latter quote focuses on some of the trends in 'globalised' organisations that have been highlighted in other studies; the demand to adapt to a global time schedule. Although this was not a frequently recurring theme in the focus groups or with managers, it generated anxiety for the long term for some of the employees and was a potential source of stress for employees who had other commitments such as family.

The ambiguity approach, involving aspects both of the opportunity and the insecurity approaches to change, was emphasised more by employees in the focus groups than among managers. Moreover, none of the focus groups advocated the business approach to change, which was frequently mentioned by managers.

The changes that had taken place in the NMC could be considered common to many multinational organisations. The typologies we have developed from the analysis of the NMC case and its employees' experiences of such changes are, however, context sensitive, a point to which we will return in the conclusion to the chapter.

Organisational change in social services

Over the past decade, there has been an overall movement towards so-called 'modernisation' of the public sector (Christensen and Lægreid, 2002, 2007; Ramsdal and Skorstad, 2004). The principles of NPM are at the heart of these reorganisations, and they are said to create more cost-efficient services in the public sector (see other chapters in this book). Changes include specialisation of services, merging of units and outsourcing of work tasks that are thought better taken care of by private sector businesses. One of the units where we carried out our case study went through a comprehensive reorganisation in 2003 and both the manager and the employees provided detailed accounts of these changes. Two branches had a similar reorganisation in 2000. These processes created increased insecurity for the employees with respect to what impact changes would have on their overall working conditions and their everyday lives. Among the changes was an increase in temporary work contracts for new employees since the outcome of the reorganisations was not clear and the end result might mean reductions in the workforce. The changes affected the everyday situation at work and at home for employees in social services. In contrast to the NMC, changes did not involve 'lifecourse' or career choices; social workers continued doing the same job but in a different unit and maybe in another part of town.

The biggest impact of changes was typically that they created new parameters for the work the employees did and as such they affected social workers' everyday life and *disrupted* an established rhythm of their lives at work and at home. Changes demanded that employees organise their work in different ways than they had before and also had considerable impact on the workload of teams and individual employees alike. As units increased in size and teams were organised according to area of specialisation, the caseloads grew but within-team cases became more similar; in short, work became more routine and familiarity with colleagues' cases was reduced.

The relationships in the workplace and to the clients were at the forefront of concerns in the social services. Change, or rather the expected outcome of change, was discussed in relation to ways in which it altered relationships in the organisation, to clients and colleagues as well as to employees' families. In contrast to the individualistic framing of organisational change in the NMC, employees in the social services tended to frame their approaches to change in a *relational* way.

However, the analysis identified subtypes of this overarching framing that concerned how different aspects of changes affected relationships within the organisation and beyond. The first was an approach that focused on *relationships between colleagues*. The second was a focus on *workload* while the third emphasised *relationships to clients and family*. On some aspects these three approaches overlapped but they are nevertheless singled out as three distinct types for the purpose of analytic clarity.

Relationships between colleagues approach

During times of change that involved mergers, the role of managers became acutely important as the following quote from a manager who had been through mergers of units demonstrates:

> *The merging led to chaos and temporariness. It became very clear that there would be problems with getting the two cultures to merge into one.... There were six social workers in one [unit] and 12 in the other, and then the administrative staff on top of that. Each unit had its routines and ideology or whatever we could call it, and this was what we were to turn into one. In a way it was*

> *unfortunate that so many chose to leave their jobs in this process. On the other hand it may have been an advantage because some of the conflicts that occurred, and some were very evident, they didn't develop into long-term situations they could have become had everyone stayed on in their jobs.* (Manager, father)

Focus group participants also discussed relationships with colleagues and how these were affected by merging two branches. In the following quote, both positive and negative aspects of these changes were highlighted:

> *There have been significant changes ... we now have twice as many colleagues, we have a new management and there has been a high turnover rate among my colleagues.... The positive thing about an increased number of colleagues is that you can be inspired and learn from more people. What is negative is that we no longer see the big picture. Earlier we knew our colleagues' tasks and what they worked with. We simply had closer contact and we followed each other up more closely. But now, I no longer have an idea of what my colleagues are doing, what cases, who the clients are etc.... But you get used to it, even though it felt strange to start with. Now I have no expectations of having this general overview ... that is the drawback. The positive thing is that you have more people to draw on, there is now a more comprehensive field of specialists.* (Mother, focus group participant)

Thus, both positive and negative effects of mergers were commented on here. Larger units provided more people and a wider variety of competence to draw from, which was regarded as positive in itself. A negative effect of the increased number of colleagues was that some felt a lack of knowledge about colleagues' work and what cases colleagues were working with. Another dimension of the mergers came up in a different focus group:

> Participant 1: *I think this is a good workplace. There's support from colleagues but I do notice a difference from when we moved and the increased workload over the past year. There's so much to do that sometimes it gets a bit tense. The mood is not as cheerful as it used to be but all in all we do have a very good workplace.*
>
> Participant 2: *If you want to create a good working environment you have to invest in it. There's no longer time for that. I feel guilty about rushing past colleagues all the time....*
>
> Participant 3: *I notice a big difference since I've been here a long time. Before if you'd been on sick leave there used to be colleagues putting flowers on your desk when you returned, that never happens now, people barely have the time to say hello as we rush past each other in the corridor. This is not about people not being nice, it's about people having more than enough with their own workload, they are nice and we*

> *have an exceptionally good workplace. It's just that....*
> (Mothers, focus group participants)

As these quotes demonstrate, there was ambivalence about the effects of the mergers. An increase in number of colleagues was regarded as helpful if there was an overall positive attitude in the workplace, and more specialist competence to draw on in the daily work. However, the increasing workload was regarded as affecting relationships between colleagues in a negative way, primarily because there was not enough time for employees to give each other the kind of caring attention that some felt used to be there before the mergers.

The workload approach

One manager of a unit expressed concern over the increased workload for the employees. This was echoed in the focus group from that unit as the following quote demonstrates:

> Mediator: *Have there been changes that have affected the length of the working hours?*
> Participant: *There were two units that merged so now I feel we are one unit doing the same amount work as two units did earlier. In spite of being fewer employees the amount of work has never been heavier.*
> (Mother, focus group participant)

In this unit the increased amount of work was not accompanied by an increase in the number of employees, which led to frustration among employees and managers alike. However, not all units that merged were affected in this way. Other dimensions of the increased workload after mergers were expressed in the following discussion:

> Participant 1: *The workload is huge but then it's been like that always. There's more work now [after the merger] but we're more people to do the work....*
> Participant 2: *On my group we're the number of social workers we're supposed to be, and that's new. It makes for a better work situation, trouble is there's not enough office space for all so some have to go looking for a free desk half the morning, and that's bad.*
> Participant 3: *On my group there are two temps and without them I don't know what we'd do.*
> (Mothers, focus group participants)

The last quote highlights another important consequence of the mergers: the increase in employees on temporary work contracts. Some of those who left their jobs after mergers had to be replaced. As managers were not sure what the total number of employees needed would be after the organisational changes had settled, employing social workers on temporary contracts became more common. This affected experiences of the overall working environment as well as the situation for individual employees:

> *Most get permanent work contracts, but we have five on temporary now, we will keep them till the number of clients is reduced. We have 2,200 clients now, if this number is reduced to 2,000 then a couple of those contracts will not be renegotiated. Such contracts are normally for one year.* (Manager, mother)

Employees on temporary contracts had different concerns about the situation:

Participant 1: *And then there's the opportunity to cut down on the working hours. Yes you can, but I don't know what rights you have if you're not permanently employed.*

Participant 2: *If you're on a short-term contract it's not something you would ask for if your contract only runs for three months, and then another three months, and so on. There are others who have the same conditions, so you don't really want to seem less attractive for the employer. It's been discussed in connection with short-term contracts that reduced working hours would mean more people could get work, but it's not easy to know how to do it.*

(Mothers, focus group participants)

Many temporary workers and a high turnover rate in the organisation are both elements that add to the workload of those who are on permanent contracts. The workload approach to change therefore encompasses viewpoints on this as well. Temporary workers are in principle entitled to the same rights as those on permanent work contracts. However, there seemed to be a widespread impression that you have to 'prove yourself' more as a temporary worker. Employees had the right to reduced working hours if their overall situation made this necessary. However, from the viewpoint of many women on permanent work contracts who worked less than full time, they felt that their commitment to work was sometimes questioned. For those on temporary contracts there was an impression that their chances of getting a permanent contract were reduced if they were employed on a full-time basis and requested to reduce their working hours.

Relationships to clients and family approach

Social workers felt a strong responsibility to their clients and to help the troubled life situations they were in. When the workload increased as a result of mergers and other changes, the negative effect this had on relationships to clients was also emphasised as a problem. Very often this was addressed as an issue in the work–family interface, involving both clients and the employee's own family.

Relationships to clients and the way they were affected by changes was commented on in the following way in one focus group:

> *What I think happens, based on my own experiences, is that we might have the same number of cases, but the cases are much heavier and more serious so in the end you have to do a less thorough job with some of them than with others. In reality you cannot do a proper job with all the cases and I think that's really regretful because we are the only security net for children in a precarious situation.* (Mother, focus group participant)

The fact that caseloads cannot be coped with during working hours or overtime, made social workers take cases home, although not in a literal sense. When they left work they had to leave the paperwork behind, but the cases stayed with them in their minds and affected their everyday lives with their families:

> Participant 1: *We can't bring our job home literally speaking but some who work with very heavy cases have it tough, and then you bring it with you and it affects you while you are at home, you'll keep thinking about the cases so you get absent minded when at home.*
>
> Participant 2: *... the weight of all the expectations ... the fact that you feel you never do enough, that you can never live up to the expectations others have, nor to your own expectations to yourself....* (Mothers, focus group participants)

The nature of the work as well as the amount of it represented sources of stress for employees in this sector:

> *But what is hard to bring home with you is all the things you didn't have time to do, and the thought of 'when in the world am I going to find time for this'. That you keep remembering this, that, and the other you'd forgotten. And that is because when you are at work you never have time to sit down and think: 'what was I supposed to do, what was it that I had to remember?'. There is no time to think because the phone is constantly ringing, something happens all the time.* (Mother, focus group participant)

The motivation behind changes in the social services was an overarching political ambition to 'modernise' the public sector according to the logic of NPM. From the perspective of employees, the results of changes included heavier workloads and more busyness. The overall approach to organisational change in social services was characterised by what we have termed a 'relational framing'. Within this wide category we have identified subtypes that are useful for analytical purposes at a more detailed level. While the boundaries between these are blurred on some dimensions, they have nevertheless proved helpful for bringing out nuances and details in the material.

Comparing employees' experiences of and attitudes to change

In the NMC, individual achievement and development were encouraged by various means, including promotion opportunities in a large internal job market. Changes that were focused on in the NMC mostly involved reorganising or closing down branches in one location without making many of the workforce redundant. In times of such changes, employees got job offers that could be accepted or rejected; it was said to be up to the individual employee to decide about their future in the company. The emphasis was therefore on personal choice and individual opportunities. The individualised framing of the situation in the organisation cannot be thought of, however, without referring to the wider context of the 'silent discourses' in the focus groups (Brannen and Nilsen, 2005). Choices that employees were offered careerwise had to be regarded in a long-term time perspective: they would affect their lifecourses and those of their families in significant ways. The typologies from the analysis must hence also be seen against variations between employees in different lifecourse phases and with varying family circumstances.

Although the social services are a public sector organisation, the changes that were ongoing were aimed at increasing cost–efficiency, thus making use of many of the NPM principles and practices that originate in businesses in the private sector. The mergers and reorganisations that took place to achieve this affected employees and their experiences. In social services the work could only be carried out in teams that worked closely together with the welfare of third parties in mind: the clients. Relationships between people therefore became centre stage. The collectivistic and relational framing of experiences with changes thus invited a focus on relationships, particularly with colleagues and clients. The timeframe within which employees discussed changes was the routine and everyday life that would affect their lives in both the short term and the long term. The changes that had occurred in the NMC were disruptive in lifecourse terms, demanding that employees move to another city or country; changes in social services during this particular time period are better described as disrupting the everyday lives and routines of employees both at home and at work.

Since this chapter only analysed data from the organisational case studies, the full impact of factors at the individual level that the interviews provide has not been brought to bear on the discussion. However, the interplay of different layers of context is demonstrated by comparing parents' experiences across organisations that operate from different logics and in different sectors of the labour market. Whereas the changes in the NMC were ongoing in a longer timeframe, adjusting to changes on the world market, current organisational change in the social services involved adopting similar principles to those with which profit-driven companies operate – budget balance and cost-efficiency. The contexts of parenthood and sector of employment are both decisive in how organisational change is experienced.

The typologies we have outlined are based on an exploratory and grounded analysis of the focus groups and manager interviews. They have been helpful for making sense of differences within and between the two organisational settings and have therefore been important for drawing out aspects of different layers of context. They are context-sensitive typologies and so is their *transferability* (Lincoln and Guba, 1985). They have pointed to systematic differences between the organisations, and are hence useful tools as an overarching frame of analysis of the data, not least with gender differences in mind. In this instance we have highlighted the different logics underpinning the ways that these organisations operate and the type of work done in each, and have paid less attention for instance to the fact that one organisation has a female-dominated workforce and the other a male-dominated one. Further analysis that combines individual biographical interviews with the focus groups from the organisational case studies will be undertaken, rooted in the considerable literature on gendered organisations (for example, Rapoport et al, 2002). However, in order to understand how mothers and fathers experience organisational change in gendered ways it is important to explore the contextual parameters in workplaces that to a large extent decide how experiences can be categorised. This chapter, with its context-sensitive analysis of the experience of change within specific organisations, is hence also a basis for further exploring parents' experiences of cobbling together the everyday of work and family life. To some extent the final chapter of this book develops these themes further and also highlights important issues for further examination.

Notes

[1] Used synonymously with the term 'new workplaces' (Ellingsæter and Solheim, 2002).

[2] This is not to say that differences between the two sectors will always follow the dividing lines we have identified here. Other studies demonstrate how relationships to clients as customers influence the way employees talk about their work in private sector enterprises (Anderson-Gough et al, 2000; Lewis, 2007). However, there are important differences between business clients (customers) and social service clients that demand different approaches from employees in the two organisational settings.

[3] The overall methodology and design of the study is described in Chapter Two.

[4] As George and Bennett (2005: 237) observe, 'the relationships among types, typologies, typological theories, and their usefulness in case study methods

for theory development are important but underdeveloped topics'. The term 'typology' can have many conceptual meanings (McKinney 1969), from the rigorous Weberian 'ideal types' to different forms of descriptive and analytic categories that can aim to be 'descriptive', 'classificatory' or 'explanatory' (Elman, 2005). In this instance we use the term 'typology' to describe analytic classifications of the experiences employees talked about in relation to organisational change. Analytical categories as typologies are not types that are fixed across contexts. They are merely analytical constructs to help organise and classify specific material in the process of analysis with the aim of comparison.

[5] In the current political rhetoric the term 'modernisation' is used to describe a process where principles of NPM and privatisation measures together are employed to change publicly funded services (Christensen and Lægreid, 2002).

TEN

Changing contexts, enduring roles? Working parents in Portuguese public and private sector organisations

Maria das Dores Guerreiro, Pedro Abrantes and Inês Pereira

This chapter discusses the two organisational case studies that took place in Portugal, one in the public sector and the other in a private company. It compares the two organisational contexts in terms of changes, their prevailing labour policies and practices and the way in which working parents with young children perceive their working and family lives. Before comparing the two organisational case studies, the chapter begins with a reference to the political, social and economic changes that Portuguese society has undergone in the last 40 years and the policies regulating labour, supporting the family and defining forms of childcare.

Portuguese pathways to modernity

The working parents who took part in the case studies were born in the 1970s, a decade marked by profound change. Up until and including the 1960s, Portugal was characterised by an agriculture-based economy, traditional cultural patterns and an authoritarian political system, including the exploitation of large colonies in Africa. In the 1970s, this system collapsed and a radical opening-up of all these spheres occurred.

In April 1974, a revolution brought democracy and Portugal experienced major structural changes. The Portuguese Constitution[1] defined the new legal framework for the changes to be made in the country. Family law was changed and the concept of the male breadwinner was abolished. Both members of a couple now had the same rights and obligations and both parents were equally responsible for supporting and caring for their children. The Constitution also promoted equal access to education and work.

Inspired by the ambition of constructing a socialist regime, this led to the nationalisation of a significant number of companies. This process culminated in a democratic capitalist regime, in which different layers of modernity and tradition continue to coexist. Broadly speaking, we may describe these structural changes as the movement from a traditional social system towards modernity (da Costa and Machado, 2000). This has happened through a set of diffuse processes taking place in new phases of modernity, characterised by global networking, deregulated financial and labour markets, and new inequalities and risks (Boltanski and Chiappello, 1996; Castells, 1996; Esping-Andersen, 1996; Beck, 2000).

After the 1970s, education was vastly increased; women entered into the labour market, reaching high levels of activity;[2] economic and cultural exchanges with European countries were massively expanded (particularly after membership of the European Union [EU] in 1986); the development of Portugal's two main cities (Lisbon and Porto) attracted investments and workers; the bases of a welfare state were laid; and a pluralist democratic society based on the service sector and increasingly on the 'new middle class' emerged (da Costa and Machado, 2000).

However, most of these modernising trends were not regulated or planned. They took place in an end-of-century world context, riven by adaptation and disturbance. Four major structural challenges affecting Portuguese society today may be discerned. While they are interrelated, each is analytically distinguishable and affects the lives of young workers who are the focus of our study and how they balance their family and working spheres.

First, there was a decline in traditional agriculture and the old industrial system, which were not competitive by new European and global standards. These are only now being partially replaced by new sectors and projects. The radical change from a closed system to an economy that is open to the world and a member of the European Economic Area has led to a double pattern of modernisation. It has enabled the emergence of highly innovative and competitive islands within a universe dominated by companies that are hardly competitive in either of the two emerging global sectors: either the high-tech knowledge economy or low-cost, large-scale mass production (Reich, 1993; Castells, 1996). In this new global working structure, services represent the most stable market in Portugal, although low-cost immigrants are increasingly employed, in particular those who speak Portuguese, for example Brazilian migrants.

New working parents have been particularly affected by this change, since the transition to adulthood has become a long and uncertain process, leading to multiple strategies and huge inequalities. The rate of long-term unemployment among young people has grown considerably over the last decade. In this context, most young people have temporary and precarious jobs; job security is a major concern during this stage of their lives since it is the main requirement for independence, marriage and parenthood (Guerreiro and Abrantes, 2003).

Second, consumer expectations have grown faster than productivity, leading to a permanent structural imbalance in the Portuguese economy (Santos, 1993). Investment by the EU in development projects and cultural convergence with European lifestyles and consumption patterns have created a tremendous change in individual patterns of living (Costa et al, 2002), far in excess of Portugal's capacity for wealth production. For instance, technology consumption patterns are in line with European ones, but productivity does not follow this trend. Ever-growing imports are consistently higher than exports, which leads to inflation and structural vulnerability in family and company budgets. With regard to public finances, the growing deficit of recent years[3] has led to non-compliance with EU standards, frequent changes of government, the privatisation of several public services and increasing taxation of consumption.

Young people and working parents feel these contradictory experiences acutely since they are the target of modern society's promotion of consumption and lifestyles. However, the necessary resources are frequently not available to them, impacting on their identities, life choices and careers. Therefore, many young people live at home with their parents until their thirties, delaying projects of living independently or as part of a couple, and of becoming parents, goals that they expect to achieve as part of a satisfactory way of life.

Third, there has been a great rise in educational qualifications, although the level of qualified people is low by European standards, bringing increased upward occupational mobility and, at the same time, integrating women into the labour market. Family patterns have also been changing: there has been a decrease in the fertility rate and an increase in the divorce rate. Together these trends have implications for the reconciliation of work and family life.

These changes also underline the growth of social inequality, and the exclusion of significant segments of the population. While some have got 'rich quick', others have been excluded. The continuing high levels of poverty and the increasing unemployment rate in a country riven by huge inequalities is a sad feature of Portuguese development in the 1990s (Capucha, 2005). It is true that globalisation, new management strategies and the deregulation of labour markets (Boltanski and Chiappello, 1996; Beck, 2000) are increasing inequality throughout the world, but inequality, poverty and exclusion rates in Portugal are particularly high and unacceptable in a European context, as they challenge social integration, economic growth and political legitimacy.

Fourth, a complex divide exists between formal publicly regulated parts of the economy and informal deregulated sectors. In recent decades, like other Mediterranean countries, Portugal has experienced notable developments in terms of establishing a welfare state (Esping-Andersen, 1996). Embryonic until the 1970s, this new provision was based on principles of social equity and complex bureaucratic procedures. However, the welfare state is now developing in an age dominated by global neoliberal deregulation and instability, since its policies often clash with cultural, political and economic traditions and structures. The inevitable outcome is a complicated, incomplete and fragmented welfare system, able to provide considerable support only for some groups and activities (usually those most connected to the public system). On the other hand, major inequality and exploitation continue as consequences of long-term unemployment, the informal economy and other types of precarious work. A large informal labour market not only affects the traditional, declining economic sectors but is also embedded in some of the modern flourishing sectors, where taxes are unpaid and state regulations and workers' rights are ignored (Rodrigues, 1995). A 'grey market' of hybrid solutions, which takes advantage of public benefits but avoids its obligations, is widespread throughout the Portuguese economy.

All these trends frame and challenge working parents' careers and family lives. New lifestyles and expectations contribute to major changes, as almost all Portuguese parents have (or at least expect to have) a full-time job even when they have small children. However, parenthood requires some kind of facilities and guarantees, including education or care for young children. Economic security and formal public support are not available for many of this generation, which leads to significant postponement of parenthood or puts parenthood at risk.

The legal and organisational contexts

Labour, employment and working conditions are regulated by Portuguese labour law, which sets out rules on pay, contracts (permanent, long term, short term, temporary, full time and part time), the regulation and organisation of working time (schedules and holidays), employee absences and redundancy procedures. In addition to general labour law, there are instruments that regulate collective work, for example company agreements, collective conventions and collective work contracts. These instruments may not, however, be used to limit an employee's rights and must give broader benefits than those provided by general labour law. A new Labour Code was introduced in 2003 by the social-democrat government, which is again being revised.

Current labour law also regulates the protection of parenthood and parents' rights to attend to their family responsibilities (see Chapter One, Table 1.1). The Portuguese welfare state is also partially responsible for childcare services that support working parents. During the late 1990s, the Portuguese government expanded childcare services considerably, a policy aimed to support working families and to provide children with education. The inclusion of preschool provision (for children aged four and five) within the educational system and the extension of childcare to all children was laid down by law and was a Ministry of Education priority. In 10 years (1997–2007), the rate of preschool provision increased from 64.3% to 77%. Moreover, the increase in crèches and childminding for younger children (under three years old), corresponding to 22% of the total number of children at that age, was supported by public funding, either directly or through outsourced private non-profit childcare organisations. Despite these recent improvements, shortages remain, leading working parents to combine public childcare with the support of family networks or other (paid) daycare facilities.

In Portugal, family support, gender equality and 'work–life balance' principles are not explicit organisational goals; few employers have policies or specific arrangements for these matters. Yet, these issues are starting to be considered in terms of good workplace practice that is part of an enterprise's social responsibility – through the improvement in working conditions, the provision of flexible work schedules and the modernisation of working patterns, as well as providing to parents some financial support for childcare facilities.

It is important to differentiate between employment in the public services, where an assortment of measures exists and where, usually, more respect is given to enforcing labour law and social policies, and employment in private companies, where work–family reconciliation is less guaranteed, as we illustrate below.

The case study organisations

The *privately owned organisation* in the study was part of a multinational consultancy company with its national head office in Lisbon. The company employed several hundred highly qualified employees (most with university degrees), who were relatively young (average age less than 30). Almost all workers had a full-time schedule, working officially from 09:00 to 18:00. Sometimes, weekly working hours had to be adjusted to suit clients' needs; most consultants carried out specific projects for clients in locations outside the company. There was also a common practice of working longer than formal hours. The work pressure was intense and it was difficult to take time off.

There was no formal policy on equal opportunities for men and women, nor were childcare facilities provided by the company. In theory, all workers were entitled to make use of workplace policies, mandated by public law. Still, in many cases, due to work intensification and job insecurity, employees had given up (or felt under pressure to give up) some of their statutory rights. Flexible work arrangements, such as part-time or flexible schedules and working from home, were rarely used by the working parents in the study but were used episodically in family crises, for example when a child was sick. Both line managers and employees agreed that it was difficult to take advantage of different schedules and options on account of factors such as workplace culture but mainly due to the intensity of work. Moreover, as other research on client-based work has shown, relationships with clients can also be perceived as reducing opportunities for flexibility (Anderson-Gough et al, 2000; Lewis, 2003b).

> *With this kind of economic activity it is difficult to have flexible arrangements. Teams work by project. They mostly work in the client's office and they must adjust to their schedule. Beyond this the clients are always making unforeseen requests that require urgent answers....* (Woman, private company, human resources manager)

In the *public sector*, we studied some of the branches of the Portuguese social services. This is a national public organisation responsible for social care for various groups of people in need of services, for example, older people, children, disabled people and poor families. Childcare institutions for children under the age of three or residential care for children at risk and for the older population are examples of these facilities.

Social services in Portugal have a four-tiered structure: national, regional, subregional and local levels. The last of these is where operational services and centres are located. It should be noted that, in the face of this hierarchical structure, for the case study we selected particular subsections of social services. Accordingly, the fieldwork was carried out in the central services (headquarters) and in some local branches of the Lisbon Department, including Lisbon City and the surrounding metropolitan area. The workforce profile was highly diversified but it was possible to identify certain patterns. The workers' average age was around 46, with a degree of variation among departments. Because of the tradition of employment security in the Portuguese public sector, the workforce was relatively stable. Hence, the age profile of the workforce was old, unlike in the consultancy organisation. Most workers remained there for the whole of their working lives. Workers were mostly women (around 79%), a fact consistent with the gender typing of social care work. Again, in contrast to the consultancy company, more than half of the employees (53%) were low skilled and a quarter (26%) were highly skilled.

Almost all workers worked full time. However, the new flexible forms of work recently implemented in public services, unusual in Portugal, are being discussed as a possibility. From 2001, the social services' managers were able to offer new employees temporary individual work contracts, instead of permanent contracts with the social benefits covered by the specific public services law. Some (15%) workers were already in this situation when the fieldwork took place. They were hired as 'green receipt' temporary workers in the second half of the 1990s, when the Socialist government introduced new social policies to fight poverty, such as a minimum income for poor families. Temporary status has been replaced by individual contracts without the status of civil servant. However, most public employees were still covered by the public service law at the time of the study (end of 2003, beginning of 2004).

The organisational structures of the private company and the public institution were also quite distinctive. The private company was small and flat in structure, composed of few hierarchical levels and departments, with the emphasis on teamwork and informal relationships. In contrast, the social services had a massive structure, composed of various hierarchical levels and departments and based on well-defined individual functions and formal relationships. This was the evidence of different patterns of work organisation. However, this did not mean that the private company was a less asymmetric organisation. Rather, power relationships were based on a more informal way of working.

As we shall show, these two organisations had different ways of interpreting and applying policies, which led to differences in daily working arrangements and career prospects. In the private sector organisation, formal legislation was interpreted more flexibly through local and individual negotiation between managers and employees in an attempt to combine the employees' entitlements and rights with the organisation's needs. Thus, a culture of informal negotiation existed in which recourse to formal entitlements was perceived as undesirable. Policy interpretation in the public sector was by all accounts much stricter. According to the public service human resource manager who was interviewed, the state as employer must accomplish the laws that are defined:

> *The law regarding workers' entitlements must be accomplished. An entitlement is an entitlement.... This is a sensitive matter in public administration.... Employees here are aware of their rights and if someone doesn't know, the colleagues tell him/her about the legislation. People try to be informed to make use of their entitlements.* (Woman, public service human resources manager)

In reality, however, the contrasts between the private and public sectors were often blurred.

Expertise, flexibility and insecurity

In recent years, both the private and public organisations in question went through very significant processes of change in attempts to adapt to changing national and international contexts. Although with varying significance and to different degrees, it should be noted that in both cases these changes occurred around the same key issues: modernisation, flexibility, specialisation and productivity. In a very broad sense, this set the stage for creating more efficiency in the organisations.

New legislation introduced changes in both private and public work organisations. The increase in working parents' benefits[4] and the decrease in weekly working hours[5] were good examples, while the individualisation of work contracts was another – controversial – change that was taking place, particularly in the *public sector*, with a potentially great impact on workplaces and workers' lives. These recent changes generated ambivalence among employees in general and working parents in particular, offering a sense of new opportunities for innovation and making use of new parental entitlements, but also the feeling of insecurity and fear of unemployment and unfairness among colleagues.

In the *social services* focus groups, parents said that these changes were felt by most public employees in the form of increasing uncertainty about the future, especially due to the lack of information about government policies related to the so-called 'modernisation of public services', the merging of several departments and the loss of civil servants' status for new work contracts. This was a major issue in some local *social services* agencies, especially those affected by restructuring processes and where employees were expecting the renewal of their current precarious contracts under new conditions. The policies were of particular concern to parents with heavy family responsibilities. Even if the managers were supportive of the policies, it was often difficult and expensive to implement them, for instance if it was necessary to assure shift teams in childcare or in eldercare residences.

> *The continuous working day is a serious problem.[6] It reduces one working hour per day. Because we have a shortage of workers, if I give permission for this short schedule, I am declaring that after all the service can go on and I will be not allowed to hire anyone.... I met with them and explained that it was*

> *impossible to organise shift teams with that time reduction.* (Woman, senior manager, eldercare service)

Participant 1: *We work with children that must be cared for [if we need a sick leave].... Today my son is sick and my husband stayed at home. I couldn't because I have already used all my time off to assist him. They need me here.*

Participant 2: *If someone cannot come to work, we have to take care of her class of children too and it is very hard.*
(Mothers, childcare educators, focus group participants)

Nevertheless, most of the parents in the public sector considered that they had the best possible working-time conditions to raise a child:

Participant 1: *We are in the public service.... One thing is the public sector, another is the private [sector].*

Participant 2: *In the private [sector] we need to work until late.*

Participant 3: *I worked there from nine to seven.*

Participant 1: *And I was fired when I became pregnant.*
(Mothers, social workers, focus group participants)

Participant 1: *We have a good work schedule. We have time to be with our children.*

Participant 2: *It's the benefits of working in a public institution.*

Participant 3: *We can combine work and family.*

Participant 2: *If we had another occupation it wouldn't be like that.*
(Mothers, social workers, focus group participants)

There was therefore a gap between objective reality and subjective experience in the *public sector* organisation. Until recently, reductions in personnel, lay-offs, cuts in wages, contract changes and so on had not occurred: those retiring had simply not been replaced by new employees, so that total employment had slightly decreased. In addition, most social services workers were established civil servants; as noted above, no more than 15% had individual contracts. The increase in the latter was a slow and progressive change but it had significant long-term effects, especially on workers' lives, creating a sense of insecurity about the future (Lewis et al, 2002).

A major problem in social services was that, both internally and externally, it was being permanently reorganised. This generated a continuous sense of confusion and uncertainty – a relative lack of order and control – that affected the organisational climate and workers' lives, from those at the top to those working in local agencies. Line managers mentioned a lack of communication and support between the different tiers of management, as well as contradictory guidance from the top managers, creating in some situations resistance to change. In some cases, permanent uncertainty was also mentioned as a reason for frustration and a lack of motivation.

The conditions for the workforce in the *private sector* were more demanding and insecure but generated more interesting careers for the workers, who had continuous training for updating their skills. On the other hand, it made for more difficult personal and family lives, if parents did not feel entitled to make full use of some of their rights, such as sick or parental leave. In the private company, insecurity was mostly experienced as an inevitable international trend occurring in all economic sectors. The company's turnover had increased significantly, bringing a considerable intensification of work pressure. Most interviewees said that they usually worked more than 10 hours a day, although they saw that as a result not only of the organisation's practices but also because of changes in the labour market. Since there were few consultancy experts in Portugal until the 1990s, in the past they could demand and expect to receive higher wages or less work pressure. The new generation was facing strong competition, which meant that their personal demands could not be met; if they did not accept greater work pressure they risked losing their jobs. Accordingly, working harder and remaining committed to the job was no longer an optional career strategy as it had been 10 years previously. It was now a survival strategy:

Participant 1: *I don't feel secure.*
Participant 2: *Me neither.*
Participant 1: *The market is so competitive, one day we can be in a stable situation and the next in a very unstable one. I think that's natural.... If we work in this profession, we know it's like that. We must accept it....*
Participant 2: *We know what we can count on, and so does the organisation. There's a high turnover. The organisation tries to maintain some workers....*
(Fathers, auditors in consultancy company, focus group participants)

On the other hand, flexibility and teamwork strategies also had advantages for workers, especially for mothers. Where there were sensitive line managers or good peer relationships, workers managed their tasks autonomously, unconstrained by rigid space and time boundaries, and could meet personal and family needs. This was common among professional groups, although increasing work pressure often meant that they used their flexibility to attend to their work demands, by working from home:

Participant 1: *Sometimes I have to finish some tasks and doing it here or at home is the same.... And at home I do it quickly, so I can stay*

> *two days at home. The importance is that I can accomplish the deadline for that project.*

Participant 2: *During my birth leave I had to interrupt it because there were some projects to be finalised.... It has been a kind of respect regarding my team colleagues who had to finish [work that I had started].*

(Mothers and fathers, consultants in private company, focus group participants)

Certain work–life policies recently introduced as a result of new national legislation protecting parenthood or the former two-hour reduction in the schedules during a child's first year are not easily implemented and there was evidence that parental leave was not always fully used on account of work pressure and insecurity. This was one of the reasons why many working mothers left successful careers in the private sector and applied to work in the more regulated (lower-paid) public sector. Some even became independent professionals.

Inequalities within the organisations

Structured social inequality and cultural difference are still fundamental elements of society today (da Costa et al, 2002) and are visible in the Portuguese labour market. The two organisational cases are no exception. Different sources of inequality had varying significance according to the organisation.

Education remains a crucial resource inside work organisations, one that intensifies with the current emphasis on modernisation, flexibility and knowledge creation. Portugal is a country riven by educational inequality, since a significant proportion of young workers are highly qualified while, in contrast, many older workers have not even completed their basic education (da Costa and Machado, 2000). In both organisations, new management approaches widened the gap between low-skilled workers and high-skilled workers. A related source of inequality concerned 'precarious contracts' and low pay. While professional workers were also experiencing insecurity, they were compensated by having high wages, knowledge and skills. Both organisations emphasised new working structures based on flexibility, teamwork, technology and lifelong training. However, in practice this mostly applied to professionals. Both in the private *and* in the public sector, low-skilled employees felt that they were not rewarded as they should be:

> *What I have learned has been with my personal effort, the company didn't give me any specific training ... If we are working here we should be recognised ... I think my wage today is comparatively less than some years ago.... They only demand work, urgent work....* (Father, clerk in the private company, focus group participant)

Participant 1:   *The situation is very complex. We have a monthly wage of €450 and I have two children. One is at school. The other, I can't afford to have in childcare and I have him with a childminder. It's expensive but the crèche would be much more expensive.*

Participant 2:   *It's always a stress. And if we ask for the welfare support, it's necessary a 'cunha', asking for someone's power to intervene. I had to ask my boss to get a place in childcare....*

Participant 1:   *I became a father when I was 19 ... I was in the private sector. And I took the risk of having two children. Then I tried to come to the public sector, I tried a regular job, because I only had a wage if the company had work for me.*

Participant 2:   *But here as a driver you don't have accident insurance....*

Participant 1:   *... I stay here because I have a stable job.*

Participant 2:   *Some days ago I was joking and told our manager that I should apply for the minimum wage.... Sometimes we must bring the minimum wages to 'gypsies' and each family earns €700 or €800. This compared with our €450 salary....! So, we should apply too!*

(Fathers, drivers in the public sector, focus group participants)

Age was also an important factor in inequality, although there were two contradictory currents. On the one hand, work insecurity had significantly increased over the last decade, mostly affecting the younger generation. This was obvious at the public institution. The year 2001 marked a new era, in which the organisation's managers were able to offer new employees temporary individual work contracts, instead of permanent contracts with their series of social benefits that are defined in the civil service legislation. In a subtle way, however, this was also happening in the private company, especially as a result of the policy of outsourcing. On the other hand, as there was a great difference between the generations as far as educational opportunities and access to new skills were concerned, the younger generation had more resources for success, promotion and in adapting to ongoing organisational change.

Gender inequalities were a key issue although they were seldom explicitly recognised by line and human resources managers or even by parents. While equal treatment and similar performances between male and female workers emerged in the discourse of the interviewees, they all recognised that motherhood had detrimental effects on the careers of women and on their availability to perform the kinds of work obligations that men perform. Mothers suffered the consequences of the gap between internal organisational demands and their external personal and family lives. Current trends in flexibility, training and work intensification were especially difficult for mothers, since a highly asymmetric division of labour in families is still part of Portuguese culture. This meant that young mothers had a particularly hard task in dealing with both organisational and family demands and expectations.

This was especially evident in the *private company* where there was greater work pressure and a more male-dominated work culture. Many women with small children left the company. Discrimination was not explicit but the whole (intensive) work system was adapted to the availability and schedules of male workers, who were not much involved in family work.

> *And then she decided to have a second child. Well, it was almost a two-year career break.... Her past – excellent; her present – so so; her future ... I saw a brilliant future for her. But under specific conditions. Then, she made her choice and left. I felt really sorry. She was a person with an excellent technical profile but then she told me – 'I have made a choice. It is clearly an option. I'm really sorry, but I can't reconcile both, so I prefer to work in a quieter place, to have more time for my family'.* (Man, senior manager, private company)

Many female *public service* employees told us that they moved from private companies to the public sector in order to raise a family, since the female-dominated public administration had stricter regulations as a result of which mothers were more protected and experienced less pressure. However, as we discovered in the interviews with managers in the social services, this was not exactly what happened with regard to the top managerial positions, since the mechanisms for advancement involved following typical male schedules and careers where the work pressure was very high. Thus, women occupying key management positions in the public administration also experienced this kind of covert discrimination: you either put your family first or join the rat-race.

> *Managers feel more pressure.... They have more responsibilities to accomplish and because of that, sometimes they can't make use of their entitlements. For instance, I have never made use of my two hours per day for feeding my children, either because of the work pressure or because I end up not having breast milk enough.... Our work pressure is really strong. We need to have longer working schedules, mainly these recent years, with all the changes introduced in public service.* (Woman, human resources manager, social services)

Daily management of work–family policies

Here we shall focus on how work and family policies are managed in the workplace on a daily basis. There are not many significant differences between the two organisations as far as formal workplace policies are concerned, as they are based on general Portuguese labour law. However, we found substantial differences in the use of these policies. Moreover, in the private sector company they were a matter for daily and informal negotiation whereas in the public sector the legislation was followed more strictly.

In *social services* there were no specific policies for work–family reconciliation except for greater access to institutional kindergartens. However, in comparison with the private sector, the social services had the following: first, a legal framework that guaranteed public workers extra privileges; second, a management that followed the law on work schedules and leave; and third, greater understanding in informal practices by line managers and supervisors. We also noted a tendency towards schedule flexibility in which the traditional nine-to-five schedule was being replaced by a multiplicity of schedules (for example, the possibility of working six hours in succession, with a shortened lunch break, and then leaving the workplace early). These processes, however, mostly occurred in administrative roles as they were more difficult to implement for frontline occupations involving the delivery of specific services.

In contrast, the interviewees from the *private company* highlighted difficulties in reconciling work and family life. The company was facing a process of work intensification, amplified by international, national and internal competition. The work organisation – small teams related to specific projects – gave considerable power to line managers, who could control daily schedules. This form of organisation, combined with the company's dependence on its clients with their own particular schedules and deadlines, also complicated the implementation of alternative ways of organising work, such as teleworking or part-time work.

The application of policies takes place at different levels. We shall illustrate this point first with data on the daily rhythm of work (working hours and schedule management) and second with respect to the use of statutory rights that help employees manage episodic 'crises' (parenthood, sickness and so on).

Regarding working hours, in the private company we found a disregard for the established schedule, as employees tended to work long hours and under high levels of pressure. With tight deadlines producing a great sense of job insecurity and periods in which there was an excessive amount of work, employees in the private company often had no option but to work long hours. An occasional absence or lack of punctuality was usually easily overlooked, but each employee tended to work, on average, more than their share/allocation of weekly hours.

This was not the case in the social services. Long working hours were not a common practice in this institution, since the number of working hours per week was laid down by law and this was accepted by employees and supervisors alike. There were, however, certain exceptions to this main trend (for example, the case of drivers, who complained about this problem in the focus groups).

A similar pattern appears when we compare, in both organisations, the use of paternity, maternity and parental leave. The private company's employees sometimes felt pressured not to use their full leave. The fact that employment in the public sector was more secure (although not always) than employment in the private company also helped to explain why employees in the latter felt greater pressure from their managers.

Thus, work–family reconciliation was usually easier for employees in the public sector than for those in the private company. In fact, both employees and managers in the social services felt that the actual implementation of legal entitlements was a great advantage, when they compared their situation to the private sector. So, although there were some complaints, most of the employees felt privileged to work in a public organisation, because, even though it did not have a specific work–family policy, there was an attempt to follow the general legislation. The promotion of work–family measures in the workplace thus follows a two-layer structure: first, the effective use of statutory policies and second, the implementation of particular policies. The fact that the first level – compliance with the legislation – is scarcely accomplished in many (private sector) workplaces, plus the fact that for many focus group participants this first level is the only one the company aims for, also explains the low sense of entitlement to work and family support among employees in the private sector organisation.

Informal negotiation, mostly with line managers, is thus a key factor that shapes parents' (mothers') work–family lives in the Portuguese case as in the other cases in this book. Beyond the basic legislative rights, other policies become constructed as 'privileges', even those that are written into the legislation. Their take-up is decided by supervisors and line managers, according to the type of activity, situational conditions and a supervisor's disposition. The case of the continuous work schedule, available in the public service, was a particular focus of discussion in some of the focus groups, since it was an important new policy. In some services it was implemented, but in other places there were problems about its implementation, as was clear in a kindergarten where some working parents in the study were sited. The important role of managers was underlined with regard to eliciting support in specific moments of crisis but it also applied to broader questions, namely workers' take-up of entitlements. During the focus group interviews, some employees used strong terms to illustrate the variable and discretionary power of managers, especially in facilitating (or not) the employees' family–work balance.

Workplace policies and practices express the organisation's goals, managers' responsibilities and employees' demands. These demands are shaped by employees' sense of entitlement and knowledge of their own rights. It was clear that some traditional workplace policies relating to weekly working hours, holidays, sick or parental leave and two hours per day to feed a child during its first year, were well known, while newer family-friendly legislation, namely paternity leave, the continuous work schedule in the public sector and timetable flexibility, was less well known.

Lifecourses, careers and attitudes towards work

Our case studies were carried out within a specific period of time (between 2003 and 2004) but the notion of continuity was present in the focus groups, mostly when respondents talked about their careers and future prospects within an organisation and how such prospects influenced the lifecourse. Life prospects and attitudes to work were, thus, two important dimensions discussed in the focus groups, in combination with notions of job insecurity and mutual trust and loyalty between employer and employee.

Although temporary contracts were not common either in the private or in the public organisation (except for supply staff in certain critical periods), a higher sense of insecurity was found among the private sector employees, which was to be expected. Private company employees had a sense of *"daily insecurity"*, resulting from a very informal and competitive situation. This led not only to difficulty in organising long-term projects, but also to a real threat of being dismissed. This permanent insecurity affected the present (for instance, the actual use of entitlements – many employees feared to request them) and, in a general sense, the definition of a career path. Still, even in the public sector, many employees felt a sense of insecurity on account of the far-reaching processes of change taking place in public organisations in which budget cuts, downsizing, outsourcing and greater efficiency was the order of the day. But this *"long-term insecurity"* was something they tolerated as it had yet to impact on them directly.

This difference between public and private employment also created distinct career attitudes in the two workplaces. Thus, on the one hand, private company employees faced greater job insecurity and had more problems with work–family reconciliation. On the other hand, they had more opportunities to progress in the company hierarchy, they earned better salaries and they usually had better physical working conditions. Thus, in this company we mostly found employees who invested heavily in their careers, usually delegating family responsibilities to their partners, relatives or external helpers. Even among these, the feeling of job insecurity was great but it was partly compensated for by the existence of training opportunities, as this company was perceived as a learning organisation in which employees gained experience or qualifications that prepared them for work elsewhere. The employees intending to stay in the organisation evaluated their organisation positively, expecting to reach a more senior position. Those who thought they would leave in the future wanted more time for their families or to find a better – and more stable – job.

> *Insecurity is a part of our activity. It could disturb everything but, strangely, it doesn't. That's a really interesting point. People have a career; colleagues in the same position compete with each other. It could disturb personal and professional relationships but it doesn't. When people join the company, they are prepared for an annual evaluation…. At the end of the year, if someone receives a negative evaluation, they know: either they improve their performance or probably must change their career.* (Man, manager, private company)

An almost opposite situation occurred in the public sector where jobs were more stable, but less well paid and with less career progression. Many employees preferred to stay in this workplace, even though they had to struggle with bureaucratic problems or face career stagnation, as public employment was considered more secure, and to leave was seen as too risky. So, within the social services it was more common to find workers who invested less in their careers but who appreciated (or needed) a stable job.

> Interviewer: *We have talked about recruitment problems; do you have problems with retaining staff?*
>
> Interviewee: *No, no. No one leaves. With civil servant status [entitlements for all permanent workers in the public sector, as defined by law], only if some employee was an asshole. No one leaves.*
> (Female, line manager, social services)

Nevertheless, it should be noted that the freeze on new contracts for public services and the spread of 'individual contracts', traineeships and outsourcing provoked far-reaching changes in the context of the public organisation, thus creating a less secure and predictable workplace. Once again, the borders between public and private sectors were blurring.

Conclusions

This chapter analysed two case studies conducted in Portugal, one in a private sector company and one in a public sector organisation. It compared the way in which working parents and their managers talked about their daily work and how they articulated their work–family life in light of the changes in workplaces, and in the context of wider transformations in Portuguese society and globally.

The main structural difference between the private company and the social services department was the smaller size and less bureaucratic nature of the former and the more complex, hierarchical structure of the latter. The private company's employee profile was relatively young and more gender balanced. The social services department had an older age structure and a predominantly female workforce.

Due to the need to remain competitive, the private company had undergone intense restructuring and downsizing, with high turnover. The employees experienced *"daily insecurity"* while recognising that it was a *"learning organisation"* that provided training and prepared its employees to easily find a new job. The public sector, which until recently was identified as a good place for a stable work–life balance, had introduced measures aimed at so-called modernisation and rationalisation of the public service. New recruits were given individual, fixed-term employment contracts without any of the rights of the traditional civil servant. The different departments were being restructured, generating *"long-term insecurity"* in employees who had not yet felt the changes directly.

Where working conditions and family-life support policies are concerned, there are sharp contrasts. These made a difference to the ways in which parents structured their work and combined it with their parental responsibilities in these two organisations. The private company abided by general labour laws and had no specific workplace policies for working parents, although it followed an informal policy of flexible hours associated with the large volume of work and the need to meet deadlines, which supposedly made it possible to deal with sporadic family problems. The interviewees mentioned considerable difficulties in reconciling their family lives and the demands of their jobs. In the public sector, full compliance with the legislation on working conditions was evident, particularly that regarding parents with small children. It also had specific policies for balancing work and family, such as a continuous six-hour working day. These policies and the civil service's traditional job security made it a very attractive sector, at least until recently.

Another topic analysed was the inequality found in work settings. Asymmetries in terms of age, education, qualifications and access to refresher training, with the resulting repercussions on pay and more or less job insecurity, were found in both sectors. However, in the private company a highly qualified workforce of 'symbolic analysts' (Reich, 1993) predominated, while this was not the case in the social services department.

Gender inequality prevailed in both organisations: mothers were assumed to have the main caring responsibilities, even though the organisations had different cultures with different attitudes towards careers. The private company had a *male-dominated work culture*, leading many mothers of small children to feel pressured by work demands and to leave the company and change careers. Meanwhile their male co-workers stayed and climbed the corporate ladder. By contrast, in the public sector, a *motherhood work culture* prevailed that was more compatible with work and family life integration in traditionally gendered families.

In conclusion, we can say that our comparison of these two case studies provides some insight into the sociocultural specificities of work in the private and public sector and the way in which they interact with macro-structural factors, generating a range of possibilities on the basis of which parents make choices and create their life paths.

Notes

[1] Published in 1976.

[2] With the colonial war and the huge male migration flux of the 1960s, female activity rates grew. They currently represent 68.4% of those aged 15-64, mostly working on a full-time basis, even when couples have children (67%).

[3] The deficit decreased to below 3% only in 2007.

[4] Since 2000, with father's leave, and later, with the 2003 Labour Code, which extended flexible non-paid parental leave and also created the following options regarding the maternity leave period: either four months on 100% of pay or five months on 80% of pay.

[5] In 1996, the private sector reduced weekly working hours from 42 hours to 40 and in 1999, the public sector introduced the continuous working day (that is, without a break) of six hours, which applies to parents with children up to the age of 12, reducing their working week from 35 to 30 hours.

[6] The continuous working day enables employees to finish work earlier.

ELEVEN

Comparing flexible working arrangements across organisational contexts

Ann Nilsen, Suzan Lewis and Julia Brannen

This chapter moves beyond discussions of single case studies and within-country cross-sector comparisons to begin to consider the broader picture, focusing on parents' need for flexible working arrangements in order to manage their everyday lives. One of the key features of the Transitions study was its focus on how *change and transitions* in organisations (but also families and societies) affected the lives of working parents with young children. Change is a major theme running through this chapter, in which we address two issues. The first is the complexity of organisational change and the particular challenges for cross-national comparison. This is illustrated with reference to some of the public sector case studies and different forms that change and 'modernisation' take. The second is the impact of organisational change and turbulence stemming from globalisations and the question of whether this renders local context more or less significant for parents. This is highlighted in a comparison of parents' experiences of flexible working arrangements in some of the private sector organisations, as they change in response to global competition. The importance of gender as a permeating feature of organisational context (Acker, 1992) is also highlighted particularly in the latter discussion, although here it is the slow pace of change that is apparent.

While gender has not been the explicit focus of all the organisational case studies, the Transitions study design took account of the gender-segregated pattern of employment that is to be found across countries, with more women employed in the public than the private sectors. The division of labour in families is also asymmetrical across contexts, albeit with marked differences. Thus, gender can be thought of as a structuring element that intersects with other variations and makes the situation for working mothers and fathers different, even when other aspects of context are similar (Harding, 1987).

The research team endeavoured to create a comparative framework for the project that could be applied across national contexts. However, as Chapter Two demonstrates, qualitative studies represent a challenge in cross-national comparisons, not least because of cultural and linguistic differences. In the following analysis the term 'flexible working' is one such concept that does not have the same meaning in different countries and contexts. However, flexibility of working hours is a key aspect of working life that many parents of young children seek in order to juggle the different tasks and responsibilities of everyday life. In some contexts, such as in the Scandinavian countries, parents of young children are, by law, entitled to work part time and can negotiate flexible working hours in the sense that they can arrive at and leave work with a degree of flexibility (an hour in the morning and in the afternoon). In other contexts, such as Bulgaria and Portugal, part-time work is very rare; here flexibility has a different connotation in that it must be negotiated individually with an employer. These differences must be taken into account in comparative analysis. In the comparison of cases within the public and private sectors respectively, we highlight how different aspects of context such as organisational change and global trends shape the possibilities for an interpretation of flexible working for mothers and fathers.

Comparing organisational change and the negotiation of flexible working arrangements in social services

First, we consider how far the public sector organisational cases embedded in their respective national contexts may be compared. Since organisations, even those with the same functions, vary across countries, different issues emerge, as the chapters throughout this book reveal. Any comparisons must take such contextual diversity into consideration. Thus, the discussion takes as its point of departure some of the various elements that arose in the case studies as presented in the chapters. These we subject to comparative attention and thereby create a 'secondary' analysis of these issues, illustrating some of the pitfalls of assuming cross-national similarity in changes that take place within one sector.

In this discussion we consider the modernisation of social services across the countries and how this shapes the organisational contexts in which working parents (mostly mothers) manage their responsibilities. However, in comparing social services in different countries it should not be taken for granted that they are modernising in the same ways. Even if the aims of change are similar across organisations and contexts, the processes involved for reaching these goals are likely to vary. The effects of these processes on workers' lives and circumstances also differ. We show the importance of both examining the trend towards modernisation of the public sector across Europe and also its impact at workplace level in terms of the organisation, employer–employee relations and the way that parents in social services manage their work–family lives.

We now consider organisational change in social services in three countries – Bulgaria, Norway and Sweden. These cases were selected on the basis of the comparability of topics raised in the previous chapters since all the case studies focused on organisational change. Social services were organised somewhat differently across the countries but all had in common a female-dominated workforce. Since the 1970s, much attention has been paid in some countries to the 'modernisation' of the public sector and welfare states. The rationale for modernisation has been framed in terms of cost-efficiency in relation to both service delivery and labour costs. A catchphrase for the ideas behind the 'modernisation' process is New Public Management in which management models and organisational practices were imported from the private sector to turn public services into 'more efficient' organisations (Christensen and Lægreid, 2002). Although the Scandinavian countries have proved more resilient to adopting these principles, the privatisation of public assets and the outsourcing of services, both key ingredients of New Public Management, are becoming more common in these countries too (Christensen and Lægreid, 2002). These trends form the backcloth for comparing social services across contexts and in particular for comparing how changing workplaces are experienced by parents in their everyday lives where flexible working arrangements are frequently needed.

In all three countries, while to some extent the ideas of cost-efficiency prevailed, the ways in which each country has sought to implement these varies. There are important differences, especially in the education and training of the workforces in social services. In particular, Bulgarian social services were still very new at the time of the study and many of its managers had not trained within the public sector but came from other parts of the economy.

'Modernising' social services: mergers and decentralisation

During the process of modernisation under way at the time of the study, the Bulgarian and Swedish social services chose a decentralisation model for organising social services, while the Norwegian social services opted for mergers of different services into larger units. In Bulgaria, following the fall of communism, social services moved from being state run to greater municipal control although the headquarters remained in Sofia. In Sweden, social services shifted from the municipal level of organisation to more local and community-based units that were organised in a web-like fashion (see Chapter Four). The Norwegian case differed significantly from these two latter cases because a major reform was about to be implemented at the time of the case study. This involved mergers of units into larger entities with different services co-located.

All three countries sought to implement changes that made the services more cost-efficient. In the Bulgarian and Swedish cases, central management was located outside the units that provided services for clients and, in the case of Sweden, even the line managers were located outside 'operating' units. In all the countries, social work was organised in teams. In the merged Norwegian organisations, unit and line managers were located within teams that provided specialised services.

The contexts in the countries varied in many aspects. Working hours were fixed and longer (no part-time contracts) in Bulgaria than in Norway and Sweden where working hours were shorter and where more formalised flexible working-time arrangements made it easier on the whole for working parents to manage their various responsibilities. Since work was organised in teams, colleagues both facilitated and constrained the flexibility of working parents in all three settings.

In Sweden, the line managers who were not located within the teams chose to take a 'hands-off' approach to the way colleagues in a team organised and shared their workloads. Thus, colleagues became the main 'negotiating partners' when parents wished to take short, especially unplanned periods of time off from work for pressing family reasons. The sharing of workloads made it more important for individual parents to take their colleagues' situations and viewpoints into consideration on these occasions. Because of the typically short periods of absence from work that were involved, no replacement personnel were sought. Thus, the overall workload for the teams increased and created tension between colleagues.

In Bulgaria, on the other hand, working hours were formally a matter to be decided by the central management in the capital. However, the line managers were located within the teams and hence played a key role in the everyday running of teams and were the key negotiating partners when time off or part-time work was needed by parents for short periods of time.[1] Line managers in Bulgarian social services tended to be sympathetic to parents' requests. By contrast, top management adopted a 'business ethics' approach, which the line managers did not share, thus strengthening the solidarity among social workers, social assistance workers and managers at the local level, creating a feeling of 'them' against 'us'.

In Norway, the outcome of the mergers in terms of number of staff needed was not clear. Consequently, more employees were on temporary contracts. The units affected by mergers also had increased sick leave rates. Relationships between colleagues in some instances became strained as the number of new colleagues increased, while the individual employees' overview and knowledge of their workplace became blurred. The employees most affected by the situation were temporary workers. If for family reasons they needed part-time work, to which they were entitled by law, they felt they could not request this since it would affect their chances of gaining permanent employment contracts later on.

The role of managers became more important during the merger period in the Norwegian social services. In some instances, two different work cultures made for a difficult transition period for managers because the burden of turning the new units into a unified workplace was on their shoulders. Managers, especially line managers, were regarded favourably by the teams. The relationship between line managers and employees has more similarities with the Bulgarian than the Swedish case. Solidarity among employees was evident. However, the increase in team size and the growth of temporary employees made some Norwegian workers feel alienated from their workplaces and their colleagues.

The informal flexibility practices common in the Bulgarian social services were supervised and coordinated by the line managers. Individual employees' needs were therefore balanced against the total workload of the teams. In contrast to the similar Swedish system, the line managers were 'hands on' in the negotiation processes and so tension between colleagues in a team was avoided. In the Norwegian case, the mergers and rapid changes at the time of the case study overshadowed the concerns that were important for employees in Sweden and Bulgaria.

It is important to bring to bear different layers of context in the interpretation of data across countries (Chapter Two). The forms of reorganisation chosen in the three countries by the respective social services were different. All sought to become more cost-efficient, but they chose different routes towards accomplishing this objective. Whereas Bulgaria and Sweden *decentralised* their social services with this objective in mind – the Swedish case was even more decentralised and specialised than the Bulgarian – the Norwegian social services were *merged* with other services in larger units to obtain the same cost-efficiency effect, although it also needs to be borne in mind that a study such as ours can only capture a moment in the process of change.

Centralisation and decentralisation of services both had their downside. In the Swedish case of decentralisation with line managers separated from teams, individual autonomy was centre stage; organisational and personnel negotiations were left to the teams themselves. While this was cost-efficient in the short run, tension was created between colleagues that put strain on the organisation in the long run, creating difficulties for working parents in particular. Line managers in the Bulgarian and Norwegian cases, even though the circumstances and contexts were different, were very important in keeping the teams running and maintaining positive relationships between colleagues. However, if Bulgarian parents needed flexible arrangements, either entitlements or concessions, the line managers had to seek the authority of more senior managers in responding to employee requests. In Norway, the issues were different and manifested themselves through the uncertainty created by the mergers that were ongoing. Here line managers were key to creating a good working environment that also allowed for flexible working arrangements. A similar situation was observed in the UK social services.

Comparing parents' experiences of flexible working arrangements in private sector organisations

We now turn to a discussion of flexible working arrangements in the private sector organisations.[2] Specifically, we explore how the private sector's greater exposure to the workplace changes associated with global competition affects the experiences of being a working mother and a working father in a climate where profit margins and shareholder interests are the main concerns for business. In addition, the focus on the private sector puts gender on the agenda in a particular way and also highlights dilemmas for both employers and employees in the implementation and take-up of flexible working arrangements.

There is much debate about the extent to which globalisation leads to homogeneity of practice or whether the local context prevails (James and Wood, 2007) and this was one of the key questions that the Transitions study set out to address. For example, do national work–family policies, such as parental leave, and organisational flexible working practices soften the impact of globalising forces or do globalising forces undermine the impact of such national, European or workplace provisions? What are the processes by which this occurs?

The companies discussed here are the UK insurance company, the Dutch banking and insurance company, the Slovenian finance organisation, the Portuguese consultancy firm and the Norwegian multinational company. We examine both similarities and differences between the contexts and the experiences of parents in the different organisations and explore the ways in which global competition interacts with national contexts to blur some of these differences.

Differences: national family policies and organisational norms and practices

There were marked contextual differences in both national and workplace policies in the organisations and in the gender assumptions about parenthood on which these are based. Statutory work–family policies vary between countries and make a difference to the ways in which both women and men can manage work and family boundaries (see Chapter One).

Other differences emerged in the prevailing views of both employers and employees on the compatibility of support for parents with business competitiveness. Differences in experiences of job insecurity were also relevant to a consideration of the experiences of flexible working since perceived job insecurity can, in some contexts, reduce take-up of entitlements.

The variations in statutory work–family policies are based on different assumptions about women and men's roles, obligations and entitlements. The Norwegian and Slovenian contexts provide an interesting contrast in this respect. In the Norwegian context, for example, gender equality has become equated in the dominant public discourse with more equity between women and men, both in the labour force and the family in terms of informal care and housework (Knudsen and Waerness, 2009). This was reflected in national policies to encourage fathers to be more involved in childcare. It was also reflected in a stronger commitment among the parents to striving for gender equity in the family (fathers taking the full quota of paternity leave) than was evident among the parents in the other countries.

Among the Slovenian parents, in contrast, the division of labour within the family remained largely traditional despite the long-established dual-breadwinning model of both partners in full-time employment, supported by state policies. Both cultural norms about gender roles and relationships and related policies were crucial factors influencing the impact of flexible working arrangements, especially which parent took them or whether entitlements were shared. In the Norwegian case, it was expected that men would take the full father's quota (four weeks at the time of the interviews). Paid parental leave was available to Slovenian fathers, in principle, but take-up was minimal and none of the interviewees mentioned the idea or practice of fathers taking parental leave.

At the workplace level, prevailing views of the compatibility of support for working parents with sustaining or enhancing organisational competitiveness, as discussed by both parents and managers, also varied across the different contexts. At one extreme, in the relatively newly privatised bank in Slovenia, parents relied on longstanding state support for reconciling work and family life. However, beyond compliance with regulations, there was limited voluntary, formal employer support and little expectation or sense of entitlement that it should be forthcoming. In fact, parents and their managers alike often considered that formal organisational support for work and family life was not operationally feasible within a market economy. In the Portuguese organisation too, reconciling work and family tended to be regarded as an individual responsibility, with an implicit assumption that supporting parents was bad for business. This was particularly evident among professionals and managers.

At the other extreme, in the Netherlands, Norway and the UK, with varying levels of state support for parents, flexible working arrangements were not necessarily considered incompatible with workplace efficiency and competitiveness. Indeed, there was often a discourse of such initiatives as increasing productivity or efficiency arising from other changes. In Peak, in the UK, for example, managers cited mergers and acquisitions as the catalyst for a drive to create a new culture based on increased flexibility and trust to enhance effectiveness, in line with a high commitment management approach (Appelbaum and Berg, 2001). In the Dutch case study, the discourses were more contradictory. The company strove to be a caring organisation and did not view supporting working parents as bad for business, but this support was not regarded as relevant to the modernisation and transformation of the company.

Differences in experiences of job insecurity were also relevant to a consideration of the experiences and take-up of flexible working arrangements. Mergers and acquisitions, restructuring and downsizing in the five private sector companies contributed to feelings of deep transition and constant change. A decline in perceived job security was reported fairly widely but was experienced differently across contexts and this potentially impacted on employees' willingness to take up flexible working options. Aspects of economic and labour market contexts underpinned differences in parents' experiences of job insecurity and its potential consequences. In Peak in the UK, for example, there was a widespread acceptance of the insecurity of jobs, but this was cushioned by the relative ease of securing new jobs at the time. In the Portuguese organisation, insecurity was also accepted by parents because they knew that they were acquiring good working experience, which would make them more employable elsewhere. However, there were cultural reasons for not taking up flexible working arrangements as employees were expected to put work before family in order to display what is a particularly male model of commitment (Rapoport et al, 2002). Thus, the organisational culture as well as the national context was significant. Although jobs at Sava in Slovenia were considered relatively secure in comparison with other Slovenian organisations, there was some fear of job loss and there was much less optimism about finding new jobs.

Overall, an ideal context would be one in which national regulations and workplace policies and practices and other contextual factors were mutually supportive of both mothers and fathers. There were some individual examples of parents – mostly but not exclusively mothers – across the organisations, who felt supported at work and at home and able to make good use of statutory entitlements and workplace policies for flexible working. However, in none of the case study workplaces was this systemic and organisation-wide.

Similarities: intensification and extension of work

These interrelated contextual variations fed into differences in parents' sense of entitlement to take up flexible working arrangements (Lewis and Smithson, 2001). There was, however, one trend that emerged consistently across the organisations: the experience of intensification – and often extension – of work. Employees in all these case studies in the diverse national contexts reported that they were working harder. This was justified, especially by managers, in terms of competitive pressures. In some contexts, they were also working longer to cope with more intense workloads. Following downsizing and reorganisations, workforces were lean and there was little or no slack in the system to provide cover if people were absent for any reason. In the face of global competition, 'efficiency' drives and associated changes in work organisation frequently put more onus on individual or team responsibility to manage demanding tasks and schedules (Burchell et al, 2002). These trends appeared to be of increasing significance for the ways in which work–family policies and practices were experienced in these organisations and contributed to a blurring of the boundaries between work and family. These trends reinforced a male model of work (Pleck, 1977; Lewis, 1997; Rapoport et al, 2002), based on assumptions that ideal workers were able to work as though they did not have major everyday responsibilities for family and care. The conditions of greedy organisations (Coser, 1974) and gendered organisations (Acker, 1992) are thus exacerbated. It is difficult for two parents to work long and hard, leaving limited time and energy for children, and in contexts where it was possible to reduce working, it was usually mothers who did so. In Peak in the UK, for example, new mothers in managerial jobs returned to reduced hours of work after maternity leave because the long hours expected of managers were not compatible with parenthood. They were, however, demoted because they no longer conformed to the gendered ideal of prioritising work over family. In this context, no fathers asked for reduced working hours.

The parents in this study were thus managing work and family commitments in particularly demanding contexts, which limited the capacity of any flexible working arrangements to challenge gendered norms. The following quotes from focus groups and manager interviews illustrate these points:

> *I think there's less people to do the same job now.* (Father, Peak, UK)

> *The absent workers are not replaced so those that remain have to do their own work plus the work of an absent person.* (Woman, manager, SAVA, Slovenia)

We demand a lot from people. All the time we think it's temporary, but there is always something new. (Man, manager, BIC, the Netherlands)

Sometimes people, mainly at a lower hierarchical level, are obliged to work on weekends and sometimes 10/11/12 hours per day, not being paid for that. (Mother, private sector company, Portugal)

I think there are two cultures, one where they work overtime and another where they work an incredibly lot of overtime [laughs]*!* (Man, professional, NMC, Norway)

Growing convergence in flexible working practices in diverse contexts

Thus far we have discussed local differences in context and growing similarities related to global competition. Below we consider processes by which the trends that transcend countries were encroaching on the particularities of support infrastructures that had been built up in particular contexts (national and/or workplace policies).

The changing organisation of work in response to global competition was resulting in convergence of experiences across national and workplace contexts. Two interrelated *processes* were involved. First, changes in the organisation of work, particularly work intensification, but also interrelated trends such as the fast pace of change, management approaches including the growth of teamworking and target setting, and in some contexts job insecurity, had the potential to undermining national policy. The effectiveness of national regulations in supporting employed parents therefore depended on how they were implemented in the workplace in the context of these trends.

Intensified workloads often undermine statutory provisions. For example, parents were often reluctant to ask for time off for family reasons to which they were in some cases entitled, because they feared they would get behind with their work or because already overburdened colleagues would have to cover for them. In Slovenia, for example, despite generous parental leave provisions developed under a banner of gender equality in the former communist regime, parents talked about pressures not to take up entitlements. In particular, they reported not taking their full entitlement for leave to care for a sick child because of workload and team pressures in the context of a tight workforce with no spare capacity. While the leave entitlements were less generous in Portugal, parents in the Portuguese organisation also talked about the subtle pressures not to take up their rights. For example, they discussed how teams thanked fathers if they gave up their five days' leave because of intense work demands on the teams, and also mentioned that some mothers did not take their full leave.

In other countries, parental leave entitlements were more established and were taken up, certainly by women but also by men. Nevertheless, intense work demands associated with global trends also undermine progressive policies such as the father's quota of parental leave in Norway, as reported in previous research (Brandth and Kvande, 2001). The Norwegian parents at NMC reported that there were no problems for fathers taking the statutory paternity leave period of four weeks, although some felt that if they asked for extended leave they would experience negative pay or career consequences. Moreover, the experience of leave taking was not always positive due to workload issues. A father who reduced his working hours by 50% after paternity leave explained that he had actually retained most of his work tasks and had to accomplish these in half the time, which he found enormously stressful. He insisted that he would never do this again. When policies are implemented without labour replacement, experiences are very negative. Thus, even where there was strong commitment to gender equality and state policies were in place to support this, work intensification could undermine fragile developments towards greater equity. So, while combining paid work and parenting may have been easier in some contexts with more generous leave schemes, the advantages were being eroded to some extent by the intensification of work.

Second, changes in the organisation of work, associated with global competition and efficiency drives, especially work intensification, have the potential to undermine not only state policies, but also workplace policies to support working parents. Again, this occurred across national contexts. There were a number of overlapping processes at play here. To begin with, intense workloads and the lack of any spare capacity undermined various forms of reduced hours working. Many parents found that reduced hours resulted in having to accomplish the same workload in less time (as in the case of the Norwegian father discussed above whose workload was not reduced during his half-time leave). Alternatively, the extra work had to be covered by colleagues.

Reduced hours schedules, available in the case study organisations in the Netherlands, Norway and the UK, although rarely in the other countries, could provide a very satisfactory arrangement for new parents in relatively affluent contexts if it was well supported by management. Such support would include ensuring appropriate workload. However, intensified workloads and lean workforces in the case study organisations frequently undermined such arrangements, especially among higher-status workers. Often managers and colleagues supported reduced hours in principle but workloads and expectations were not reduced in proportion to the reduction in work hours, or work was redistributed to other team members, resulting in overload for part-time workers and/or their colleagues. This occurred even in national contexts where there was policy and cultural support for part-time work.

The growing prevalence of largely autonomous teams in the context of intensive workloads, could also undermine flexible working policies, as was the case in the public sector organisations discussed earlier. Team dynamics often included providing informal cover for family emergencies, for example, but colleagues could also become agents of social control as parents strove to avoid putting extra demands on their already overloaded colleagues.

A major factor affecting the take-up and experience of workplace flexible working arrangements in all the case studies was management support and this varied within as well as across the five cases. There are a number of influences on management attitudes to and support of working parents (Lewis, 2003a). Intensification of managers' own workloads and the need to achieve demanding targets with limited human resources influenced many of the managers in all the case studies.

Thus, the intensification of workloads and related trends, through processes involving non-replacement of labour, team dynamics under pressure and influences on managers' decision making and support, reinforced gendered ideal worker assumptions that took little account of parental commitments, even in the organisations where the discourse was relatively 'family friendly'.

To return to the question of the relative impact of local and global processes, it was clear that there were local differences in relation to state and workplace support for work and family commitments. It is important to take account of these differences when examining parents' experiences. At the same time, however, it was also evident that workplace trends associated with responses to global competition, particularly although not exclusively in the private sector, were beginning to blur these differences. Local contexts may therefore become increasingly irrelevant to the experiences of working parents in the face of the spread of unregulated capitalism. If so, one of the casualties is likely to be progress towards gender equity.

Concluding remarks

In this chapter we have drawn out some trends across the public and private sectors and have compared parents' experiences of their everyday responsibilities in the context of the changes taking place in and across these sectors. The aspects of comparisons have varied. In the first section we considered modernisation and cost-efficiency drives in social services and how organisational change manifested itself and impacted on mothers' and fathers' possibilities for working flexibly. We have argued that although changes across these cases (set in their own national contexts) had the same goal, the effects of changes for working parents varied according to the particular context, whether at the public policy level or the level of the particular work organisation. In the second part of the chapter we compared private sector companies in several countries with a view to highlighting the similar ways in which globalisation impacted on the conditions for working mothers and fathers, in particular the opportunity for flexible working arrangements. While we found that work in the private sector companies was generally more intensive compared with the public sector, we also found that some public sector managers and professionals also reported intensive workloads, reflecting the New Public Management ideas borrowed from the for-profit sector. The latter finding suggests a growing convergence between the two sectors. Similarly, the increased emphasis on work–life policies and practices for parents in some of the private sector organisations – at least in principle – can be interpreted as a trend that strengthens the case for convergence.

The impact of context on working parents is mediated by gender. However, although flexible working arrangement is the overarching topic for both sections of the chapter, the approach to this is different in the two sectors and hence gender issues become more explicit in the discussion of the private sector. Women form the majority of the workforce in the public sector social services across countries. The reforms that have occurred here thus impact more on mothers than on fathers. Increased workloads and work intensification in the private sector affect both mothers and fathers but are likely to impact negatively on the already asymmetrical division of labour in families whereby mothers take greater responsibility for children than fathers in all the countries. Moreover, the intensification of work was reported to be undermining both public and workplace policies that support working parents, making it difficult for both mothers and fathers of young children to reconcile two demanding jobs with equally intense and pressing parental demands.

The conclusions to be drawn from this evidence suggest that, in so far as parents have choices, these are increasingly likely to be between sustaining or returning to a highly gendered domestic division of labour, on the one hand, or limiting the number of children, on the other. Another scenario is to forgo parenthood altogether. The current trend towards the intensification of workloads reinforces a male model of work, designed for employees who take on a male-breadwinner or dual-worker role (Lewis and Giullari, 2005). While these demands are also found in the public sector, especially in managerial and professional jobs, private sector organisations tend to be even more 'greedy' (Coser, 1974). This is one of the factors sustaining gender segregation between public and private sector jobs. Moreover, since the latter are usually better paid, this also maintains the gender gap in earnings. Hence, despite the modernising trends in the workplace and policies intended to support working parents, the gendered separation of the public and private spheres of family and work remains entrenched.

Notes
[1] For longer periods of leave, Bulgarian parents in social services tended to take the generous state leave given for sick children and did not fear losing their jobs since competition for this poorly paid work was low.

[2] Here, in addition to drawing on the chapters of the book, we draw on the national case study reports to inform our comparisons across contexts.

TWELVE

In conclusion

Julia Brannen, Suzan Lewis and Ann Nilsen

In this final chapter we will consider what can be learned from the case studies about how national public policy is implemented and supported, or undermined, by workplace practices and trends in particular workplaces that were broadly comparable across countries. Employing organisations affect employees' opportunities and strategies for integrating work and parenting, by the supports they provide and also by the demands that they make on parents. We noted in Chapter One that the literature suggests a growth in what are often called 'family-friendly', 'work–family' or 'work–life balance' policies and what is typically referred to as 'flexible working' arrangements. This volume provides evidence to support this in both the public and the private sector but not in all countries. However, it also shows how the existence of support at organisational and national levels does not necessarily produce a sense of entitlement and enable parents to take advantage of these policies. Moreover, even if parents do take up policies, the impact is not always positive and unproblematic. In this chapter, we make some comparisons across the organisational case studies and make sense of the disparate picture they suggest.

Comparing formal policies across countries

A key question addressed by the case studies in this book is how formal policies at national (public policy) and/or organisational policy levels support working parents and their need to fulfil their responsibilities to their children in particular contexts. In short, how do such policies play out in practice in parents' lives and how does this vary across the countries we have studied?

As set out in Chapter One, in some of the seven countries under study the national policies are generous and provide in principle substantial time flexibility, substantial amounts of leave and financial remuneration for parents with responsibilities for younger children – Norway and Sweden representing by far the 'best cases' in this study. However, other countries provide parents with some formal rights. In Portugal, for example, new – albeit small – changes were introduced through the Public Law to enable Portuguese parents to work continuous shifts and so allow them to shorten their working day. In the Netherlands, the Dutch government expects social partners (that is, the employers' associations and trades unions) to extend public policy entitlements by offering additional support under collective agreements: the result is that most Dutch employers offer at least one work–life policy that supplements statutory provision.

In contrast, under UK law, the laws are framed in such a way that the onus is placed *not* on employers or trades unions but on individual 'parents' – a gender-neutral term – to make *requests* to their employers/managers for time flexibility, particular types of leave and hours reduction. The UK government 'advocates' organisational support for parents and other carers but as long as it is not prejudicial to business interests. As a result, parents' entitlement is limited to the public policies and an embedded workplace culture of rights is absent. UK public sector employers, however, offer rather better conditions of service and, at least on paper, better policies for working parents than the private sector. Nevertheless, some private sector companies, including small- and medium-sized companies, develop innovative policies and practices (Lewis and Cooper, 2005); for example, the private UK company described in Chapter Seven endeavoured to build a workplace culture that was supportive to parents.

In many ways, these differences reflect the history of maternal employment and welfare policy in the different countries. Sweden represents a long tradition going back to the early 1970s of child-oriented and woman-friendly policies involving a reconceptualisation of motherhood and a gender-equal dual-breadwinner model. Historically, in Norway, the Scandinavian model took other forms; for example, the history of daycare provision has been much less impressive than in Sweden and Denmark (see Leira, 1992). In contrast, the Netherlands and the UK were late in enabling women to continue working when they have young children. Until the late 1980s, mothers in the UK gave up work at the birth of their children and returned to new, usually part-time employment subsequently; the UK only began to develop policies to support 'parents', that is, mothers, in the late 1990s (Moss, 2003). Moreover, from 1979, the UK's neoliberalism, which prioritised market forces, meant minimal labour market regulation and largely private childcare provision. However, with a change of party in government in 1997, childcare and education are increasingly being integrated although formal remunerated leave is still limited, and although couched in gender-neutral terms such policies do little to change the established gender order.

The situations of former Eastern European countries are different again and their policies at the time of the study were shaped both by the era of communism and by the subsequent abrupt transition to a market economy. Bulgaria has a system of public childcare and generous long-paid parental leave including for sick children, albeit the pay is at a low rate. There are no family-friendly workplace policies as such – no part-time working for example. The term 'parents' in these contexts is also not a gender-neutral term but is explicitly assumed to refer to mothers. Employees in general are governed by the statutory provisions fixed in the National Labour Code (valid for all employment contracts in the country). In Slovenia, the transition to a market economy was accompanied by a recession, which bottomed out in 1993, bringing a period of intensive economic restructuring. Slovenian public policies to support working parents, which also date back to the communist era and to a paternalistic strong state, are generous. Slovenia's provision for parents remains in many ways close to the Swedish model despite the fact that in the post-socialist period the state is promoting neoliberalist policies. However, unlike in the Scandinavian contexts, the promotion of equal opportunities for both men and women in the labour market and in family life is absent even though the dual full-time workers pattern still predominates. In both Slovenia and Bulgaria, work–family policies target mothers only. The state is strong and paternalistic and care provision for parents with young children is considered a public matter.

Comparing parental practices across sectors and countries

Where policies exist at national and European Union [EU] level, they are intended to apply equally to public and private employment sectors. However, management's implementation of these policies is unequal across sectors, with greater implementation in the public sector. However, this is not to say that constraints are absent in the public sector. Indeed, as we argue (Chapter Eleven), the gap between the sectors is diminishing as both are subject to similar international/global trends. This in turn affects the take-up of policies by parents (mothers). To return to our case studies, we now consider how implementation of public and organisational policies compares across the sectors and countries in which the case studies in this book are located and the consequences for the take-up of both policies by parents (see Table 12.1).

The Scandinavian cases (Norway and Sweden) in our study represent public and private sectors. In the Swedish social services (and other local authority work), in addition to the generous state policies, extra compensation for parental leave is offered, such as two days' paid time off to attend childbirth classes or medical examinations related to pregnancy. Even though the Swedish social services prided themselves on looking after their employees and employees took up some of the extensive paid parental leave to which they were entitled, when the social workers (the focus of the Chapter Four) returned to work they seldom were offered reduced or restructured workloads; if they did reduce their working time there was no replacement and so the work was redistributed to colleagues. Instead, it was up to the social worker teams to find their own solutions; they were expected to make arrangements for cover when a colleague needed time off from work. Because of the strong interdependence placed on the non-hierarchically structured teams, team members who were parents of younger children – nine out of 10 of whom were women – mentioned a reluctance to overburden their colleagues, given already intensified workloads. This, they said, led them to take less parental leave than they might have done, for example. However, as the authors of the chapter on the Swedish case argue, other factors come into play, namely the nature of the work. Swedish social workers hold high professional status (in contrast, for example, with the status of social workers in the UK): they are expected to shoulder responsibility for clients and are given considerable

Table 12.1: Public and organisational policies, parental sense of entitlement to take up policy provisions and perceived obstacles to take-up, by organisational case

	Public policy	Parents' sense of entitlement to public policy	Organisational policy/culture	Obstacles mentioned by parents to take up public and organisational policies
Norway private	Strong	Strong	Weak	Many
Norway public	Strong	Strong	Strong	Some
Sweden public	Strong	Strong	Strong	Many
Portugal private	Weak	Weak	Weak	Many
Portugal public	Weak	Moderate	Moderate	Few
UK private	Weak	Weak	Moderate	Many
UK public	Weak	Weak	Moderate	Many
Netherlands private	Moderate	Moderate	Moderate	Some (ambivalence)
Bulgaria private	Strong	Weak	Weak	Many
Bulgaria public	Strong	Strong	Moderate	Some
Slovenia private	Strong	Moderate	Weak	Many

discretion to manage their own heavy workloads, making it harder to draw the boundary between work and home life and to prioritise their own needs over those of clients. These factors create a situation in which parents (mothers) who returned to work after taking parental leave, for example, felt constrained to take full advantage of the public policy and workplace policies. Indeed, many sought to change to less-pressured work, for example downshifting into routine work or going part time.

The Norwegian private company, by contrast with the social services in Norway and Sweden, did not always comply with the public policy, while it had no workplace policies (in addition to those provided by the state) to enable parents to meet family responsibilities. Some of the Norwegian parents (sic mothers) in the private company did not take up their full statutory entitlement to parental leave. The experience of these workers was not too dissimilar to that of the social workers in the Swedish case but for very different reasons. The private Norwegian company was in a heavily male-dominated sector. It was also facing a process of work intensification, amplified by international, national and internal competition. The work organisation – small teams devoted to specific projects – was such that considerable power was vested in line managers to control daily schedules. This form of organisation, combined with the company's intensive demands of its clients, meant that the workforce had to work to clients' schedules, often to tight deadlines. Managers were therefore unwilling to implement supportive policies for working parents such as the right (in law) to part-time work. The climate of work intensification and change produced considerable job insecurity among the workforce as well creating an excessive amount of work at particular times. This made employees reluctant to take up full statutory leave and led to a culture of long hours working. The situation was very different in the Norwegian and Swedish social services. Yet in the context of intensification, the impacts of autonomous teams in the Swedish case and the power of line managers in the private Norwegian company on take-up of policies were not dissimilar.

Policy implementation in the Portuguese social services was by all accounts much stricter than in the private finance Portuguese organisation: formal legislation (Labour Law) was interpreted more flexibly through local and individual negotiation between managers and employees in an attempt to combine the employees' entitlements and rights with the organisation's needs. Thus, in the private sector company a culture of informal negotiation existed in which recourse to formal entitlements was perceived as undesirable. Comparing the public and private cases, we see some similarities both between and across sectors; in practice, differences between the private and public sectors were often blurred. The Portuguese private company was in some respects like the case of the Swedish social services (social workers). Its workforce was younger (although more gender balanced) and the local organisation was small. The Portuguese parents in this organisation worked in small non-hierarchical autonomous groups and were under considerable pressure from their clients to deliver. However, in the case of the Portuguese company, this pressure derived from global market competition and not from needy citizens. In both the Portuguese private company and the Swedish social services, parents (mothers) were reluctant to take the full parental leave. However, unlike the Swedish social workers, the Portuguese parents lacked specific workplace policies and only had recourse to basic entitlements. They accepted insecurity as a fact of working in a global company and the need to work long hours. The Portuguese workers in the social services were better provided for than parents in the Portuguese private sector and they recognised their comparative advantage: greater security, not having to work long hours and more entitlements (because they worked in the public sector). Indeed, one strategy that some Portuguese mothers mentioned was to move out of the private sector when they had children. But, as in UK social services, there was a shortage of workers because of financial constraints; thus, in practice, parents were not able to take up the entitlement to shorten their working day.

In the UK, public and private sector workplace policies offered parents and staff the opportunity to work flexibly, while formal state provision for parents was poor, especially by comparison with the Scandinavian cases. In social services, there were major financial constraints on public spending especially since the case study was a hard-pressed local authority serving a needy population. Major organisational restructuring was also taking place in the public sector as part of New Public Management and the modernisation of government. Managers and workers alike, particularly those who delivered frontline services, mentioned the constraints on parents who sought to work flexibly. Reasons included the operational requirements of the work setting to provide full-time cover and the lack of a budget to provide for extra staff.

In the insurance company, a number of changes were under way, instigated by global change in the finance sector. In this context, a move away from a formalised to an informal 'trust-based' flexitime system was introduced as a more modern approach – influenced more by 'new management theory'. There was also an increased emphasis on autonomous, self-managing teams, as occurred in other cases (the Portuguese company and the Swedish social services). However, in both sectors, with respect to the opportunity to work in more flexible ways, many staff described this as being subject to their line managers' discretion. As a consequence they had to justify, for example, working from home and wanting time off, which created a pressure to be visible in the organisation, a feeling of not being trusted and a low sense of entitlement to support. In both social services and the finance company, implementation depended crucially on negotiations between individual workers and line managers. While there were some supportive managers in both workplaces, having a supportive manager was seen as a lottery. The conditions in the two sectors were different, however. In social services, a tension existed between a new 'enlightened' management approach (adhered to by some new senior managers who were themselves mothers and had negotiated flexible packages) in which meeting staff needs was seen as a productive strategy for enhancing the commitment of the workforce to the employer, and an ethos of central economic control in which managers sought to guard scarce resources. In the insurance firm, there was also a tension between new-style and old-style managers. New-style managers advocated a business case for supporting parents while old-style managers still considered that there were inherent tensions between a supportive culture and the organisation's business goals. In social services, the situation was interpreted by many parents as an erosion of the former advantages of working in the public sector, while some of the insurance company staff also felt that their conditions had deteriorated as informality replaced formal policies, leaving more discretion to managers.

In the Dutch finance organisation (no Dutch social services took part in the study), a similar situation was identified as in the UK finance company. Major changes in the organisation's structure were taking place and, in a highly competitive global culture, business goals revolved around efficiency, transparency and accountability. Although the company implemented work–family policies and tried hard to be a decent and caring organisation, these policies were given a relatively low priority and were often regarded as conflicting with the organisation's business goals. For example, work–family issues were not discussed in the boardroom when important strategic issues were at stake. This created scope for managerial discretion as in many of the other organisations and was likely to lower the employees' sense of entitlement to work–family provisions and the extent to which they used them. While parents felt legally entitled to claim them, those who took advantage of them, for example the opportunity to work part time, were women. In all the case studies but less so in the Scandinavian cases, work–family policies were assumed to be a women's issue. One of the most significant consequences of take-up in this Dutch finance company that parents reported was the detrimental consequence for careers in the organisation. Thus, managers saw mothers who took advantage of work–family policies as prioritising their families over their careers, the antithesis of the widely held 'ideal worker' norm (Rapoport et al, 2002; Gambles et al, 2006). As in other case studies, where there were no budgets or standard replacement procedures to cover parental leave or flexibility, the utilisation of work–family policies was interpreted as a threat to the solidarity among co-workers.

In the Slovenian private sector organisation (Chapter Six), there were no workplace policies to support parents (mothers); parents relied instead on the state's generous policies. Moreover, instigated by the integration into a global market economy, structural, functional and technological changes were taking place in this company along with the expansion of services. Parents saw these as having negative effects on the organisation's culture, in particular (as in other finance organisations in the Transitions study) creating considerable intensification of work and, unlike in the UK finance company for example, less flexible work patterns. Notions about flexible working favoured the employer rather than the employee/parent; in particular, as the Slovenian case study notes, the bank's operating hours were changed so that workers had to work two split-shifts. This made for a longer working day, creating problems for parents of young children. Unlike some other contexts (the UK private company for example), the procedures for making even slight changes to the standard pattern of the working day were heavily bureaucratic. Like other contexts, requests for changes also required the support of line managers for approval. As a consequence, for example, mothers refrained from taking the full amount of allowable leave for sick children, and often took their own annual leave instead.

Comparing this private sector organisation with a public sector organisation (the Bulgarian social services discussed in Chapter Five), all working parents in the Bulgarian social services used the public policy of lengthy paid parental leave and the state-funded childcare centres introduced under the former communist regimes. But they considered them insufficient for a satisfactory work–life balance. They blamed the state for low salaries, attitudes that reflect the reality: both low and high expectations of the state under communism and the post-communist realities of unsuccessful economic reforms. Moreover, in the social services, working schedules and the hours of public childcare were inflexible and did not support workers in the face of work intensification and the pressures of bringing up families in a stressful situation of managing on a low income. (Bulgaria was the poorest country in the EU at the time of the study, and public service employees were very low paid and unemployment was high.) Managers who dealt with employees' requests for more flexible work–family boundaries had to balance them against issues of costs and efficiency. Line managers were more sensitive to such requests while higher levels of management were driven by organisational goals. As a result, social benefits once organised at the enterprise level (under communism) such as opportunities for family holidays, free workplace canteens, health and childcare, and subsidies covering transport expenses and work clothes, were a thing of the past. Flexible working options such as part-time work, job sharing and working from home were not yet on the agenda in Bulgaria. In this context, many parents employed in social services relied on a wide range of different types of intergenerational support from their kin in addition to using public provision such as formal childcare.

The two cases described from Slovenia and Bulgaria are similar in some respects to cases in other countries. Both were experiencing work intensification though the extent and causes differ according to sector. These cases also stand out from the others notably in respect of greater rigidity in the structure and methods of management and the bureaucratic procedures that governed employees when they made requests for support from their managers, making the reconciliation of work and family life very difficult. However, this was also to some extent true in the social services in the UK and Portugal. In addition, the wider patterns of low income, high unemployment and heavily gendered roles in relation to family life in a country such as Bulgaria create an extremely challenging context for working parents (mothers).

Concluding remarks

In this chapter we have addressed a dominant concern in these case studies, namely how public and workplace policies are implemented and how they affect parents' sense of entitlement and take-up by mothers and fathers. We found that in most contexts such policies were heavily gendered in terms of assumptions underlying them and their outcomes. In Bulgaria and Slovenia, liberalisation and new pro-market ideologies favoured employers but brought about rising unemployment and less employment protection. However, we also found that all the organisations in this study were subject to some degree of workplace change and transition. As discussed in Chapter Eleven, private sector organisations fall within a continuum in terms of their support for parents within increasingly competitive contexts.

The public sector organisations were more likely to characterise themselves as caring organisations and generally sought to be more supportive of parents than the private sector, although this was less apparent in practice. Efficiency drives and New Public Management discourses were driving change but were not necessarily leading to a diminution in bureaucratic procedures and structures. As we set out in Chapter Eleven, policy and practice to support parents, whether at state or workplace levels, tended to be undermined in all contexts by trends such as the intensification of work and, in some cases, poor management support.

In all the countries (to varying degrees), policies for combining paid work and family care were primarily, or only, for women. This gender assumption was often made by managers at all levels, as well as by many of the parents themselves. This phenomenon mirrors and interacts with the persistence of gender asymmetry in family involvement and the division of domestic labour. Line manager support, or lack of it, was of crucial significance for working parents' options for negotiating both their paid work and their family responsibilities. While this was true in all the case studies, it was particularly so in the countries with fewer supportive national regulations, or a shorter history of take-up of family supportive initiatives, and in organisations where there are limited resources to cover absent personnel (for example in sections of the social services organisations in Bulgaria and the UK). Changing conditions including heavy workloads and targets for managers reinforced task- rather than people-centred management styles in many contexts. Middle- and lower-level managers in particular had to negotiate intensified targets, changing working practices and parents' expectations of support. There were also wide differences among managers within the same organisations, particularly between new-style managers who embraced change and those who clung to old ways of working. In some contexts, new-style managers were more supportive of parents and of flexible working arrangements, while in others, for example in the Slovenian private sector organisation, parents found new-style managers to be less supportive. Moreover, management strategies of delegating responsibility for managing team members' work and family boundaries to workgroups created their own tensions, which the teams often lacked the resources to resolve.

While differences emerged between the public and private sectors, some of the distinctions between the two sectors were blurring since the traditionally better (non-material) conditions and higher job security in most of the public sector organisations were being eroded, and as private organisations (in some countries) became more attuned to flexible working and part-time working practices. For example, parents in the Norwegian and UK social services felt that the growing focus on cost-efficiency eroded the benefits formerly associated with public service work.

Yet it is not all doom and gloom. At different levels – global, European, national and organisational – there is evidence of some positive change. Moreover, change comes in many guises as it has many causes: international competition, technological advances and changing gender relations, demographic trends, migration patterns and so on. Changes at some of these levels are positive and at others they are negative. However, change is not a uniform process; change at one level may be accompanied by negative change at another, as we have discussed in Chapter Eleven. For example, improvements in labour laws can be associated with outsourcing and 'offshoring' with a range of consequences. State work–family policies may change for the better with the passing of new legislation while gender equality may advance more slowly and may take generations. The direction and pace of change are not predictable as the collapse of the global financial system that has taken place since this study was carried out testifies. Changes at different levels do not work together. The outcomes of their interaction are unstable. They are also inequitable across different social groups that make up society and the workforce of high- and low-skilled workers and across the divisions of gender.

Social and economic forces can be powerful levers for change, positive and negative. We have seen in this volume that transformations such as the spread of global competitive capitalism have created many other changes that can undermine national and EU policies to support working families and children. As discussed in Chapter One, there is recognition at the EU level that the drive for competitiveness of national and organisational economies should not be at the expense of quality of working life and quality of life more generally (Eurofound, 2002, 2008; EU, 2007). It is argued that economic performance has to be balanced with socially sustainable forms of work organisation (Webster, 2004). However, in these discussions the economic sustainability associated with contemporary ways of working tends to be taken for granted. The global recession that has occurred since this study was completed challenges these assumptions. Working practices that are often incompatible with family life are not socially sustainable, but neither have they ensured economic sustainability. The global recession will result in even greater pressures for employees who survive layoffs. But it might also provide the opportunity for rethinking the ways we value family life and employment.

The participation of women in the labour force is essential for both economic and social sustainability in all European countries. Social reproduction is also essential for national welfare in the long term. Parents and children need support to sustain current and future communities and workforces. There is a need for focused debates and initiatives on these issues. This should involve collaboration across governments, employers, trades unions, non-governmental organisations and others, at EU and national levels, and confronting big questions about European goals and values. How can we address the long-term impacts of contemporary working hours and practices on parents, on children's health and well-being, on fertility rates and sick leave rates, on community well-being and other social indicators? How can we achieve the multiple goals of sustainable economic growth that benefits all, and benefits families? How can we generate social equality, including gender equity and partnership? These questions urgently require strategies for change. Neither governments nor employers alone can bring about the necessary changes, as the case studies in this volume have shown. A long-term strategic approach is needed and gender equity has to be at the forefront of change. Without such a strategic approach, national policy and local workplace policy contexts may become increasingly irrelevant in the face of the forces of global capitalism.

Appendix

Table A1: Characteristics of private organisations

	Bulgaria	Nether-lands	Norway	Portugal	Slovenia	UK
Status	7 offices	National division	Onshore branch	National agency	2 branches	Regional office
Size[a]	Extra large	Extra large	Extra large	Large	Large	Large
Workforce age (whole organisation)[b]	Middle	Middle	Middle	Young	Middle	Middle
Gender	Mostly women	Mostly men	Mostly men	Balanced	Mostly women	Balanced
Skills of most workers	High	High	High	High	Medium/high	High
Part-time work	Unusual	Usual	Unusual	Unusual	Unusual	Usual
Trade union membership	High	Low	High	Low	High	Low

Notes: [a] Medium: 51–250; large: 251–1,000; extra large: over 1,000 employees.
[b] Young: most workers under 30; middle: most workers between 30 and 45; old: most workers over 45.

Table A2: Characteristics of public social services

	Bulgaria	Norway	Portugal	Sweden	UK
Status	Regional (16 town agencies)	Municipality (4 units)	Regional district	2 submunicipal districts	Metropolitan borough
Size of workforce[a]	Medium	Medium	Extra large	Large	Extra large
Workforce age (whole organisation)[b]	Middle	Middle	Old	Middle	No data available
Gender	Mostly women	Mostly women	Mostly women	Mostly women	Mostly women
Skills of most workers	High	High	Low	High	Intermediate
Part-time work	Unusual	Usual	Unusual	Usual	Unusual
Trade union membership	Medium	High	High	High	Medium

Notes: [a] Medium: 51–250; large: 251–1,000; extra large: over 1,000 employees.
[b] Young: most workers under 30; middle: most workers between 30 and 45; old: most workers over 45.

Table A3: Details of the manager interviews and focus groups

	Number of manager interviews	Number of focus groups (total number of members)	Focus group size (2, 3–4, 5+)	Number of mixed-sex focus groups	Whether manager present at focus group
UK finance	6	6 (24)	1, 3, 2	4/6	5/6
UK social services	11	11 (28)	9, 2, 0	5/11	4/11
Sweden social services	5 human resources + 2 focus groups (n=13)	6 (26)	0, 2, 4	5/6	0/6
Bulgaria finance	7	5 (37)	0, 2, 3	1/5	0/5
Bulgaria social services	7	4 (26)	0, 0, 4	2/4	2/4
Portugal finance	2	9 (24)	4, 5, 0	5/9	0/9
Portugal social services	3	7 (24)	0, 7, 0	2/7	0/7
Norway other[a]	6	4 (15)	0, 3, 1	3/4	0/4
Norway social services	4	4 (18)	0, 2, 2	2/4	0/4
Netherlands finance	8	4 (32)	0, 1, 3	4/4	0/4
Slovenia finance	7	8 (29)	0, 6, 2	4/8	0/4
Total	68	68 (283)	14, 33, 21 (21%, 49%, 30%)	37/68 (54%)	7/68 (10%)

Note: [a] In Norway, a company in a sector other than finance was studied.

Table A4: Characteristics of focus group members in the public sector (social services)

	Number in focus group	Number who work part time	Number from minority ethnic groups	Number aged 40+	Number with a child aged 11+	Number of fathers	Number of lone parents	Number of agency workers	Number educated to degree/upper secondary/ lower level
UK	28	6/28	18/28	7/28	5/28	7/28	8/28	2/28	14, 3, 9[a]
Sweden	26	4/26	1/26	1/26	1/26	8/26	2/26	0/26	19, 6, 1
Bulgaria	26	0/26	1/26	0/26	5/26	2/26	3/26	0/26	21, 5, 0
Portugal	24	2/24	0/24	0/24	0/24	6/24	1/24	0/24	12, 2, 10[a]
Norway	18	5/18	0/18	5/18	4/18	2/18	1/18	0/18	16, 2, 0
Total	122	17 (14%)	20 (16%)	13 (11%)	15 (12%)	25 (20%)	15 (12%)	2 (2%)	81, 18, 19 (66%, 15%, 16%)

Note: [a] Two unknown.

Table A5: Characteristics of focus groups participants in the private sector (finance)

	Number in focus groups	Number who work part time	Number from minority ethnic groups	Number aged 40+	Number with a child aged 11+	Number of fathers	Number of lone parents	Number of agency workers	Number educated to degree/upper secondary/ lower level
UK	24	6/24	0/24	4/24	2/24	10/24	3/24	0/24	12, 3, 9
Bulgaria	37	0/37	0/37	0/37	3/37	8/37	1/37	2/37	29, 8, 0
Portugal	24	0/24	0/24	1/24	0/24	11/24	1/24	0/24	14, 8, 2
Netherlands	32	23/32	0/32	2/32	0/32	12/32	0/32	0/32	14, 17, 1
Slovenia	29	2/29[a]	0/29	4/29	5/29	7/29	0/29	0/29	16, 12, 1
Norway[b]	15	1/15	0/15	3/15	2/15	7/15	2/15	0/15	14, 1, 0
Total	161	32 (20%)	0 (0%)	14 (9%)	12 (7%)	55 (34%)	7 (4%)	2 (1%)	99, 49, 13 (61%, 30%, 8%)

Notes: [a] In Slovenia, two people worked six hours per day.
[b] In Norway, a company in a sector other than finance was studied.

References

Abrahamsen, B. (2002) *Heltid eller deltid: Kvinners arbeidstid i kvinnedominerte og mannsdominerte yrker* [*Full-time or part-time: Women's working hours in female and male dominated occupations*], Oslo: Institute for Social Research.

Acker, J. (1992) 'Gendering organisational theory', in J. Mills and P. Tancred (eds) *Gendering organisational analysis* (pp 252-4), London: Sage Publications.

Ahrne, G. and Hedström, P. (1999) *Organisationer och samhälle: Analytiska perspektiv* [*Organizations and society: Analytical perspectives*], Lund: Studentlitteratur.

Alasuutari, P., Brannen, J. and Bickman, L. (2008) 'Introduction', in P. Alasuutari, L. Bickman and J. Brannen (eds) *Handbook of social research* (pp 193-223), London: Sage Publications.

Allard, K., Haas, L. and Hwang, P. (2007) 'Exploring the paradox: experiences of flexible working arrangements and work–family conflict among managerial fathers in Sweden', *Community, Work and Family*, 10 (4): 475-95.

Allen, T. (2001) 'Family supportive work environments: the role of organizational perceptions', *Journal of Vocational Behaviour*, 58 (3): 414-35.

Anderson, S. E., Coffey, B. S. and Byerly, R. T. (2002) 'Formal organizational initiatives and informal workplace practices: links to work–family conflict and job-related outcomes', *Journal of Management*, 28 (6): 787-810.

Anderson-Gough, F., Grey, C. and Robson, K. (2000) 'In the name of the client: the service ethic in two professional services firms', *Human Relations*, 53 (9): 1151-74.

Appelbaum, E. and Berg, P. (2001) 'High performance work systems and labor market structures', in I. Berg and A. L. Kalleberg (eds) *Sourcebook of labor markets*, (pp 271-94) New York, NY: Kluwer.

Appelbaum, E., Bailey, T., Berg, P. and Kalleberg, A. (2005) 'Organizations and the intersection of work and family: a comparative perspective', in S. Ackroyd, R. Batt, P. Thompson and P. S. Tolbert (eds) *The Oxford handbook of work and organizations* (pp 52-73), Oxford: Oxford University Press.

Bäck-Wiklund, M. and Bergsten, B. (1997) *Det moderna föräldraskapet* [*Modern parenting*], Stockholm: Natur och Kultur.

Bäck-Wiklund, M. and Plantin, L. (2004) 'Analysis of organizational case study – Sweden', www.workliferesearch.org/transitions

Bäck-Wiklund, M. and Plantin, L. (2005) 'Biographical interviews: report from Sweden', www.workliferesearch.org/transitions

Bäck-Wiklund, M. and Plantin, L. (2007) 'The workplace as an arena for negotiating the work-family boundary: a case study of two Swedish social services agencies', in R. Crompton, S. Lewis and C. Lyonette *Women, men, work and family in Europe* (pp 171-89), Basingstoke: Palgrave Macmillan.

Bailyn, L. (1993) *Breaking the mould: Women, men and time in the new corporate world*, New York, NY: Free Press.

Bailyn, L. (2006) *Breaking the mould: Redesigning work for productive and satisfying lives,* Ithaca, NY: Cornell University Press.

Bailyn, L. and Harrington, M. (2004) 'Redesigning work for work–family integration', *Community, Work and Family,* 7 (2): 199-211.

Beck, U. (2000) *The brave new world of work,* Cambridge: Polity Press.

Bergmark, Å. and Lundström, T. (2005) 'En sak I taget? Om specialisering inom socialtjänstens individ- och familjeomsorg I' ['One thing at a time? On specialization within the social services', *Socialvetenskaplig Tidskrift,* 12: 125-48.

Blair-Loy, M. and Wharton, A.S. (2002) 'Employees' use of work–family policies and the workplace social context', *Social Forces,* 80 (3): 813-45.

Bloor, M., Frankland, J., Thomas, M. and Robson, K. (2001) *Focus groups in social research: Introducing qualitative methods,* London: Sage Publications.

Blumer, H. (1956) 'What is wrong with social theory?', *American Sociological Review,* 19 (1): 3-10.

Blumer, H. (1969) *Symbolic interactionism: Perspective and method,* Upper Saddle River, NJ: Prentice Hall.

Bø, I. (2001) *Hjem–barnehage–arbeidsplass: Daglige overganger og gjensidige tilpasninger* [*Home–nursery–workplace: Daily transitions and reciprocal adjustments*], Høgskolen i Stavanger, Norway: Arbeidsrapport.

Boh, K., Bak, M., Clason, C., Pankratova, M., Qvortrup, J., Sgritta, G. B. and Waerness, K. (eds) (1989) *Changing patterns of European family life,* London and New York, NY: Routledge.

Boltanski, L. and Chiappello, E. (1996) *Le nouvel esprit du capitalisme* [*The new spirit of capitalism*], Paris: Gallimard.

Bond, S., Hyman, J. and Wise, S. (2002) *Family friendly working? Putting policy into practice,* York: Joseph Rowntree Foundation.

Bourdieu, P. (1983) 'The forms of capital', in J. G. Richardson (ed) *Handbook of theory and research for the sociology of education* (pp 241-58), New York, NY: Greenwood.

Boxer, D. and Cortes-Conde, F. (1995) 'From bonding to biting: conversational joking and identity display', *Journal of Pragmatics,* 27 (3): 275-94.

Brandth, B. and Kvande, E. (2001) 'Flexible work and flexible fathers', *Work, Employment and Society,* 15 (2): 251-67.

Brandth, B. and Kvande, E. (2002) 'Reflexive fathers: negotiating parental leave and working life', *Gender, Work and Organization,* 9 (2): 186-203.

Brandth, B. and Kvande, E. (2006) 'The Norway report', in P. Moss and M. O'Brien (eds) *International report of leave policies and related research* (pp 172-79), Employment Relations Research Series, No 57, London: DTI.

Brannen, J. (2004) 'Working qualitatively and quantitatively', in C. Seale, G. Gobo, J. Gubrium and D. Silverman (eds) *Qualitative research practice* (pp 312-27), London: Sage Publications.

Brannen, J. (2006) 'Being a working mother in context', Paper given at the international conference 'The effects of the European Union on the socio-economic development of women', Izmir, Turkey, 22-24 June.

Brannen, J. and Nilsen, A. (2005) 'Individualisation, choice and structure: a discussion of current trends in sociological analysis', *The Sociological Review*, 53 (3): 412-28.

Brannen, J. and Nilsen, A. (2006) 'From fatherhood to fathering: transmission and change among British fathers in four generational families', *Sociology*, 40 (2): 335-52.

Brannen, J. and Nilsen, A. (forthcoming) 'Ideals and practices in case-based comparative research: a European study of working parents in context'.

Brannen, J. and Pattman, R. (2005) 'Work–family matters in the workplace: the use of focus groups in a study of a UK social services department', *Qualitative Research*, 5 (4): 523-42.

Brannen, J., Lewis, S., Nilsen, A. and Smithson, J. (2002) *Young Europeans, work and family: Futures in transition*, London: Routledge.

Brante, T. (2003) 'Konsolidering av nya vetenskapliga fält – exemplet forskning i socialt arbete' ['The consolidation of new scientific fields – research in social work as an example'], in Högskoleverket (2003) *Socialt arbete: En nationell genomlysning av ämnet* [*Social work: A national review of the scientific field*], (pp 133-96), Report No 2003:16 Stockholm: Högskoleverket.

Bryman, A. (1988) *Quality and quantity in social research*, London: Routledge.

Bryman, A. (2001) *Social research methods*, Oxford: Oxford University Press.

Buehler, C. and Philipov, D. (2005) 'Social capital related to fertility: theoretical foundations and empirical evidence from Bulgaria', MPIDR Working Paper WP 2005-016, available at www.demogr.mpg.ed

Burchell, B., Lapido, D. and Wilkinson, F. (eds) (2002) *Job insecurity and work intensification*, London: Routledge.

Caproni, P.J. (2004) 'Work/life balance: you can't get there from here', *Journal of Applied Behavioural Science*, 40 (2): 208-18.

Capucha, L. (2005) *Os desafios da pobreza* [*The challenges of poverty*], Oeiras, Portugal: Celta Editora.

Castells, M. (1996) *The rise of the network society*, (Information Age: Economy, Society and Culture, Vol I), Cambridge, MA: Blackwell.

Černigoj Sadar, N. (1985) 'Izkušnje plačanega dela in družine' [Experiences of work and family life], *Družboslovne Razprave*, 3: 55-65.

Černigoj Sadar, N. (1989) 'Psychosocial dimensions of paid work and family life', in K. Boh, M. Bak, C. Clason, M. Pankratova, J. Qvortrup, G. B. Sgritta and K. Waerness (eds) *Changing patterns of European family life* (pp 141-71), London and New York, NY: Routledge.

Černigoj Sadar, N. (2000) 'Spolne razlike v formalnem in neformalnem delu' [Gender differences in formal and informal work], *Družboslovne Razprave*, 16 (34): 31-52.

Černigoj Sadar, N. (2007) 'Uvajanje certifikata družini prijazno podjetje v Sloveniji' [Introduction of 'family friendly enterprise certificate' in Slovenia], in A.Kanjuo-Mrčela and N. Černigoj Sadar (eds) *Delo in družina: S partnerstvom do družini prijaznega delovnega okolja* (pp 100-12), Ljubljana: Fakulteta za družbene vede, Knjižna zbirka OST.

Černigoj Sadar, N. and Lewis, S. (eds) (1996) *Balancing employment and family life: The role of employers*, Ljubljana: Faculty of Social Sciences – Centre for Welfare Studies, University of Ljubljana.

Černigoj Sadar, N. and Verša, D. (2003) 'Zaposlovanje žensk' [Employment of women], in I. Svetlik, J. Glazer, A. Kajzer and M. Trbanc (eds) *Politika zaposlovanja* (pp 398-433), Ljubljana: Fakulteta za družbene vede, University of Ljubljana.

Černigoj Sadar, N. and Vladimirov, P. (2002) 'Work/personal life arrangements in organisations', in Proceedings of the 2nd International Conference 'Human Resource Management in Europe: Trends and Challenges', 17 October, Athens University of Economics and Business.

Christensen, T. and Lægreid, P. (2002) *New Public Management i norsk statsforvaltning* [*New Public Management in Norwegian state management* (pp 67-95)], Særtrykk. Bind nr: nr 2(2002), Bergen: Institutt for administrasjon og organisasjonsvitenskap, Universitetet i Bergen.

Christensen, T. and Lægreid, P. (eds) (2007) *Transcending new public management: The transformation of public sector reforms*, Aldershot: Ashgate.

Cohen, D. and Prusak, L. (2001) *In good company: How social capital makes organisations work*, Boston, MA: Harvard Business School Press.

Coleman, J. (1988) 'Social capital in the creation of human capital', *American Journal of Sociology*, 94, Supplement: Organisations and Institutions: Sociological and Economic Approaches to the Analysis of Social Structure: S95-S120.

Connell, R. W. (1995) *Masculinities*, Cambridge: Polity Press.

Coser, L. (1974) *Greedy institutions: Patterns of undivided commitment*, New York, NY: Free Press.

Crompton, R. (2002) 'Employment, flexible working and the family', *British Journal of Sociology*, 53 (4): 537-58.

Crompton, R. (2006) *Employment and the family: The reconfiguration of work and family life in contemporary societies*, Cambridge, MA: Cambridge University Press.

Crompton, R., Dennett, R. and Wigfield, A. (2003) *Organisations, careers and caring*, Bristol: The Policy Press.

Crompton, R., Lewis, S. and Lyonette, C. (2007) *Women, men, work and family in Europe*, London: Palgrave.

Crozier, M. (2000) *À quoi sert la sociologie des organisations?* [*What is the sociology of organisations for?*], Paris: Éditions Seli Arslan.

da Costa, A.F. and Machado, F.L. (2000) 'An incomplete modernity: structural change and social mobility', in J.M. Viegas and A. Firmino da Costa (eds) *Crossroads to modernity: Contemporary Portuguese society* (pp 15-40), Oeiras, Portugal: Celta Editora.

da Costa, A.F. da, Mauritti, R., da Cruz Martins, S., Machado, F. L. and Ferreira de Almeida, J. (2002) 'Social classes in Europe', *Portuguese Journal of Social Science*, 1 (1): 5-39.

Dellgran, P. and Höjer, S. (2005) 'Rörelser I tiden: professionalisering och privatisering i socialt arbete' ['Current trends: professionalization and privatization in social work'], *Socialvetenskaplig Tidskrift*, 12 (2-3): 246-67.

den Dulk, L. (2001) *Work–family arrangements in organisations: A cross-national study in the Netherlands, Italy, the United Kingdom and Sweden*, Amsterdam: Rozenberg Publishers.

den Dulk, L. and de Ruijter, J. (2005) 'Werk/privé cultuur en de houding van managers ten aanzien van werk/privé beleid in de financiële sector' ['Work–life culture and the attitudes of managers concerning work–life policies in the financial sector'], *Gedrag en Organisatie*, 18 (5): 260-75.

den Dulk, L. and Peper, B. (2007) 'Working parents' use of work–life policies', *Sociologia*, 53: 51-70.

den Dulk, L. and van Doorne-Huiskes, A. (2007) 'Social policy in Europe: its impact on families and work', in R. Crompton, S. Lewis and C. Lyonette (eds) *Women, men, work and family in Europe* (pp 35-57), London: Palgrave.

den Dulk, L., Peper, B. and van Doorne-Huiskes, A. (2005) 'Work and family life in Europe: employment patterns of working parents across welfare state', in B. Peper, A. van Doorne-Huiskes and L. den Dulk (eds) *Flexible working and organisational change: The integration of work and personal life* (pp 13-38), Cheltenham: Edward Elgar.

DfEE (Department for Education and Employment) (2000) *Work–life balance: Changing patterns in a changing world*, London: DfEE.

Dikkers, J., Geurts, S., den Dulk, L., Peper, B. and Kompier, M. (2004) 'Relations among work–home culture, the utilization of work–home arrangements, and work–home interference', *International Journal of Stress Management*, 11 (4): 323-45.

Dikkers, J., Geurts, S., den Dulk, L., Peper, B., Taris, T. W. and Kompier, M. (2007) 'Dimensions of work–home culture and their relations with the use of work–home arrangements and work–home interaction', *Work & Stress*, 21 (2): 155-72.

DiMaggio, J. P. and Powell, W. W. (1991) 'The Iron Cage revisited: institutional isomorphism and collective rationality in organisational fields', in W. W. Powell and J. P. DiMaggio (eds) *The new institutionalism in organisational analysis* (pp 1-38), Chicago, IL: University of Chicago Press.

Dominelli, L. (1997) *Sociology for social work*, Basingstoke: Macmillan.

Domsch, M.E. and Ladwig, D.H (2000) *Reconciliation of family and work in Eastern European countries*, Frankfurt am Main: Peter Lang.

Douglas, A. and Philpot, T. (1998) *Caring and coping: A guide to social services*, London: Routledge.

Driessen, H. (1997) 'Humour, laughter and the field: reflections from anthropology', in J. Bremmer and H. Roodenburg (eds) *A cultural history of humour: From antiquity to the present day* (p 224), Cambridge: Polity Press.

DTI (Department of Trade and Industry) (2001) *Work–life balance: The business case*, London: DTI.

Eaton, S. C. (2003) 'If you can use them: flexible policies, organizational commitment, and perceived performance', *Industrial Relations*, 42 (2): 145-67.

Eborall, C. and Garmeson, K. (2001) 'Desk research on recruitment and retention in the social care and social work', COI communications for the Department of Health, www.doh.gov.uk/scg/workforce/coidesk.pdf

Edwards, R. (2004) 'Present and absent in troubling ways: families and social capital debates', *Sociological Review*, vol 5, no 1, pp 1-21.

Eitrheim, P. and Kuhnle, S. (2000) 'Nordic welfare states in the 1990s: institutional stability, signs of divergence', in S. Kuhnle (ed) *Survival of the European welfare state* (pp 39-57), London: Routledge.

Ellingsæter, A. L. (1999) *Gender mainstreaming and employment policy: Norway report*, Report 99.11, Oslo: Institute for Social Research (ISF).

Ellingsæter, A. L. (2003) 'The complexity of family policy reform: the case of Norway', *European Societies*, 5 (4): 419-43.

Ellingsæter, A. L. and Solheim, J. (eds) (2002) *Den usynlige hand: Kjønnsmakt og moderne arbeidsliv* [*The invisible hand: Gender power and the modern working life*], Oslo: Gyldendal akademisk.

Elman, C. (2005) 'Explanatory typologies in qualitative studies of international politics', *International Organisation*, 59 (2): 293-326.

Engan, E. T. and Kvande, E. (2005) 'Kontantstøtten og arbeidslivets fedre', in B. Brandth, B. Bungam and E. Kvande (eds) *Valgfrihetens tid: Omsorgspolitikk for barn møter det fleksible arbeidslivet* [*The time of freedom of choice: Care policies for children meet the flexible working life*] (pp 124-37), Oslo: Gyldendal Akademisk.

Esping-Andersen, G. (ed) (1996) *Welfare states in transition: National adaptations in global economies*, London: Sage Publications.

EU (European Union) (2007) *A more cohesive society for a stronger Europe: The European Union's commitment to social protection and social inclusion*, Brussels: EU.

Eurofound (2002) *Quality of work and employment in Europe: Issues and challenges*, Dublin: European Foundation for the Improvement of Living and Working Conditions.

Eurofound (2008) *Annual review of working conditions in the EU*, Dublin: European Foundation for the Improvement of Living and Working Conditions.

Eurostat (2001) *The social situation in the European Union 2001*, Brussels: European Commission.

Evans, J. (2001) 'Work/family reconciliation, gender wage equity and occupational segregation: the role of firms and public policy', *Canadian Public Policy/Analyse de Politiques*, 28, Supplement: Occupational Gender Segregation: Public Policies and Economic Forces: S187-S221.

Fagnani, J., Houriet-Ségard, G. and Bédouin, S. (2003) *Transitions research report #1: Context mapping for the EU Framework 5 funded study 'Gender, parenthood and the changing European workplace'*, Manchester: RIHSC, Manchester Metropolitan University.

Fleetwood, S. (2007) 'Why work–life balance now?', *International Journal of Human Resource Management*, 18 (3): 351-9.

Forth, J., Lissenburgh, S., Callender, C. and Millward, N. (1997) *Family friendly working arrangements in Britain, 1996*, Research Report No 16, London: Policy Studies Institute, Department for Education and Employment.

Fried, M. (1999) 'Parental leave policy and corporate culture', *Women and Work*, 1: 11-26.

Fukuyama, F. (1995) *Trust: The social virtues and the creation of prosperity*, London: Hamish Hamilton.

Gambles, R., Lewis, S. and Rapoport, R. (2006) *The myth of work–life balance: The challenge of our time: Men, women, and societies*, Chichester: Wiley.

Geertz, C. (2000 [1973]) *The interpretation of cultures: Selected essays*, New York, NY: Basic Books.

George, A. L. and Bennett, A. (2005) *Case studies and theory development in the social sciences*, Cambridge, MA: MIT Press.

Glaser, B. and Strauss, A. (1967) *The discovery of grounded theory: Strategies for qualitative research*, Chicago, IL: Aldine.

Grahl, J. (2007) 'The Bolkestein Directive', in P. James, I. Roper and G. Wood (eds) *'Modernising' work and employment in public services* (pp 29-48), London: Palgrave.

Granovetter, M. (1973) 'The strength of weak ties', *American Journal of Sociology*, 78: 1360-80.

Griffiths, L. (1998) 'Humour as resisitance to professional dominance in community health terms', *Sociology of Health and Illness*, 20(6): 874–95.

Grootscholte, M., Bouwmeester, J. A. and de Klaver, P. (2000) *Evaluatie wet op het ouderschapsverlof: Onderzoek onder rechthebbenden en werkgevers* [*Evaluation of the law on parental leave: Analysis of claimants and employers*], The Hague: Ministerie van Sociale Zaken en Werkgelegenheid.

Grover, S. L. and Crooker, K.J. (1995) 'Who appreciates family-responsive human resource policies: impact of family-friendly policies on the organizational attachment of parents and non-parents', *Personnel Psychology*, 48: 271-88.

Guerreiro, M. das Dores and Abrantes, P. (2004) *Transições Incertas: Os jovens face ao trabalho e à família* [*Young generations facing work and family*], Final Report, Lisbon: CIES-MTSS.

Haas, L. and Hwang, P. (1995) 'Company culture and men's usage of family leave benefits in Sweden', *Families Relations*, 44 (1): 28-36.

Haas, L. and Hwang, P. (1999) 'Parental leave in Sweden', in P. Moss and F. Deven (eds) *Parental leave: Progress or pitfall? Research and policy issues in Europe* (pp 45-68), Brussels: NIDI/CBGS Publications.

Haas, L. and Hwang, P. (2000) 'Programs and policies promoting women's economic equality and men's sharing of child care in Sweden', in L. Haas, P. Hwang and G. Russell (eds) *Organizational change and gender equity: International perspectives on fathers and mothers at the workplace* (pp 133-61), London: Sage Publications.

Haas, L. and Hwang, C.P. (2007) 'Gender and organizational culture: correlates of companies' responsiveness to fathers in Sweden', *Gender & Society*, 21(1): 52–79.

Haas, L., Alldred, K. and Hwang, P. (2002) 'The impact of organizational culture on men's use of parental leave in Sweden', *Community, Work and Family*, 5 (3): 319-42.

Hammare, U. (2004) *Kompetens i den sociala professionen* [*Competence in the social profession*], Stockholm: Socialstyrelsen, www.sos.se

Hammersley, M., Gomm, R. and Foster, P. (2002) 'Case study and theory', in R. Gomm, M. Hammersley and P. Foster (eds) *Case study method: Key issues, key texts* (pp 234-58), London: Sage Publications.

Hantrais, L. (1999) 'Contextualisation in cross-national comparative research', *International Journal of Social Research Methodology*, 2: 93-108.

Hantrais, L. (2009) *International comparative research: Theory, methods and practice*, Basingstoke: Palgrave Macmillan.

Hanžek, M. (ed) (1998) *Human development report – Slovenia*, Ljubljana: Zavod za makroekonomske analize in razvoj.

Harding, S. (1987) 'Introduction', in S. Harding (ed) *Feminism and methodology: Social science issues* (pp 1-14), Bloomington, IN: Indiana University Press.

Hasenfeld, Y. (1983) *Human service organizations*, Engelwood Cliffs, NJ: Prentice Hall.

Hellberg, I. (1978) *Studier I professionell organisation*, Göteborg: Sociologiska Institutionen: Göteborgs Universitet.

Hochschild, A. (1997) *The time bind: When work becomes home and home becomes work*, New York, NY: Metropolitan Press.

Hooker, H., Neathey, F., Casebourne, J. and Munro, M. (2007) *The Third Work–Life Balance Survey*, London: Department of Trade and Industry.

Humer, Ž. (2004) 'Tracing the act on equal opportunities for women and men – the case of Slovenia', in S. Sevenhuijsen and A. Švab (eds) *The heart of the matter* (pp 123-46), Ljubljana: Peace Institute.

Ignjatovič, M. and Svetlik, I. (2005) 'HRM of low intensity', in I. Svetlik and B. Ilič (eds) *HRM's contribution to hard work* (pp 25-58), Berlin and New York, NY: Peter Lang.

Jacoby, S. and Ochs, E. (1995) 'Co-construction: an introduction', *Research on Language and Social Interaction*, 28 (3): 171-83.

James, P. and Wood, G. (2006) *Institutions, production, and working life*, Oxford: Oxford University Press.

Jämo (1999) *Jämställdhetsplanens betydelse för jämställdheten: Resultat från en enkätundersökning bland företag och myndigheter hösten 1999* [*The importance of an equality plan for gender equity: Results of a survey among companies and governmental organizations during the autumn 1999*], Stockholm: Jämo.

Jogan, M. (2001) *Seksizem v vsakdanjem življenju* [*Sexism in everyday life*], Ljubljana: Fakulteta za družbene vede.

Johansson, G. (2002) 'Arbete, familj och flexibilitet' [Work, family and flexibility'], in *Hela folket i arbete?* [*All people in the workforce?*], Arbetslivsforum 2002, Stockholm: Fas.

Johansson, R. (2002) *Nyinstitutionalism inom organisationsanalysen: En skolbildnings uppkomst, spridning och utveckling* [*New institutionalism in organizational analysis: The origin, dissemination and development of a school form*], Lund: Studentlitteratur.

Johansson, S. (2005) 'Socialtjänstens organisation som forskningsobjekt' ['The organization of the social service as a field of research'], I *Socialvetenskaplig Tidskrift*, Nr. 2-3, pp 108-25

Kanjuo-Mrčela, A. (2003) 'Employee ownership in Slovenia at the beginning of the millennium', Paper presented at the EFES Central and Eastern European employee ownership network conference, Brdo, Slovenia, 28-29 March.

Kanjuo-Mrčela, A. and Černigoj Sadar, N. (2006) *Telefonska anketa o usklajevanju dela in starševstva/zasebnega življenja mladih v Sloveniji* [*Balancing work and parenthood/ private life of young people in Slovenia*] (Results of a telephone survey), Kanujo Ljubljana: Fakulteta Za Družbene Vede [Faculty of Social Sciences].

Kirby, E.L. and Krone, K.J. (2002) 'The policy exists but you can't really use it: communication and the structuring of work–family policies', *Journal of Applied Communication Research*, 30 (1): 50-77.

Knijn, T. and Kremer, M. (1997) 'Gender and the caring dimension of the welfare states: towards inclusive citizenship', *Social Politics*, 4 (3): 328-61.

Knudsen, K. and Waerness, K. (2009) 'Shared or separate? Money management and changing norms of gender equality among Norwegian couples', *Community, Work and Family*, 12 (1): 39-55.

Kovacheva, S. (2000) *Sinking or swimming in the waves of transformation? Young people and social protection in Central and Eastern Europe*, Brussels: Youth Forum.

Kovacheva, S. (2002) 'Work flexibilisation and its impact on family relationships in Bulgaria', in G. Dimitrov, G. Fotev, I. Tchalakov, K. Koev, L. Deyanova and P.-E. Mitev (eds) *The social world in the 21st century: Ambivalent legacies and rising challenges*, Special Issue of the journal *Sociological Problems*, XXXIV: 196-212.

Kovacheva, S. (2004) 'The role of family social capital for young people's transition from school to work in Bulgaria', *Sociologija*, (Belgrade), XLVI (3): 211-26.

Kovacheva, S. (2006) 'Youth transitions and family support in a transforming social context – reflections from the new member states', in W. Lutz, R. Richter and C. Wilson (eds) *The new generations of Europeans: Demography and families in the enlarged European Union* (pp 145-76), London and Sterling, VA: Earthscan..

Kovacheva, S., Matev, A. and Demireva, N. (2004) *Transitions: Organisational case studies – Bulgaria*, Plovdiv: Plovdiv University.

Kvande, E. (1998) 'Kjønn og makt i forførende og grådige organisasjoner' [Gender and power in seductive and greedy organisations], in *Kjønn i endring: Institusjoner, normer, identiteter* [*Changing gender: Institutions, norms and identities*] (pp 28-40) Konferanserapport, del 2, Oslo: Norges forskningsråd.

Lee, M., MacDermid, S. and Buck, M. (2000) 'Organizational paradigms of reduced load work: accommodations, elaboration and transformation', *Academy of Management Journal*, 43 (6): 1211-36.

Leira, A. (1992) *Welfare states and working mothers*, Cambridge: Cambridge University Press.

Lewis, J. and Giullari, S. (2005) 'The adult model worker family, gender equality and care: the search for new policy principles and the possibilities and problems of a capabilities approach', *Economy and Society*, 34 (1): 76-101.

Lewis, L. and den Dulk, L. (in press) 'Parents' experiences of flexible work arrangements in changing European workplaces', in K. Christensen and B. Schneider (eds) *Workplace flexibility: Realigning 20th century jobs to 21st century workers*, Ithaca, NY: Cornell University Press.

Lewis, S. (1996) 'Sense of entitlement, family friendly policies and gender', in H. Holt and I. Thaulow (eds) *Reconciling work and family life: An international perspective on the role of companies* (pp 9-17), Copenhagen: Danish National Institute of Social Research.

Lewis, S. (1997) 'Family friendly policies: organisational change or playing about at the margins?', *Gender, Work and Organisations*, 4: 13-23.

Lewis, S. (2001) 'Restructuring workplace cultures: the ultimate work–family challenge?', *Women in Management Review*, 16 (1): 21-9.

Lewis, S. (2003a) 'The integration of work and personal life: is post industrial work the new leisure?', *Leisure Studies*, 22: 343-55.

Lewis, S. (2003b) 'Flexible work arrangements: implementation, outcomes, and management', in C. L. Cooper and I. Robertson (eds) *International review of industrial and organisational psychology* (pp 1-28), Chichester: John Wiley.

Lewis, S. (2007) 'Working time, client time, and family time: accounting for time in the accountancy profession', in T. van der Lippe and P. Peters (eds) *Competing claims in work and family life*, London: Edward Elgar.

Lewis, S. and Cooper, C. L. (2005) *Work–life integration: Case studies of organisational change*, London: Wiley.

Lewis, S. and Haas, L. (2005) 'Work–life integration and social policy: a social justice theory and gender equity approach to work and family', in E.E. Kossek and S.J. Lambert (eds) *Work and life integration: Organizational, cultural, and individual perspectives* (pp 349-74), Mahwah, NJ: Lawrence Erlbaum Associates.

Lewis, S. and Smithson, J. (2001) 'Sense of entitlement to support for the reconciliation of employment and family life', *Human Relations*, 54 (11): 1455-81.

Lewis, S., Gambles, R. and Rapoport, R. (2007) 'The constraints of a "work–life balance" approach: an international perspective', *International Journal of Human Resource Management*, 18 (3): 360-73.

Lewis, S., Smithson, J. and Kugelberg, C. (2002) 'Into work: job insecurity and changing psychological contracts', in J. Brannen, S. Lewis, A. Nilsen and J. Smithson (eds) *Young Europeans, work and family* (pp 69-88), London: Routledge.

Lin, N. (2001) *Social capital: A theory of social structure and action*, Cambridge: Cambridge University Press.

Lincoln, Y. and Guba, E. (1985) *Naturalistic inquiry*, Beverley Hills, CA: Sage Publications.

Linstead, A. and Thomas, R. (2002) 'What do you want from me? A poststructuralist feminist reading of middle managers' identities', *Culture and Organization*, 8 (1): 1-20.

Lipsky, M. (1980) *Street-level bureaucracy: The dilemmas of the individuals in public services*, New York, NY: Russell Sage Foundation.

Lobel, S.A. and Googins, B.K. (1999) 'The future of work and family: critical trends for policy', *Human Resource Management*, 38 (3): 243-54.

Macnaghten, P. and Myers, G. (2004) 'Focus groups', in C. Seale, G. Gobo, J. Gubrium and D. Silverman (eds) *Qualitative research practice* (pp 65-80), London: Sage Publications.

McAuley, A. (1993) 'Economic justice in eastern Europe', in S. Ringen and C. Wallace (eds) *Societies in transition: East-Central Europe today* (pp 29-44), Prague papers on social responses to transformation, vol 1, Prague: CEU.

McKinney, J. C. (1969) 'Typification, typologies, and sociological theory', *Social Forces*, 48 (1): 1-12.

Mangen, S. (1999) 'Qualitative research methods on cross-national settings', *International Journal of Social Research Methodology*, 2 (2): 109-24.

Metcalfe, B. and Afanassieva, M. (2005) 'Gender, work and equal opportunities in Central and Eastern Europe', *Women in Management Review*, 20 (6): 397-411.

Mikhailov, D. (2005) *Civil society without citizens*, Sofia: CIVICUS.

Mitchell, J.C. (2002) 'Case and situation analysis', in R. Gomm, M. Hammersley and P. Foster (eds) *Case study method* (pp 165-86), London: Sage Publications.

Molyneux, M. (2002) 'Gender and the silences of social capital: lessons from Latin America', *Development and Change*, 33 (2): 167-88.

Morgan, D.L. (1996) 'Focus groups', *Annual Reviews of Sociology*, 22: 129-52.

Moss, P. (2003) 'Getting beyond childcare: reflections on recent policy and future possibilities', in J. Brannen and P. Moss (eds) *Rethinking children's care*, Buckingham: Open University Press.

Nilsen, A. and Brannen, J. (2005) *Negotiating parenthood: Consolidated interview study*, Report for the EU Framework 5 funded study 'Gender, parenthood and the changing European workplace', Research Report No 8, Manchester: Research Institute of Health and Social Change, Manchester Metropolitan University.

Nilsen, A., Sümer, S. and Granlund, L. (2004) *Case studies national report: Norway*, for the EU Framework 5 funded study 'Gender, parenthood and the changing European workplace', Bergen: Department of Sociology, University of Bergen, www.workliferesearch.org/transitions

O'Brien, M., Brandth, B. and Kvande, E. (2007) 'Fathers, work and family life', *Community, Work and Family*, 10 (4): 375-86.

OECD (Organisation for Economic Co-operation and Development) (2002) *Babies and bosses: Reconciling work and family life* (Vol. 1), Paris: OECD Publications.

Office for Equal Opportunities (2007) *Očetje v Sloveniji [Fathers in Slovenia]*.

Official Journal of Republic of Slovenia (2000) *National social protection plan*, no 31/7.4.2000, Ljubljana: Official Journal of Republic of Slovenia.

Peper, B., van Doorne-Huiskes, A. and den Dulk, L. (2005) *Flexible working and organisational change: The integration of work and personal life*, Cheltenham: Edward Elgar.

Perrow, C. (1986) *Complex organizations: A critical essay*, New York, NY: Random House.

Pettersson, U. (2001) *Socialt arbete, politik och professionalisering: Den historiska utvecklingen I USA och Sverige [Social work politics and professionalization: The historical development in USA and Sweden]*, Stockholm: Natur och Kultur.

Pfau-Effinger, B. (1998) 'Gender cultures and the gender arrangement – a theoretical framework for cross-national comparisons on gender', in S. Duncan (ed) 'The spatiality of gender', Special issue of *Innovation: European Journal of Social Sciences*, 11 (2): 147-66.

Plantin, L. (2001) *Mäns föräldraskap: Om mäns upplevelser och erfarenheter av faderskapet [Men's parenting: On men's perceptions and experiences of fatherhood]*, Göteborg: Institutionen för Socialt Arbete.

Plantin, L., Månsson, S.-A. and Kearney, J. (2003) 'Talking and doing fatherhood: on fatherhood and masculinity in Sweden and England', *Fathering: A Journal of theory, research and practice about men as fathers*, 1 (1): 3-26.

Pleck, J. (1977) 'The work–family role system', *Social Problems*, 24 (4): 417-27.

Powell, G. N. and Mainiero, L. A. (1999) 'Managerial decision making regarding alternative work arrangements', *Journal of Occupational and Organizational Psychology*, 72: 41-56.

Przeworski, A. and Teune, H. (1970) *The logic of comparative inquiry*, New York, NY: Wiley.

Putnam, R. (1993) *Making democracy work*, Princeton, NJ: Princeton University Press.

Putnam, R. (2000) *Bowling alone: The collapse and revival of American community*, New York, NY: Simon & Schuster.

Raiser, M.C., Haerpfer, T., Nowotny, T. and Wallace, C. (2001) 'Social capital in transition: A first look at the evidence', EBRD Working Paper No 61.

Ramsdal, H. and Skorstad, E. (2004) *Privatisering fra innsiden: Om sammensmeltingen av offentlig og privat organisering [Privatisation from inside: On the fusion of public and private organisation]*, Bergen: Fagbokforlaget.

Rapoport, R., Bailyn, L., Fletcher, J. K. and Pruitt, B. H. (2002) *Beyond work–family balance: Advancing gender equity and workplace performance*, London: Jossey Bass.

Reich, R. (1993) *O trabalho das nações [The work of nations]*, Lisbon: Quetzal Editores.

Remery, C., van Doorne-Huiskes, J. and Schippers, J. (2003) 'Family-friendly policies in the Netherlands: the tripartite involvement', *Personnel Review*, 31 (4): 456-73.

Remery, C., Schippers, J. and van Doorne-Huiskes, A. (2002) *Zorg als arbeidsmarktgegeven: Werkgevers aan zet* [*Care as labour market aspect: Employers on move*], Tilburg: OSA Publicatie.

Rigné, E. M. (2002) *Profession, science and the state*, Göteborg: Department of Sociology, Göteborg University.

Rodrigues, M. J. (1995) *O sistema de emprego em Portugal: Crise e mutações*, Lisbon: Dom Quixote.

Rostgaard, T., Christoffersen, M. N. and Weise, H. (1999) 'Parental leave in Denmark', in P. Moss and F. Deven (eds) *Parental leave: Progress or pitfall? Research and policy issues in Europe* (pp 25-44), Brussels: NIDI/CBGS Publications.

Sacks, H. (1992) *Lectures on conversation*, vols I and II, Oxford: Blackwell.

Sainsaulieu, R. (1997) *Sociologie de l'entreprise* [*Sociology of the enterprise*], Paris: Presses de la Fondation Nationale des Sciences Politiques.

Santos, B. de Sousa (ed) (1993) *Portugal: Um retrato singular*, Porto: Edições Afrontamento.

SCB (Statistics Sweden) (2005) *Arbetskraftsbarometern 05: Utsikterna på arbetsmarknaden för 70 utbildningar* [*The labour barometer 2005: Future prospects on the labour market for 70 different educations*], www.scb.se

SCP (Sociaal Cultureel Planbureau) (2004) *Werkt verlof? Het gebruik van regelingen voor verlof en aanpassing van de arbeidsduur* [*Do leaves work? The use of policies for leave and working time adjustement*], The Hague: SCP.

Senge, P. (1990) *The fifth discipline: The art and practice of the learning organization*, New York, NY: Doubleday.

Senge, P., Kleiner, A., Roberts, C., Ross, R., Roth, G. and Smith, B. (1999) *The dance of change: The challenge of sustaining momentum in learning organizations*, New York, NY: Doubleday.

Sevenhuijsen, S. (2003) 'The place of care: the relevance of the ethics of care for social policy', in S. Sevenhuijsen and A. Švab (eds) *Labyrinths of care: The relevance of the ethics of care perspective for social policy* (pp 13-41), Ljubljana: Peace Institute.

Simon. A., Owen, C., Moss, P. and Cameron, C. (2003) *Mapping the care workforce: Supporting joined-up thinking: Secondary analysis of the Labour Force Survey for childcare and social care work*, London: Institute of Education.

Simoneti, M., Bohm, A., Rems, M., Rojec, M., Pavlič Damijan, J. and Majcen, B. (2001) *Secondary privatisation in Slovenia: Evolution in ownership structure and company performance following mass privatisation: Case reports*, Warsaw: CASE.

Smithson, J. and Stokoe, E. (2005) 'Discourses of work–life balance: negotiating gender blind terms in organizations', *Gender, Work and Organization*, 12 (2): 147-68.

Smithson, J., Lewis, S. and Cooper, C. (2004) 'Flexible working and the gender pay gap in the accountancy profession', *Work, Employment and Society*, 18 (1): 115-35.

Sørensen, B. A. (1998) 'Den nye organisasjonsera' [The era of new organisations], in *Kjønn i endring: Institusjoner, normer, identiteter* [*Changing gender: Institutions, norms, identities*] (pp 6-15), Konferanserapport, del 2, Oslo: Norges forskningsråd.

Stake, R. E. (2002) 'The case study method in social inquiry', in R. Gomm, M. Hammersley and P. Foster (eds) *Case study method* (pp 19-26), London: Sage Publications.

Stebbins, R. (2001) *Exploratory research in the social sciences*, Thousand Oaks, CA: Sage Publications.

Stolle, D. and Lewis, J. (2002) 'Social capital – an emerging concept', in B. Hobson, J. Lewis and B. Siim (eds) *Contested concepts in gender and social politics* (pp 195-229), Cheltenham: Edward Elgar.

Sümer, S., Smithson, J. das Dores Guerreiro, M and Granlund, L. (2008) 'Becoming working mothers: reconciling work and family at three particular workplaces in Norway, the UK and Portugal', *Community, Work and Family*, 11 (4): 365-84.

Švab, A. (2003) 'Does the state really care? The conceptualisation of care in family policy in Slovenia', in S. Sevenhuijsen and A. Švab (eds) *Labyrinths of care* (pp 53-77), Ljubljana: Peace Institute.

Švab, A. (2004) 'Caring about family and work: the concept of reconciliation of family and work in Slovenian family policy', in S. Sevenhuijsen and A. Švab (eds) *The heart of the matter* (pp 47-68), Ljubljana: Peace Institute.

Svetlik, I. (2005) 'Introduction: cracks in the success story', in I. Svetlik and B. Ilič (eds) *HRM's contribution to hard work* (pp 9-24), Berlin and New York: Peter Lang.

Swedish National Agency for Education (2005) *Barn, elever och personal – Riksnivå. Sveriges officiella statistik om förskoleverksamhet, skolbarnomsorg, skola och vuxenutbildning* [*Children, pupils and personnel – at a national level. Swedish official statistics on preschool, school and adult education*], Del 2, Rapport 260, 2005, Stockholm: Skolverket.

Sztompka, P. (1996) 'Trust and the emerging democracy: lessons from Poland', *International Sociology*, (11) 4: 133-48.

Thomas, L. and Ganster, D. (1995) 'Impact of family supportive work variables on work family conflict and strain: a control perspective', *Journal of Applied Psychology*, 80: 6-15.

Thompson, C. A., Beauvais, L. L. and Lyness, K. S. (1999) 'When work–family benefits are not enough: the influence of work–family culture on benefit utilization, organizational attitudes and work–family conflict', *Journal of Vocational Behaviour*, 54: 392-415.

Thompson, C. A., Jahn, E. W., Kpelman, R. E. and Prottas, D. J. (2004) 'Perceived organizational family support: a longitudinal and multilevel analysis', *Journal of Managerial Issues*, 16 (4): 545-66.

Toš, N. (ed) (2004) *Vrednote v prehodu III* [*Values in transition III*], Dokumenti SJM 10, Ljubljana: Fakulteta za družbene vede, Inštitut za družbene vede –CJMMK.

Toš, N., Hafner-Fink, M., Uhan, S., Malnar, B., Štebe, J., Kurdija, S., Švara, S., Bešter-Falle, Ž. and Kovačič, M. (2003) *Mednarodna raziskava o družini: Pregled in primerjava rezultatov* [*International survey on family*], Ljubljana: Fakulteta za družbene vede, Inštitut za družbene vede – CJMMK.

Toš, N., Trampuž, C., Mlinar, Z., Markič, B., Roter, Z., Klinar, P., Hafner-Fink, M., Štebe, J., Malnar, B., Uhan, S. and Kurdija, S. (1994) *Vrednotenje družine* [*International social survey programme 1993: family*], Ljubljana: Fakulteta za družbene vede, Inštitut za družbene vede – CJMMK.

Tronstad, K.R. (ed) (2007) *Fordelingen av okonmiske ressurser mellom kvinner og menn: Inntekt, sysselsetting og tidsbruk* [*The distribution of economic resources between women and men: Income, occupation and time use*), Report, Oslo: Statistisk sentralbyrå (Central Bureau of Statistics).

Tronto, J. (1993) *Moral boundaries: A political argument for an ethic of care*, London and New York, NY: Routledge.

TUC (Trades Union Congress) (2001) *Changing times: TUC guide to work–life balance*, London: TUC.

Tyrkkö, A. (2001) 'Samspelet mellan arbetsliv och familjeliv' ['The interplay between work life and family life'], in L. Gonäs (ed) *Könssegregering i arbetslivet*, [*Gender segregation in work life*] Stockholm: Arbetslivsinstitutet.

UNDP (United Nations Development Report) (2001) National Human Development Report Bulgaria, *Citizen participation in governance: From individuals to citizens*, Sofia: UNDP.

van der Lippe, T. (2004) 'Emancipatiegezindheid van werkgevers' [*Emancipation inclination of employees*], in SCP, *Emancipatiemonitor 2004* (pp 226-50), The Hague: SDU.

van Doorne-Huiskes, A., den Dulk, L. and Peper, B. (2005) 'Organisational change, gender and integration of work and life', in B. Peper, A. van Doorne-Huiskes and L. den Dulk (eds) *Flexible working and organisational change: The integration of work and personal life* (pp 39-61), Cheltenham: Edgar Elgar.

Vike, H. R., Bakken, A. H., Brinchmann, H., Haukelien, R. and Kroken, K.J. (2002) *Maktens samvittighet: Om politikk, styring og dilemmaer i velferdsstaten* [*The conscience of power: About politics, management and dilemmas in the welfare state*], Oslo: Gyldendal Akademisk.

Walby, S. (1997) *Gender transformations*, London/New York: Routledge.

Wallace, C. and Pichler, F. (2007) 'Bridging and bonding social capital: which is more prevalent in Europe?', *European Journal of Social Security*, 9 (1): 29-54.

Webster, J. (2004) *Working and living in the European knowledge society: The policy implications of developments in working life and their effects on social relations*, Report for the project 'Infowork', Dublin: Department of Sociology, Trinity College, Dublin.

White, M., Hill, S., McGovern, P., Mills, C. and Smeaton, D. (2003) 'High performance management practices, working hours and work–life balance', *British Journal of Industrial Relations*, 41 (2): 175-95.

Williams, J. (2000) *Unbending gender: Why family and work conflict and what to do about it*, New York, NY: Oxford University Press.

Winchester, R. (2003) 'Stay or go?', www.communitycare.co.uk

Wingfors, S.S. (2004) 'Socionomyrkets professionalisering' ['The professionalization of the social worker'], Doctoral thesis, *Göteborg Studies in Sociology*, Nr 20.

Yeandle, S., Phillips, J., Schreibl, F., Wigfiled, A. and Wise, S. (2003) *Line managers and family-friendly employment: Roles and perspectives*, York: Joseph Rowntree Foundation.

Yin, R. K. (2003a) *Case study research: Design and methods* (3rd edition), London: Sage Publications.

Yin, R. K. (2003b) *Applications of case study research* (2nd edition), London: Sage Publications.

Index